Recalibrating
the Labor Market

Second Edition

JOHN CREA

DEDICATION

To the love of my life Susan,
for her encouragement,
her patient indulgence,
and not the least – her editing skills.

Contents

Introduction to Second Edition   -1-

PART I   BACKGROUND

Chapter 1   Why We Work – A Brief Historic Overview   -21-

Chapter 2   Our Occupation – Our Identity   -39-

Chapter 3   The Insatiable Drive for Wealth   -69-

PART II   TODAY'S LABOR MARKET

Chapter 4   The Beneficial Impact of Technology   -89-

Chapter 5   The Global Labor Market   -133-

Chapter 6   Employer vs. Employee   -155-

Chapter 7   The Central Contradiction of the Labor Market   -173-

PART III   TOMORROW'S LABOR MARKET

Chapter 8   The Need for Market Regulation   -195-

Chapter 9   Managing the Change   -217-

Chapter 10   Caregivers and Service Providers   -235-

Chapter 11   The Many Benefits of a Shorter Workweek   -253-

Chapter 12   A Remedy for a Broken Labor Market   -281-

Endnotes   -299-

Index   -308-

Introduction to Second Edition

I STOOD ON THE PATIO, high above the sparkling grey expanse of the Pacific, the morning sun behind me rising up over the mountains, steaming mug of coffee in hand, content in the knowledge that this would be another fine day in paradise. We were on vacation in Puerto Vallarta. When you are from Minnesota, and you are on vacation in Mexico, and it's January, that automatically feels like paradise.

The plush setting only added to my contentment. We were in the penthouse apartment of a small condominium building in an older part of the city. It was a large apartment – more than enough room for my wife and I and her two brothers and their wives. There was the owner's suite, plus multiple guest bedrooms and baths, a large kitchen and commons area, and best of all, a large open-air patio with its own private pool and a view to die for. Quite opulent.

The owner of the apartment was a good friend of my sister-in-law, and we were there as her guests. She broke the year up between her home in Wisconsin and this palace in Puerto Vallarta. She was always hustling – a writer, she also owned gift and apparel shops in town – she was a bit of a workaholic. But we were on vacation, and she went out of her way to make us comfortable. As I said, *contentment* best describes what I was feeling that morning.

Gazing out over the ocean, what I saw next brought me back down to earth a bit. A work crew was setting up at the building just down the hill from us. There was some repair work needed on the roof, and I watched as they pulled an extension ladder off the top of their truck, rachet it up one-two-three stories high, and prop it up against the wall. They then started humping bags of tools and materials up this ridiculously long and rickety ladder.

Watching the long ladder bounce and sway with each step kind of gave me the creeps. I could never do that! They seemed not to mind, though, each making a couple trips up that ladder loaded with gear. With everyone and everything safely up on the roof, they could now get to work on the repairs. I would have watched that work from my vantage point on our patio, well above their rooftop, but it was time for breakfast.

The image of those workers climbing that ladder has stayed with me all these years. I can't help thinking how much easier and SAFER it would have been for that crew if they had a cherry picker lift at their disposal. This episode jarred me from my happy morning stupor, and is indeed one of the reasons I tackled the subject of labor market reform in the first place.

YEARS OF SEARCHING FOR VOCATIONAL OPPORTUNITIES for adults with intellectual/developmental disabilities provided an even greater reason. These individuals are all eligible for SSDI benefits.

None of them have to work. Yet all of them WANT to work. They seem to understand, perhaps intuitively, that working is important to everyone and helps make them a more complete person. They also like to shop, so it's important to have a few bucks of their own in their pocket. They took great pride opening their pay checks every two weeks!

Their appreciation for work was not lost on me. They helped me see just how important it is to be able to work. Important for the money we earn, of course. But for much more than that. The work we do helps establish our role in society.

If work is so vital to us, if it indeed helps establish our very identity, we have to make sure there is enough work to go around. That is not always the case. With constant changes in the workplace and the utilization of new technology (like a cherry picker for the roofing crew down the hill), we can get more work done with fewer workers. That seems to leave us with only one alternative – lay people off.

But there is another. We could all work a little less, leaving enough work to go around. That's what we should be striving for. It IS still work, after all. And there are many other things we can do with our time. Enjoying breakfast in the warm January sun on a patio in Mexico comes to mind!

THE TWELVE READERS FAMILIAR with the first edition of *Recalibrating the Labor Market* will know that I opened the book with the challenge to *wave a magic wand* and imagine what a blessing it would be to add sixteen hours of extra free time to a typical workweek. That challenge still remains, but I am now proposing that we do this step-wise, with an eight-hour reduction in the workweek at this time.

Nowadays, it is a treat when a rare holiday comes around and we get a three-day weekend. Why not make that the norm? Imagine what a blessing that extra day would be each week – how much easier to get everything done at home. This would be true for everyone – male and female, rich and poor, urban and rural.

I don't believe in magic wands. But I do believe in the power of logical reasoning. And I believe that if we set our minds to it, we can change our lives and become less consumed by our culture of paid work.

It is time to **recalibrate the labor market**, dropping the standard fulltime workweek from 40-hour to 32-hours. That belief is based on these core convictions:

1. Work is important to all of us; therefore, it is important for all of us to have the chance to work.

    While that sounds trite on the surface, the reader should understand that the meaning of work goes well beyond just 'making a living'. Human beings are social animals who live together in cooperative communities. It is through work that we establish our role in the community, and it is through work that we contribute to society. The compensation we receive for paid employment is simply one measure of our value to the community.

2. Oftentimes, there are not enough jobs to go around.

    Advances in technology and automation make each generation of workers more productive than the last, yet each generation stubbornly sticks to the 40-hour workweek. This frequently leaves us with more people seeking paid employment than there are jobs available.

3. We have a seriously imbalanced labor market.

    The combination of increased productivity with no corresponding decrease in the number of hours worked results in almost regular bouts of high unemployment. This creates a mindset in the labor market where employers hold an unfair advantage over employees when it comes to hiring and compensation decisions.

    There is a solution to this dilemma that doesn't call for a mythical magical wand. Just a little common sense.

WE NEED TO GO BACK and look at how we ended up in this situation in the first place. The 40-hour workweek was established over 80 years ago, during the great depression, with the enactment of the Fair Labor Standards Act in 1938.* This move to limit the length of the workweek was based on fairness, and was an antidote to the severe unemployment that was manifest at that time in America and around the globe. The idea was very simple. With only so much work to go around, the shorter workweek would force employers to hire a greater number of workers to run their factories and their shops.

This ruling had a profound impact on the labor market. Forty hours a week became the normal fulltime job, and Monday through Friday the normal workweek. This standard became culturally ingrained, not just in America, but across the industrialized world.

---

* The FLSA ruled that hourly workers who put in more than 40 hours in a week get time-and-a-half for the overtime worked.

AS IT TURNS OUT, we've seen just a few changes in the workplace since the 1930's:

80 years ago	Today
Some farmers were still using horses to plow their fields, and all the cows were milked by hand.	Farmers employ 200 HP tractors to plow their fields, and milking a cow by hand is considered a quaint activity reserved for county fairs.
80 years ago	**Today**
Factories were grimy places filled with thousands of lunchbox-toting production workers who were forced to keep up with the assembly line. They hammered away at repetitive tasks all day long, feeding parts into noisy machines. The factory workers themselves were essentially replaceable cogs in a giant production machine.	Factories are spic-and-span facilities filled with automated machines and robots. There are a handful of humans around, but they are no longer mere extensions of the machines. Production workers are now highly skilled technicians who schedule runs, program the machines, optimize productivity and ensure QC.
80 years ago	**Today**
An office of any size had a receptionist who answered the phone and greeted guests. There were secretaries, book-keepers, clerical workers, and managers. Secretaries took dictation using shorthand and translated that cryptic scrawl into legible documents using	The receptionist is long gone from the front of the office. The remaining workers have jobs that are much more integrated, vertically and horizontally. They are called analysts or coordinators or customer service reps who strive for titles like supervisor or manager or

typewriters and carbon paper. Bookkeepers with green eyeshades manually filled in ledger books with credits and debits. Documents were stored in miles of filing cabinets, and retrieving an old record was a physical activity that took a clerk into a remote file room.	director. There is a personal computer on every desk, and each office worker is capable of being many, many times more productive than their previous selves. (Except perhaps when it comes to retrieving an old record – now hopelessly lost in someone's mislabeled file folder.)
80 years ago	**Today**
We routinely worked 40 hours per week.	We routinely work 40 hours per week (many of us much more!).

<u>None</u> **of the benefits of increased productivity and labor-saving devices have translated into any free time for the workers**.

THERE HAVE BEEN some solid efforts to reduce the workweek (e.g. the 30-hour workweek at Kellogg's). Back in the 1930's, John Maynard Keynes predicted that we'd all be working 15 hours a week by the year 2030, and that after putting in a three-hour workday we could turn our thoughts to **more important tasks** of art, culture, and religion. Keynes and others believed there were philosophical and cultural reasons to strive for a shorter workweek that went well beyond the primary economic intent to maintain full employment. (I strongly agree with that sentiment.)

Economists of the day (the 1930's) recognized that technological advances in factories had produced huge productivity gains, and that these were bound to accelerate in the future. Therefore, it was inevitable that the standard workweek would shorten substantially.

But it didn't happen. Once the 40-hour week was effectively codified by the FLSA, it became more than the law of the land. It became culturally established, and was then steadfastly retained by both unions and corporations.

When WWII came around, any thoughts of a shorter workweek were quickly forgotten. The demand for goods to support the war effort skyrocketed, and while working-age men rushed off to join the military, Rosie the Riveter was enlisted to fill in gaps in the workforce.

Following the war, there was an immediate need for reconstruction in Europe and Asia to repair damage wrought by the war. Here at home, there was pent up demand to meet the needs for housing, autos, and such for the returning soldiers and their new spouses as they went about procreating the baby boom. The soldiers went back to work in factories and offices, and Rosie went home to raise the kids. The economy kept humming and the overall demand for manufactured goods remained high.

But baby booms don't last forever, and this one petered out around 1965. About that time, Rosie remembered that there were parts of going to work that she liked. She liked getting out of the house. She liked the social connections. She liked having an opportunity to prove herself professionally. She liked getting her own paycheck

With the slowing economy and with the influx of millions of women in the workforce, we might've expected unemployment to really skyrocket in the late 1960's. However, the Vietnam War gave the economy a boost, as did spending on the cold war. And more than anything else, the boys on Madison Avenue had mastered the art of advertising, and we became a very materialistic society with consumers keeping the demand strong for just about everything new under the sun.

The oil crisis in the 1970's did throw us for a loop, but eventually we fought back, turning our automobile fleet of dirty gas hogs into lean, green machines. Around this time the positive economic impact of globalization kicked into high-gear (more jobs worldwide and lower consumer prices), with strong demand from consumers in two-worker households keeping the economy on the move.

The tech bubble burst in the late 1990's and set us back some, but the combination of deficit spending and the housing bubble kept the economy in motion. When the housing bubble burst in 2007-08, the economy was severely damaged, and the impact of the great recession was felt around the world for a long time. But we recovered from that economic disaster, and the global economy, with all its warts, appeared as resilient as ever.

THEN **COVID-19** CAME ALONG EARLY IN 2020. The disruption to our lives was profound. As this new corona virus was making itself at home in human respiratory tracts, we found ourselves not just <u>able</u> to spend more time at home. We were <u>confined</u> to our own homes. No going to work. No going to school. No going out at all unless absolutely necessary. And over 20 million U.S. workers lost their jobs almost overnight.

Thinking back to the beginning of 2020, pre-COVID, it seemed that the economy was swimming merrily along, with an unemployment rate down around 3% and inflation well in check. But hidden beneath all the rosy statistics were some serious problems, and when COVID hit and as businesses and institutions began to shut down, many inexcusable economic inequities came to light. Lower-wage workers were the first to be laid off, and it became clear that they had not seen a real raise in decades. Meanwhile, those at the top, particularly at the very top, had seen their compensation grow by leaps and bounds. And throughout the income spectrum, women were still paid less than men, and Blacks less than Whites.

Acknowledgement of these underlying problems was amplified by the cold-blooded murder of George Floyd by a cop in Minneapolis. That, in turn, led us to the uncomfortable realization that racial injustice and economic inequities often go hand-in-hand. Many of us who had previously been satisfied with the status quo came to the undeniable realization that large parts of our population have been systematically abused by a smaller contingent of those in charge.

At one point, we thought that COVID itself might be a racially-driven killer, with a disproportionate number of people of color getting seriously sick and dying. But when we looked deeper, we found that social determinants of health were being overlooked. These included poverty, geography, and most important for the purposes of this study, occupation.

A lot of our workers, who we would come to label as essential, were exposed to crowded workspaces and situations where the spread of any disease is enhanced. Add to that the greater chance of exposure when a low-wage worker is forced to hold down two or more jobs. With or without racial injustice, there is no justification for paying any worker so little that they must hold down second and third jobs just to survive. This ought to be *especially* true for someone we call an *essential worker*!

Some of those essential workers are employed at facilities often hidden from public view. Eyal Press's book *Dirty Work* gives us a gritty look at who is performing this work and what this work entails.[1] The next section offers one ugly example:

MOST OF THE NATION'S SLAUGHTERHOUSES are now located in smaller cities, far from the center of our largest metropolitan areas. (That is a change from 80 years ago when the largest meat packers were found within eyesight of downtown Chicago and other large midwestern cities.) Consequently, few of us personally know anyone who wields in a knife in a meat packing plant. American consumers of meat products had become blissfully ignorant of anything that happened to the animal flesh prior to it appearing neatly wrapped in cellophane in the cooler at the grocery store.

That ignorance was pierced a bit when the slaughterhouse workers did receive some well-deserved attention during the pandemic. News coverage showed them working shoulder-to-shoulder in massive cutting rooms at large packing plants. The grind and the hazards of this work were apparent even without the threat of the new corona virus. With COVID, which at the time we thought had spread from animals to humans, all those workers crammed in on the packing room floors seemed even more at risk.

How did the nation respond to the threat to these workers? Shamefully, not too well. In fact, the Trump administration invoked the Defense Production Act to classify meat packing facilities as essential infrastructure that must stay open in spite of the high incidence of the disease.

And who were the essential workers getting sick at these facilities? A CDC report in May 2020 documented that 87% of the COVID-related illnesses and deaths were borne by Hispanic, Black, and Asian workers. The reason for the lopsided number of minorities getting sick is simple – that's who works in those facilities. For a good summary of the problems at the nation's largest meat packers, see Eric Schlosser's article in *The Atlantic,* 5/12/20[2].

MANY PEOPLE WOULD CLAIM that inequities found in the labor market are not due to deliberate sexist or racist policies. Just a reflection of the value of a skilled vs. unskilled workforce. But let's focus on that skilled/unskilled divide for a minute. Please find me a job with a greater need of skills and empathy and compassion than a home health care worker. Or how about a day care worker? If I am the father of young children or the son of an elderly and infirm parent, I cannot think of any worker more important to my family's well-being. So why are these two of the lowest paid professions in America?

These were also two of the hardest hit occupations for lay-offs. The corona virus saw to that, as lay-offs everywhere reduced the need for these services. Other hard-hit occupations were in the hospitality industry – hotels, restaurants, entertainment venues. Most of the jobs eliminated were hourly – cooks, waitresses, maids, janitors. Many employed in salaried positions at these businesses were considered essential to the continued operation of an enterprise. These fortunate individuals were not only able to hold their jobs. They were allowed to do much of their work from home.

As these two charts from the Bureau of Labor Statistics show[*], unemployment rates spiked in March and April 2020 as over 20 million jobs were lost.

---

[*] BLS News Release, 2/4/2022

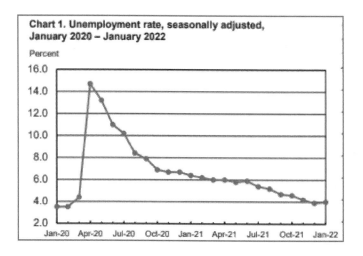

Chart 1. Unemployment rate, seasonally adjusted, January 2020 – January 2022

Over the course of the last two years, we've recovered about most of all the jobs lost to COVID, but the labor market has been on a very bumpy ride At one point the market suffered from the so-called COVID Paradox, were we simultaneously had a shortage of jobs and a shortage of workers.

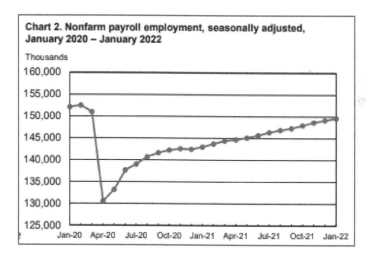

Chart 2. Nonfarm payroll employment, seasonally adjusted, January 2020 – January 2022

Early in the pandemic, with unemployment still ski-high, we saw workers afraid to get back in the workforce because of COVID exposure at work. (Not afraid just for the themselves. Afraid of bringing the disease back home to their families.) There were workers afraid to accept a new job because of uncertainty about being called back to their old jobs. There were workers unable to leave children home alone. (With distance learning in many school districts, thousands of school-age children were at home instead of in school.) And there were geographic mismatches where the workers don't live near the work that was available (not unique to COVID, but amplified by it).

To overcome some of the fear or returning to work, many companies found that it was necessary to raise the wages they paid their workers. (Neel Kashkari, president of the Minneapolis Federal Reserve, had this comment for companies complaining about labor shortages: *If you're not raising wages, then it just sounds like whining.*)[3]

When vaccinations became freely available, we began to see the COVID paradox fade away. We are now (March 2022), two years after the pandemic hit, back to within 2 million jobs of our peak employment.

I BELIEVE THERE WAS A SILVER LINING within the dark COVID cloud. Restrictions involving social distancing gave us the chance to rediscover the importance of family life.

While millions of less-fortunate hourly employees were laid off, millions of more-fortunate salaried employees were able to keep their jobs and work from home. (It was really quite an eye-opener to discover just how little office work needs to be performed in the office, and which does not. With laptops, internet access, and the occasional zoom meeting, nearly all administrative business can be conducted remotely.) And millions of school-aged children were at home distance-not-learning. We had so many people at home for so many hours, we were running out of toilet paper!

With everyone in the house, there were far more opportunities for family interactions. Like all family dynamics, these were sometimes good and sometimes not. But on balance, this was a very positive development. And it got people thinking about their **work/life balance**. Therefore, I believe the pandemic has the potential to be a truly positive disruption to the labor market – not just a cyclical correction.

THE RECESSION WE SUFFERED from COVID restrictions got the government thinking about direct payments to individuals as a way to stimulate the depressed economy. Cash payments to everyone – no questions asked – and the country did not go to hell in a socialist handbasket. Imagine that!

The COVID-19 pandemic has forced us to think about how our actions impact everyone else. We had to wear face masks which not only protected us from our neighbors, they protected our neighbors from us. Hmmm. So we're in this together?

Wearing a face masks no fun! But it sure beat getting sick and dying. That's why it was such a relief to have the vaccines developed so quickly. And that's why it is such a disappointment to see so many people refusing to take the vaccine.

Eventually, as new vaccines are developed to handle the Delta, Omicron, and who-knows-what's-next variants of the COVID virus, we will be allowed to take off the masks and stop with the social distancing. We will again be allowed to travel to distant lands and gather in large groups. We will be allowed to hug and shake hands. (Although I can see the fist-bump replace shaking hands for the most casual of greetings.) If you are reading this and you haven't been vaccinated yet, please go get the shot.

The vaccines also allow us to get back to work. But perhaps we don't need to work quite so much?

THROUGH ALL THE PERIODS of boom and bust over the last 80 years, the wisdom of a 40-hour workweek was seldom questioned, even with both husband and wife now in the workforce. I believe the reasons for this are rooted in our culture, and I'll try to cover that ground in **Part I** of the book. I look first at what work is, at what it means to us individually, and why we work so damned much!

In **Part II**, I examine the state of the Labor Market today, and how it has changed over the last 80 years. This includes improvements from technology and automation and the impact of a global labor market. All beneficial, in my opinion. But these are counteracted by a darker side of the labor market. We have developed an adversarial relationship between employer and employee. Or as Adam Smith called them, between *master* and *servant*.

Nonetheless, I am an optimist. In **Part III**, I look at what the future may hold for the Labor Market. I look at occupations which ought to be held in high esteem and which should endure far into the age of robotics. I see a shorter workweek and all the great benefits that will bring to workers and their families. And I see a role for the government to play as we transition away from paid employment into the next phase of our development as a species. Finally, I propose that 32-hours becomes the new standard for a fulltime job with no loss in pay to the worker from the reduction in hours.

I CAN HEAR the loud screams of protest from here – from business owners, from production managers, and from HR directors everywhere. From fans of Ronald Reagan who told us government is not the solution to the problem, government IS the problem. I openly admit this recalibration is not meant for your benefit. The owner/manager class <u>will</u> take a short-term operational hit as every employer is forced to adjust to the new reality of a shorter workweek. It will be the hourly employees who are the primary beneficiaries of this proposal in the short-term.

But longer-term, I believe we shall <u>all</u> benefit, as the pervasive impact of trickle-up economics and greater leisure time for everyone takes effect, and as we all remember how to work to live, not live to work.

PART I

BACKGROUND

CHAPTER 1

Why We Work –
A Brief Historic Overview

WHAT IS WORK? A mechanical engineer will tell us that work, in the most fundamental sense, is applying sufficient force to an object to cause its displacement. W = F * d. By that definition, Mother Earth has been hard at work forever – slamming continental plates into each other and blasting molten rock through holes in the crust. Wouldn't it be great if we could go all the way back to Day 1 as a spectator, grab a catbird seat high above our planet, and compress time so that we could observe the entire 4.5-billion-year history of the Earth's tectonic activity in just a few minutes? We would see a very active planet with non-stop earthquake and volcanic activity – continents crashing into each other one minute and ripping apart the next. Mother Earth hard at work, rearranging the deck chairs for her inhabitants, so-to-speak.

But, reverting to real time, the scene becomes much more placid, especially if we peel away the hyperactive layer of atmosphere. The tectonic plates, almost jelly-like in condensed time, now look rock solid. There are occasional volcanic eruptions and rumbling earthquakes, but most of the time and in most places, the surface of the Earth is quite calm. There's a lesson here for all living organisms: If you want to live to be 4.5 billion years old, get lots of rest.

Plants and animals at work

Most living organisms on our fair planet don't have that luxury, of course. In the relatively compressed layer of the biosphere, there is nonstop competition for air, water, and nutrients. Any species that does not work efficiently and diligently will be swept aside, and others will come along and take its place.

Plants work hard to grow and to stay alive, pushing roots deep into the ground to gather water and to reach nutrient-rich soils. They cling tenaciously to rocky slopes, penetrate blacktop, find tiny crevices in cement. Trees and vines work to send branches soaring into the morning sky to gather needed sunlight. Flowering plants work feverishly to produce visually attractive blooms – scented displays of eggs and sperm – all designed to enhance the chance of pollination. Plants adapt to their environment and do whatever is necessary to gain a foothold.

Animals, just like plants, work hard to survive. Our animated kin work to find water and food, work to protect themselves from the elements and from predators, and work to reproduce. Reproduction for many animals involves the work of giving birth to live babies (we even call it "going into labor") and actively raising their offspring: nursing the young, bringing them food, protecting them from predators, teaching them to forage and hunt.

All animals that live together in groups, all social animals, take the concept of work a significant step further by engaging in activities that benefit the whole group, not just their immediate families. Edward O. Wilson's book titled *The Social Conquest of Earth*[4] is a marvelous study of the strength of groups in evolution.

His focus is on highly social species of animals, those he refers to as *eusocial*, with group members from multiple generations prone to perform altruistic acts as a part of their division of labor.

Many 'higher' order animals that live in herds and packs (including humans) are highly social, but we are late-comers to the scene. Insects predate mammals by 400 million years or so, and some (ants, termites, bees, and wasps) carry out their eusocial duties to a degree that makes us look like bumbling amateurs. Wilson studied ant colonies extensively, and found that the division of labor is absolute. Whether an ant is gathering food or defending the nest, she will do so "all out" with complete disregard for her personal comfort or safety. All her actions are aimed at the survival of the colony.

Regarding insects' defense of their nests, Wilson states

> *the more elaborate and expensive the nest is in energy and time, the greater the fierceness of the ants to defend it.*[5]
> k(Something humans can certainly relate to, in spite of the way sunk costs are handled in the accounting dept.)

Homo sapiens – social and biological evolution

Wilson compares the evolution of social insects to that of social humans, and he goes to great lengths to reassure us that we are more than just worker ants. *Homo sapiens* have benefitted from <u>social evolution</u> in concert with biological evolution. We have evolved as both selfish individuals and as altruistic members of groups.

Referring to human development, Wilson states that an iron-clad rule exists in natural selection and genetic social evolution:

> *It is that selfish individuals beat altruistic individuals,*

while groups of altruists beat groups of selfish individuals. The victory can never be complete; the balance of selection pressures cannot move to either extreme. If individual selection were to dominate, societies would dissolve. If group selection were to dominate, human groups would come to resemble ant colonies.[6] He goes on *We can expect a continuing conflict between components of behavior favored by individual selection and those favored by group selection.*[7]

Wilson attributes multi-level natural selection (based on behavior that is part-selfish and part altruistic) for the rapid ascent of *Homo sapiens* to our current lofty state, with godlike powers to change our environment and to rule over all other species. Multi-level natural selection means that at a higher level, traits favoring cooperative group behavior are chosen. At the lower level, traits favoring self-serving behavior are chosen. The opposition between the two levels of natural selection has resulted in a *chimeric genotype* in each person. It renders each of us part saint and part sinner.[8]

Biological and social evolution have rendered each of us part saint and part sinner.

--E.O. Wilson

Given this dichotomy, part saint and part sinner, what role does work play in our lives? As it turns out, there are plenty of reasons why we work, both selfish and altruistic.

ANTHROPOLOGISTS tell us that the genus *Homo* has been around for over 2 million years.[9] For the great majority of that time (over 99% of our existence) we lived in what we refer to as the Stone Age, a prolonged period marked by the use of the stone tools to enhance hunting and gathering expeditions. (We can safely assume that wooden, leather, and plant-fiber tools were used side-by-side those made of stone, but artifacts made from stone are the only ones to survive the thousands of centuries.)

As Wilson points out, there was both biological and social evolution during the 2 million years of the Stone Age. The social structure of groups would have evolved. Our ancestors came to live in highly structured clans with divisions of labor designed to benefit the overall wellbeing of the entire clan. We can guess that there would have been chiefs (probably the alpha males) that served as leaders for the clans. There would have been matriarchs managing the camps and the child-rearing activities. There would have been fearless warriors to lead raids of other camps. And there would have been skilled hunters and gatherers to lead foraging expeditions.

All the work performed by members of the clan, on hunting/ gathering expeditions, and back at camp, contributed to the security and wellbeing of the clan. It would have been important for all workers to carry their weight (part saint). Most likely, any slackers (part sinner) would not have been tolerated for long. They would've been quickly identified, perhaps given a chance to mend their ways, and ultimately, if unable to contribute to the welfare of the clan, ostracized from the group. Thus, social evolution occurred.

Prehistoric man

About 200,000 years ago, the species *Homo sapiens* evolved within the genus Homo. We have no written record to guide us, but we can make some pretty good guesses on human attitudes about "work" in prehistoric times. We were always highly social animals, of course. Early members of our species, like our primate cousins, went out as teams on cooperative hunting and gathering trips. Successful expeditions resulted in bounty to be shared with the rest of the clan. Other clan members not participating on hunting or foraging expeditions would be engaged in work activities back at camp that benefitted the group – child-bearing, child-rearing, and defense of the "nest". These cooperative activities, aimed at survival of the group, were probably not thought of as work, just as living.

But the life of these early humans was not meant to stay so pure and simple. The clans were hierarchal, and it is easy to imagine scenarios where certain individuals (maybe the tribal chiefs, maybe the priests) ordered those lower in the pecking order to do things for them. The alpha males may order underlings to fetch food and water, to gather material for shelter, probably even to enforce intra-group discipline on their behalf. The underlings would comply because the elite had more important things to do – higher "value-added" governing or spiritual activities.

SOMEWHERE ALONG THE LINE, these early human subordinates, quite capable of introspective thought, probably <u>did</u> start to think of subservient duties as <u>work</u>, an activity they'd rather not be engaged in if they had a choice.

While some of the workers probably rendered these services quite willingly (just happy to be associated with the big dog!), others probably grumbled along the way. Either way, I am guessing they thought of these activities in service to higher ranking individuals in a manner quite differently from the everyday hunting, gathering, and childrearing tasks that they associated with life itself. We can imagine that at least some of these subservient activities were thought of with a negative connotation.

AS ALL THIS WAS HAPPENING, other lines of work were being born. Certain individuals would have been recognized as especially good tool makers, tools made of stone, wood, and leather. They fashioned hammers from rocks that made it easier to crack open bones and nuts. They chiseled spears and knives from stone that made the hunt more lethal and skinning the animals easier. Those weapons that were made for the hunt were also very useful for offensive raids on other clans and for defense of the home camp.

These technological advancements made the tribe more efficient as hunters and gatherers, and made life on the savannah that much easier. The tribe was better off to have the stone-cutters and leather-workers stay home and make more tools that all could use than to send these artisans out on hunting expeditions. The specialization of labor was born. This division of labor resulted in more weapons for everyone which made the clan a stronger force and more secure within their territory. The tool makers would have thus earned esteem for their skills and effort, and respect for their handiwork. Was this the birth of the mercantile class?

Tool making would have become a designated "occupation" for those skilled in the craft, and that work would have been thought of much differently from those jobs in direct service to the tribal elite.

My guess is that very early on, humans took the concept of WORK (activities performed to benefit the clan that fall outside those normally associated with life itself) and began to assign value to it. Greater value for some work (hammering out spear points), lesser value for other (fetching wood for the fire). While all this work was important for the survival of the clan, there was probably a greater appreciation for the contribution of the stone cutters than for that of the firewood gatherers.

The tool-makers would've gravitated to that specialty because they were good at the job and they enjoyed their creative work. During times of abundance, instead of going out on hunting expeditions, they probably had the freedom to stay home and keep puttering around the rock quarry to see what other new and different items they could come up with. The iPhone maybe.

THIS "PRIMITIVE" LIFESTYLE for the various *Homo* species went on for about 2 million years, remember. It was only with the onset of agriculture about 12,000 years ago that life for *Homo sapiens* began to resemble what we now think of as normal.

At some point back in that timeframe, agricultural practices became more important than hunting/gathering, and with that development permanent settlements began to appear. This would've resulted in an explosion of occupational specialties, each carrying more or less social and self-esteem than the next. All of this is conjecture, of course. It would be another 10,000 years before we started writing things down.

The ancient world

HERBERT APPLEBAUM produced a comprehensive study of the role of work in our lives in a book titled *The Concept of Work*.[10] The book chronologically tracks the meaning of work from the ancient world, through the middle ages, to modern times. Applebaum relies on the written record for his commentary, though he admits

> *People who work are mostly humble, with no voice in the recorded pages from which histories are written. It is mostly the leisured or the recipients of the state's or a patron's largesse who have the time, energy, and training to produce written works.*[11]

With that disclaimer, it is nonetheless instructive to look back at how work was perceived throughout history.

Applebaum begins his study of the concept of work with Homeric Greece. Two occupations were held in greatest esteem – farming and soldiering. Craftsmen were next in the hierarchy. At the bottom were traders and merchants – those engaged in commercial activities between households. The notion was that the agrarian households were supposed to be self-sufficient, therefore commercial trading between the farms was probably seen as a necessary evil, and somehow ancillary to the core activities needed for the survival of the household.

Slavery was deeply embedded in those ancient economies, but that was a status of non-citizenship and subservience, not an occupation. A slave may have been a teacher, a craftsman, a servant, a soldier, or all of the above; and their relative status would have reflected the work they performed on behalf of their master. Indeed, many slaves were probably more secure in life than many free working people. After all, the masters had quite an investment in slaves that they owned as they kept them fed, clothed, and sheltered so they could continue to perform their duties. But the free merchants in the market were on their own, and if they fell on hard times, they had no one else to depend on for their livelihood.

FARMERS AND SOLDIERS were also held in high esteem in the Roman Empire. To understand why this would've been true, look at parallels in Wilson's eusocial ant colonies: with human farmers analogous to foraging ants, and with soldiers of both species defending the nest. For the human soldiers, the "nest" being defended grew from the Greek city-state to the Roman Empire. Whether farming or soldiering, these most basic survival activities were not thought of as servile work, but as essential survival skills, critical for the life of the community. They were, therefore, placed on a higher plain than mercantile trade activities.

But highly esteemed or not, all work that contributed to the welfare of the community would've been considered important, and all community members would've been expected to participate. Even the nobles performed work on their family estate, perhaps to set a good example for the working class slaves and freemen if nothing else.

The middle ages

AS WE MOVED into medieval times, Applebaum shows that the attitude toward work in the middle ages is dominated by Jewish and Christian philosophy. In the very first book of the bible we are taught that God himself (God referred to as *him* in the bible) worked for six straight days to create our world before resting on day seven. Down here on Earth, Applebaum tells us that the Jews

> *respected the free workers, and treated the slave with consideration. They taught that a man is entitled to his wages on the same day he worked and that it is a sin to defraud a man of his wage.*[12]

This general attitude toward work is carried forward by the early Christians, and they viewed all work as important, including manual labor. They stressed the responsibility for all community members to contribute to the general welfare of the community. Indeed, in St. Paul's second letter to the Thessalonians, we find this edict:

> *Now we command you brethren, in the name of our Lord Jesus Christ, that you keep away from any brother who is living in idleness...* (II Thessalonians 3:6).

St. Augustine carried this attitude quite a step further, introducing the concept of working explicitly for charitable purposes (*it is more blessed to give than to receive*). For St. Augustine, economic gain is never an end in itself.

> *Any fruits of work over and above those which suffice for a frugal life, should not be allowed to accumulate, but should be given to the indigent.*[13]

Throughout the middle ages, religious monasteries became the most socially significant institutions in many localities. Monastic life was highly structured, governed by strict schedules of prayer and work:

> *The* Rule of St. Benedict *legislated minutely for the employment of every hour of the day according to the season of the year. It prescribed the time for work, prayer, reading, dinner, a siesta, and meditation. The weak and the strong must work, although consideration is given to the weak in the selection of the appropriate work for them.*[14]

The raison d'être of the monasteries was to serve God, and when the monks did their chores diligently, they became servants of God. The disciplined approach to life made the monasteries models of domestic efficiency. And if the highly structured day was good for many of the monks, it was certainly good for the abbot, making management of the monastery a much easier task.

These lessons were not lost in the secular world. Steady hard work equaled economic progress.

The modern world

THE RENAISSANCE in Europe moved us into the modern world – artistically, scientifically, and philosophically. Our attitude toward work moved forward as well, significantly shaped by the Protestant Reformation and the teachings of Martin Luther and John Calvin. According to the writings of Applebaum:

> *Luther's originality was in his idea that one best serves God by doing most perfectly the work of one's trade or profession. With this idea, Luther swept away the concept that there was a distinction between spiritual work and secular work—a belief which was prevalent in the middle ages.*

> *All work contributes to the common life of mankind. Hence, no one is more necessary than another to piety and blessedness.*[15]

Appelbaum tells us that Calvin added substantially to Luther's proclamation, giving us the backbone of the protestant work ethic:

> *With Calvin comes a new attitude toward labor. All men, including the rich, must work because to work is the will of God. But they must not lust after the fruits of their work. With*

this new creed comes a new type of man—strong-willed, active, austere, and hard-working from religious conviction. Idleness, luxury, prodigality—everything that softens the soul—is shunned. Dislike of work is a sign that one is not destined for salvation.

Puritanism—which developed from Calvinism—goes further, teaching that it is one's duty to extract the greatest possible gain from work. Success, which is proven by profit, is the certain indication that the chosen profession is pleasing to God.[16]

Switching from Applebaum's teachings to Richard Donkin, from Donkin's book *Blood, Sweat & Tears,* we learn that two hundred years after Calvin, Thomas Carlyle wrote about the *goodness* of work in and of itself:

All true work is sacred; in all true work, were it but true hard labor, there is something of the divineness.

While Carlyle's attitude about work agreed closely with Calvin's, this wasn't universally accepted by later philosophers. Donkin tells us that about a century later, John Stuart Mill thought this attitude was nonsense. He wrote:

Work, I imagine, is not a good in itself. There is nothing laudable about work for work's sake.[17]

(For me personally, if I'm engaged in work on behalf of someone else, my attitude toward work lies squarely in the Mill camp. On the other hand, if I'm putzing in the garden on my own, I think I understand what Carlyle was saying.)

In any event, the modern world brought new political realities into being as well. We were no longer locked in a feudal system where everything produced belonged to the Lord and Lady of the estate, and everything they produced belonged to the King and Queen. John Locke argued for *universal birthrights* which granted each citizen the right to defend his *life, health, liberty, and property* from the divine-rights claims of royalty. Thomas Jefferson leaned on Locke's convictions when he added his trio of *universal rights* to the Declaration of Independence: *life, liberty, and the pursuit of happiness.*

These social developments regarding personal property laid the groundwork for the industrial revolution.

The industrial revolution

ABOUT 200 YEARS after Martin Luther published his 95 theses in a letter to his superior (apparently, he did not defiantly nail them to the church door in Wittenberg, but perhaps posted them on a bulletin board for discussion)[18], the first machines of the industrial revolution sprang into life. Thereafter, life for factory workers would never be the same. Prior to the industrial revolution, the need for workers was defined by natural rhythms, day-to-day, and throughout the year. With industrialization came large, mechanically powered and artificially lit factories. These were capital intensive facilities, and as such it was economically prudent to keep them running as much as possible.

If the protestant reformation gave us the spiritual reasons to work (to serve God), it was the industrial revolution that *allowed* us to work around the clock. The foundation for modern capitalism is thus laid.

Working conditions for many in the early years of the industrial revolution were brutishly nasty. (For a flavor of what life was like, read Charles Dickens.) Yet men, women, and children subjected themselves to these awful conditions because 1) they had little choice in the matter, and 2) employment offered a chance (a remote chance) to escape their wretched status in life.

Man, as machine

In the late nineteenth and early twentieth centuries, Frederick Winslow Taylor and other proponents of *scientific management* did their very best to reduce the tasks of factory workers to the clockwork of machinery. Taylor looked back at progress made in the previous century of the industrial revolution and recognized that machines were responsible for the tremendous growth in productivity, and the steady rise in prosperity for the common man. Furthermore, he concluded that the closer we could get factory workers to behave as reliably as machines, the better off everyone would be. He was convinced that this would not happen automatically. Just the opposite, Taylor expected factory workers to slack off, if given the chance.

Taylor's approach was to reduce every manual labor task to discreet steps that could be standardized, measured, and timed. With the scientific management of labor, the output of factory workers could be as predictable as that of the machines they tended.

Taylor was indubitably right – the factory owners and consumers would be far better off. The factory workers, on the other hand, were reduced to well-oiled pieces of machinery, and the employees in those factories now had just as much autonomy as the machines.

Why did production employees put up with this kind of abuse? I'll spend a good part of the book trying to answer that question. For now, suffice it to say that at least part of the answer lies in the fact that the producers of factory goods are also the consumers of those goods.

This mentality – factory workers as cogs in a machine – held firm throughout the first half of the twentieth century. It wasn't until post WWII that this cold and calculated treatment of employees began to be seriously examined.

Man, as master of machine

During WWII, the dire need for wartime production completely outweighed any concern for the niceties in the work environment. But once the war was over and the soldiers and sailors returned to the workforce, concern for the social welfare of shop-floor workers began to take root.

Many were unhappy with the single-minded mechanistic processes of Taylorism, including, quite notably, Abraham Maslow. Maslow's assumptions about workers were diametrically opposed to Taylor's:

> *Assume that everyone is to be trusted.*
>
> *Assume the preference for working rather than being idle.*
>
> *All human beings prefer meaningful work to meaningless work.*[19]

This trust in the worker and the focus on their welfare was long overdue. We'll spend more time on that topic in the next chapter.

Conclusion

Why do we work? Just like all the other plants and animals we share this planet with, we work to live, to survive and to thrive. For over 99% of our existence, that meant hunting and gathering for our food, clothing and shelter needs. In times of abundance, that work was easy, and we probably did not think of these activities as work at all – just as living. In challenging times, when the environment turned inhospitable, working just to survive would have been very hard indeed.

In both good times and bad we were engaged in other kinds of work beyond hunting and gathering expeditions, other activities that benefitted the whole clan, not just ourselves and our families; these included shared cooking, shelter-building, and child-rearing activities. The work of our esteemed tool makers was offered as example.

There was another kind of more subservient work – personal service offered by lower-ranking clan members to the clan superiors. We can assume that at some point, well before recorded history, that type of work took on religious overtones, as in: *your service to the priest is also service to god himself.* And the priest, of course, would constantly remind everyone that keeping the gods happy would benefit the whole community. Throughout ancient times, the concept of work would have included all those activities we perform that benefit the whole community, not just ourselves.

As we moved into the agricultural period and the increasing complexity of permanent settlements, the types of work performed on behalf of the whole community would've evolved substantially. To keep track of the relative value of everyone's contributions, we moved beyond barter systems, beyond the use of cattle and grain as mediums of exchange. We invented money. We now had a handy mechanism to keep track of commercial trade, and a useful method of retaining excess profits. This allowed us to create personal wealth that went beyond one's status at birth.

With technological development (going all the way back to the Bronze Age 5000 years ago), the demand for manufactured products created a need for production workers. This really blossomed with the industrial revolution (300 years ago) and work became an avenue for lower class families to accumulate wealth and move into a more comfortable middle class lifestyle. For a fortunate few, work was an avenue to upper class comfort.

THROUGHOUT RECORDED HISTORY, work has been a means of *serving. Self-serving,* of course, but also serving the *community*, and in many cases, service to *god and country*. Work is an important way to establish our self-worth and our contributions as a member of the community. Our occupation has become a crucial part of our very identity.

CHAPTER 2

Our Occupation – Our Identity

IT IS SUCH A JOY to see and hear children on a playground. The shouts and shrieks that echo off the school building are so full of life, uninhibited, and unencumbered by the stress of our adult world. Yet role-playing as an adult is a favorite activity among children everywhere. And the specific occupations they chose tell us a lot about ourselves. Teachers, naturally, are a favorite because most kids like their teachers, and the teacher gets to be boss! Other roles you might hear the kids playing are police officer and fire fighter, positions with authority and respect, plus they have those cool uniforms.

Children will choose many adult roles to play because they sound fun, and because the jobs carry an air of respect. Jobs like astronaut (far out!) and archeologist (cool!). Kids understand, intuitively, that an occupation is an important part of establishing one's identity and status within the community. They look up to teachers and fire fighters and astronauts; and they want the other kids to look up to them.

What will you not hear out on the playground? You will not hear the kids assuming the role of a down-trodden welder who lost their job when the shipyard closed last year. Nor a laid-off factory worker, nor a down-sized office worker, nor an overworked and underpaid retail clerk. Not fun and not cool.

The mysterious process of selecting an occupation

WHAT KIND OF CAREERS young children dream about will depend a lot on the accident of their birth. A boy from the Dominican Republic may grow up with dreams of becoming a major league baseball player, but probably not an NHL hockey star. That's a trivial example, but we can think of another, just as telling, and more insidiously limiting: A young girl from a public housing high-rise may imagine herself growing up to be a hair stylist, but without any first-hand knowledge of adults who are executives in the business world, it's unlikely that she'll dream about growing up to become a bank president. And that's too bad because she would probably make an excellent bank president if given half the chance. But the types of jobs kids will initially role-play will be limited to those within the scope of their family's personal experience, and what they are exposed to on the school playground.

What role does gender play in all of this? While male and female genders occur quite naturally, society's concept of gender still needs to be learned. Children are taught that girls can grow up to be engineers and boys to be nurses, and that mothers can be the primary breadwinners and fathers the main homemakers. But kids take their cues from what they see, with girls watching their mothers and boys their fathers. Which will hold greater sway? What they hear or what they see?

As children grow older, they meet more kids and other families, and this broadens the scope of careers they can aim for. Likewise, through our culture (television, movies, books), children are exposed to an ever-growing selection of occupations. The possibilities of what a child can grow up to "be" should expand greatly as they get older.

Almost all this process, I believe, happens informally. There are guidance counselors in schools. But my sense is that their impact on a student's career selection is quite uneven. I believe the influence of family and classmates plays a bigger role.

When it comes to occupational options, there should be no limitations on what is possible. But we see, quickly, a sorting out of students by academic achievement level. Some will master reading, writing, and math skills with ease. Others will struggle. Those who struggle will respond in one of two ways. They'll push themselves even harder, attempting to keep up with their peers. Or they'll realize, with dejection, that some careers and some paths in life may not be an option for them.

This sorting-out occurs all through the school years, and is accelerated as a child moves from elementary school to middle school to high school. Once young adults reach college, the occupational choices still under consideration will influence greatly what classes they take. The course selection is designed to prepare students for anticipated jobs once they get out of school, or to get ready to enter grad school in a specific field.

But there are still many college students, as I can personally attest, who traipse blissfully through four years of liberal arts education without a clue what they want to do when they 'grow up'.

That's OK. There are now literally hundreds of potential careers to choose from. Almost 800 in fact. And if a person is curious enough, the U.S. Department of Labor tracks unique occupations – everything from Accountants to Zoologists.[20] DOL keeps a treasure trove of statistics on each occupation. How many are employed, where they are employed, who employs them, and average annual salaries. The DOL data is amazingly detailed and freely accessed. Just reading through the list should get one's imaginative juices flowing. Actuary? There's a career you can count on. Audiologist? I hear that's a good job. (feel free to groan)

The three largest categories in the 2019 DOL database are Retail sales person (4.4M), Fast food counter workers (4.0M) and Cashier (3.6M). Unfortunately, these occupations are on the low end of the scale for median annual wages: $27K, $24K and $25K respectively. Furthermore, the retail and fast food world is rife with bad jobs. Not only is the pay low relative to most other parts of our economy. The schedules of work are among the poorest and the least reliable. Lots of these businesses are open 24/7, and you often end up working evenings and weekends when everyone else is off the clock.

And if that weren't bad enough, you can't even depend on the lousy schedules that you get. You may be on the schedule to work the coming weekend, but you could get a call from your boss at the last minute telling you that they don't need you after all. (Hope you didn't have that planned-for paycheck spent quite yet.)

THE DEPARTMENT OF LABOR constantly updates the list of unique occupations it keeps tabs on. As new occupations are added, others are dropped, some very quickly. For instance, you won't find any Keypunchers on employment rolls today, while as recently as 1980 you could still find that position featured on workflow charts.

The DOL forecast for the largest single occupation in 2029 is home health and personal care aides, adding over 1 million jobs between 2019 and 2029. These are vital services, and the work is unlikely to be eliminated by automation. And although we have seen substantial growth in the salaries of these jobs in recent years, choosing this noble career still leaves one toward the bottom of the pay scale with a median annual wage of around $27K. More about the impact of this later.

A final word on when the process of choosing an occupation occurs. A couple generations ago, the expectation was that you would choose a job coming out of school and stick with that career throughout your working life. Now, that is quite rare. Workers can expect not only to change their place of employment, but to jump into entirely new career paths as they mature and enter different phases of life.

Types of work arrangements and connections between employer and employee

MOVING ON from how occupations are selected, I want to spend a moment now to discuss the various modes of employment, the ways in which one can be a participant in the workforce: as a slave, an indentured servant, an intern, an employee, an independent contractor, or as self-employed. (Volunteers do a ton of work for society, and they create great economic value for their organizations. But because they are not reimbursed for their efforts, and they do this work freely of their own accord, that "work" is not included in my analysis.)

At the very bottom of the employment pyramid we find slavery – an institution still accepted in certain backwater parts of the world. Slaves are literally owned by their employees. As such, they can be sold or traded like any other economic resource. Slaves have no say in the tasks they are asked to perform on the job. They cannot choose where they work, who they work for, or what they do. It is easy to see why those trapped in slavery will risk life and limb to escape.

Other than slaves, and their economic cousins indentured servants, most of us in the workforce are there by choice. We are employees, and we come in dozens of flavors: hourly and salaried; tipped and non-tipped; permanent, seasonal, and temporary; fulltime and part time; with full benefits and no benefits; those with and without profit sharing or employee stock purchase plans. Employers design compensation packages to attract and retain good employees and to reward them for their service to the company. It is pretty much a cold economic transaction – my labor in exchange for your compensation. It wasn't always so.

Benjamin Disraeli wrote a fine novel about England during the industrial revolution. In his book *Sybil, or The Two Nations,* we read about Mr. Trafford, an enlightened factory owner

> *With gentle blood in his veins, and old English feelings, he imbibed, at an early period of his career, a correct conception of the relations which should subsist between the employer and the employed. He felt that between them there should be other ties than the payment and the receipt of wages.*

Trafford established housing for the workers where they could live for a reasonable fee, and his own home was right in the middle of the village:

> *And what was the influence of such an employer and such a system of employment on the morals and manners of the employed? Great: infinitely beneficial. The connexion of a labourer with his place of work, whether agricultural or manufacturing, is itself a vast advantage. Proximity to the employer brings cleanliness and order, because it brings observation and encouragement.* [21]

But lest we think the situation in England in 1837 idyllic,

Disraeli makes this observation on the open design of Trafford's factory:

> *the child works under the eye of the parent, the parent under that of the superior workman; the inspector or employer at a glance can behold all.*

(It is the *child works* part caught my eye. In the modern world, we do not allow children in the workforce anymore. No moral ambiguity about that in my mind. But we should acknowledge, this is a relatively recent development.)

Disraeli's intimate, paternal relationship between employer and employee is a far cry from that between employer and employee today. Indeed, companies are apt to hire workers on "alternative work arrangements" nowadays rather than as employees with a full suite of benefits. In a column by Robert Samuelson, we learn that these include workers in four categories:

1. *Independent contractors and freelancers, usually self-employed, from writers to software engineers*
2. *On-call workers who have designated days when they may (or may not) be summoned on the job—a practice common in fast food*
3. *Workers from temporary work agencies*
4. *Workers provided by contract firms—cafeteria and security services being examples.*[22]

These "alternative" workers are a rapidly growing segment of the workforce, from 10.7% of all jobs in 2005 to 15.8% in 2015. Roughly one out of six new hires at that time. Probably much more now. Other than the first category of independent contractors, it seems unlikely that many of the other workers are intentionally choosing those routes. More likely, these are workers that large and small companies can hire and fire on a whim, and to whom they don't have to pay benefits.

Again, this is a cold, hard economic calculation. Nothing paternalistic about these arrangements.

Self-employed is a unique employment status. Being both boss and underling, employer and employee, one hopes to be truly in charge of their own destiny. Many of the self-employed who become successful drive themselves relentlessly, and like authors and artists, they can be their own worst critics.

But this book is not about or for the self-employed. This book is about employees, and interns, and those four categories of alternative workers listed above. The book focuses on the quality of these jobs, on the number of hours of labor these workers put in, and the compensation they receive for their efforts.

Specialization

WE SPECULATED in the last chapter about skilled toolmakers being asked to stay back from hunting expeditions so they could make more arrowheads for the hunting parties to use. To allow them to spend more time on their stonework would benefit the whole tribe.

Moving forward to modern times and to DOL's list of 800 careers to choose from; theoretically, as an individual's job description becomes more and more specialized, the organization that employs that worker makes more efficient use of their unique talents and capabilities. By extension, the larger economy and the entire community benefit as well.

But a high degree of specialization can also result in certain pitfalls. An individual's job may become so narrow, so focused on minutia, that it becomes hard to keep the big picture in mind. The worker may find themselves wondering: *Why does all this even matter?*

Employees who have a broader range of job responsibilities, those who *wear many hats* at work, are in a naturally better position to keep the overall mission of the organization in mind, and of finding their job to be meaningful. This is easy to see in a high-tech start-up where a handful of brilliant engineers may put in 60 – 80-hour workweeks creating a new product. Early on, all are gung-ho. But as the start-up morphs into a successful, mature company, the engineers' individual jobs probably become much more defined, more constrained; and unfortunately for some, less personally meaningful. Yet, that 60 – 80-hour workweek mentality persists.

Small jobs

BEING A TINY COG in a giant machine is one form of specialization, I guess, but not one most workers strive for. Before the advent of the industrial revolution, things were made by hand by craftspersons. The shoemaker started with a piece of tanned leather. They cut and stretched and shaped and sewed, until they ended up with a pair of shoes. That had to be a quite satisfying as a vocation.

With the industrial revolution, we started to make things with machines, in large factories, with lots of workers. Human labor became an extension of machine power. Men, women, and children were employed to load and unload machines. Keeping up with the pace of the machine was their only task. A lot of us would find these factory jobs mind-numbingly boring:

1. *Grab part from bin and place in the machine.*
2. *Push button.*
3. *Pull finished part from machine and place in another bin.*
4. *Repeat.*

Karl Marx referred to this as the *immiseration* of factory workers stuck on the same task day in and day out.

Frederick Taylor reduced the study of these simple tasks to a science, with the output of the worker scrutinized the same way as the powered equipment. With this kind of knowledge, manufacturers were able to design assembly lines – complex "machines" that employed whole line-ups of workers on narrow, repetitive jobs.

The immiseration of factory workers has been covered by several authors. Richard Donkin tells us about one of the characters in Studs Terkel's great book *Working* who put the workers' condition like this:

> *Most of us, like the assembly line worker, have jobs that are too small for our spirit. Jobs are not big enough for people.*"[23]

Jobs that are too small seem all too commonplace in the economy today. Chris Farrell found another way this can be expressed in his book *Unretirement* with this wonderful quote from H. L. Mencken:

> *If he got no reward whatsoever, the artist would go on working just the same; his actual reward, in fact, is often so little that he almost starves. But suppose a garment worker got nothing for his labor: would he go on working just the same? Can one imagine his submitting voluntarily to hardship and sore that he might express his soul in 200 more pairs of ladies pants?* [24]

Farrell is not dismissing the importance of work – just small jobs. In a column for the NY Times[25], he writes that working longer can result in better health outcomes. He's not talking about working longer hours each day, but longer into life, into what had previously been thought of as retirement years. Keeping the body and brain active is good for us, of course. More important are the benefits of continued social interactions – with your boss, co-workers, suppliers, and customers. But these 'soft' benefits from working are not automatically present. Smaller jobs (those without cognitive challenge and with fewer positive human interactions), will be much less beneficial to our mental health.

Eliminating *cog-in-the-machinery* jobs wherever possible will be good for the human spirit. One hundred years after Frederick Taylor's "scientific management" and Henry Ford's assembly line, the factory worker is no longer just a well-oiled piece of machinery. He is now CNC literate, studies 6-sigma quality methods, and squeezes every last pound of productivity out of every ounce of input. The factory worker, much like the shoemaker before the industrial revolution, once again has a meaningful job. That's the good news. The bad news is that while it used to take hundreds of workers to keep a factory running, it now takes just a handful.

A lot of those factory jobs have shifted to the retail sector. That's the focus in Zeynep Ton's book *The Good Jobs Strategy*[26]. She divides the retail world, rather definitively, into two parts: companies who pursue a *good jobs strategy,* and companies who follow a *bad jobs strategy*. Companies in the first group understand that their employees are valuable partners who need and deserve good jobs. Those in the second think of employees only in terms of their cost to the operation, and the less attention spent on them, the better.

One of the most egregious sins of companies in the *bad jobs* camp is their cavalier attitude about employees' work schedules. Amy Lindgren, with the St. Paul Pioneer Press, covered this ground beautifully in a heartfelt column on the importance of reliable work schedules.[27] Lindgren asks: without knowing when we are supposed to be working, how can anyone live their lives? Specifically, how can anyone schedule activities that have a chance of improving their economic status? Activities that are especially important to low-income workers – like going to school, looking for a better job, or holding down a second job? A schedule that bounces around from week-to-week, or worse yet, a requirement to be available on-call just in case you are needed to work, make it extremely difficult for the working poor. Lindgren wraps up the column by saying:

No one can climb a career ladder when someone keeps moving the base around.

--Amy Lindgren

Career advancement

IF WE WORK in a large company, the position we hold within the organizational hierarchy carries a lot of weight: supervisor—manager—director—president—CEO. Each of these titles represents a succession of greater responsibility and authority; each step with a larger paycheck and higher level of prestige. When it comes to climbing corporate ladders, how high is high enough? It's a very personal thing, but for some ambitious individuals there is no such thing as "high enough". Ayn Rand put it this way:

> *Man's ego is the fountainhead of human progress.*
>
> *--Ayn Rand*

Climbing up the employment ladder is important for all of us as we enter the workforce – for financial reasons, and for the honor and prestige associated with our job title. In extreme cases, career advancement itself becomes the raison d'être for the ambitious worker. (*Think about that a minute. That worker is not interested in the mission of the organization except insofar as it benefits him personally. He's driven by his personal career advancement.*) We may personally feel that we are above that sort of single-minded ambition, but it does explain how climbing the corporate ladder has become competitive sport.

An entry-level employee may be pretty satisfied with their brand new job. But if they find themselves in the same position some years down the road, their level of satisfaction will drop off substantially. On the other hand, if they make some progress advancing within the organization, and at least keep up with their peers, they will most likely be satisfied with their careers.

Like many things in life, your perception of a successful career is relative. It will depend on your personal expectations and those of your immediate circle of friends and family. If you hope that somewhere down the road you make the rank of foreman, and one day you achieve that goal, you will call that a successful career. But if you are convinced that nothing short of plant superintendent is acceptable, achieving the rank of foreman after a long, dedicated career just won't cut it.

IT USED TO BE that young adults would start out at "the plant" or "the firm" shortly after completing high school or college. It was expected that they would work hard, play by the rules, and climb the corporate ladder rung-by-rung, all the way up to the point where the Peter Principle kicked in. If a person didn't play by the rules and tried to skip a rung or two, he'd probably be labeled "*not a team player*" and get knocked down a peg or two. If a person didn't exhibit the proper amount of drive, he'd be marked "*lacks ambition*", an even more damning status.

Nowadays, careers are not nearly so linear. First, we seldom see anyone staying with a single company throughout their working lives. Second, career moves can be up, down, sideways. This is now commonplace, and there is no longer the same stigma associated with a "step down".

Not just our ego is at stake when it comes to career advancement. The size of our paycheck is directly impacted by how far we advance within our field of work. In an ideal world, our paycheck should be a direct reflection of our value to the company. As everyone knows, we do not live in an ideal world. In later chapters, I address what I believe are inequities in the way workers are compensated.

Meaningful jobs

MEANINGFUL JOBS AND GOOD BOSSES go hand-in-hand. The easiest way to see this is in the position of domestic servant. In these one-on-one employment arrangements, you might, if you are lucky, find yourself with a boss you'd be willing to give your life for. Or if you are not so lucky, you may have a boss you feel like strangling several times a day. In a love-hate employment relationship, this may be the same guy. Your job as their servant certainly has meaning in either event.

Most of us are not in one-on-one employment situations like this. We work for companies that employ tens, hundreds, even thousands of workers; all engaged to make the products and provide the services that the company offers. If we know what the company does, and why – if we understand the overall mission of the organization we work for and find that to be in sync with our personal beliefs – it will be much easier to feel that our jobs are meaningful. If not, the job is just a source of income, perhaps one we are dispassionate about, perhaps one we hate. And like being stuck in a job with a boss we don't relate to, this is bound to cause some personal discord.

It is the responsibility of everyone in a supervisory position to do more than just show how the work is to be done. It is every supervisor's responsibility to explain why the work is being done, to make sure every worker knows the mission of the company, and how, in a larger sense, the organization contributes to the welfare of the community. Without this knowledge, there is a danger that we find our jobs to be unimportant except for the paycheck, and not worthy of our sincerest efforts.

Given a company that provides goods and services useful to society, we then look for these attributes of a meaningful job (from Hackman and Oldham): *1) the chance to use a variety of skills, 2) the chance to see the job through from beginning to end, and 3) the chance to do something that makes a difference.*[28]

Let's go back to the pre-industrial revolution shoemaker again. He employs a number of skills in his craft and transforms a shapeless piece of leather into a pair of shoes – a very important pair of shoes indeed for whoever the lucky customer is. Compare that with performing a single task on a long assembly line.

I am not a Luddite. I don't believe we should go back to making shoes by hand, except perhaps as a wonderful craft. But that is not how to make sure all seven billion of us have access to an affordable pair of shoes. And building machines to manufacture our shoes and shirts and trousers doesn't mean we can't find some way for all of us to be engaged in meaningful work.

Cleaning an office building can be meaningful work if you have the right attitude, the right boss, and you work in the right environment. Dan Teran, the chief executive of a cleaning service company called *Managed by Q*[29], may be the right boss. Teran, with a tip of his hat to Zeynep Ton's 'good jobs strategy', pays his cleaners more than the prevailing wage. He knows happy employees make a better workforce. While *Managed by Q* is primarily a building cleaning service, they offer other, higher value-added services too. Teran knows that his cleaners are the ones in contact with his customers, becoming, in effect, everyday sales reps for his firm. The other contracts they win (for cleaning supplies, for pest extermination, for furniture moving and assembly) more than pay for the higher wages he pays the cleaners.

Teran believes

> *that decades of rising inequality and stagnant wages in America are not an inevitable byproduct of capitalism; instead, they come from a simple misunderstanding about how to best deploy workers and recognize the value they bring to the company.*[30]

Good bosses and bad bosses can make all the difference. A good supervisor can make any job feel worthwhile, be it working on an assembly line, at a retail checkout counter, or cleaning offices.

To summarize, we find this very succinct definition of *meaningful work* from Barry Schwartz in a column in the NY Times:

Of course, we care about our wages, and we wouldn't work without them. But we care about more than money. We want work that is challenging and engaging, that enables us to exercise some discretion and control over what we do, and that provides us opportunities to learn and grow. We want to work with colleagues who we respect and with supervisors who respect us. Most of all, we want work that is meaningful – that makes a difference to other people and thus ennobles us in at least some small way.[31]

Unemployment

IT IS PRECISELY the ennobling aspect of work that makes the status of unemployment so devastating. Wherever we find ourselves in our work careers, relatively high up on the totem pole or down at ground level, just having a job is critical to our well-being.

Buckminster Fuller had other ideas about this. In an interview back in 1970, he said:

We should do away with the absolutely specious notion that everybody has to earn a living. It is a fact today that one in ten thousand of us can make a technological breakthrough capable of supporting all the rest. The youth of today are absolutely right in recognizing this nonsense of earning a living. We keep inventing jobs because of this false idea that everybody has to be employed at some kind of drudgery because, according to Malthusian Darwinian theory, he must justify his right to exist. So we have inspectors of inspectors and people making instruments for inspectors to inspect inspectors. The true business of people should be to go back to school and think about whatever it was they were thinking about before someone came along and told them they had to earn a living.[32]

Fuller was on the right track, but I think he was missing some of the fundamental reasons why we all feel the need to work. We work for more than Darwinian *red in tooth and claw* reasons of survival. We are, after all, *partly saint*, and we actually <u>do</u> feel the need to justify our right to exist. There are social reasons why we feel the need to work. (See E. O. Wilson)

Ironic as it sounds, it is exactly because work is so important in our culture that we should all work a little less. This gives everyone a better chance to avoid unemployment and keep a paid position during down-turns in the economy, during labor markets thick and thin.

Economists tell us that bouts of high unemployment hit some classes of workers much harder than others. Younger workers suffer more than older. Less-educated more than those with more education. Blacks and Hispanics more than whites. And some industries are hit harder than others (for example, construction workers are typically laid off more than government workers). Until recently, women were hit with more unemployment than men, although that has reversed itself in the last few decades

Unemployment is not an equal-opportunity employer.

--George Borjas

George Borjas, in his textbook *Labor Economics*, classifies unemployment by types:

- **Frictional**. The natural result of the labor market being in a constant state of flux. There's always some delay when a worker leaves one job (whether voluntarily or not) and signs up for another.
- **Seasonal**. Agricultural unemployment an easy example. Retail unemployment following the Christmas shopping season another.
- **Cyclical**. An imbalance in the number of workers and the amount of work available as we enter a recession.
- **Structural**. As automation eliminates whole classes of jobs, and as old industries fade away, there is a surplus of workers in certain fields and a mismatch between the skills that workers bring to the table and the skills employers are looking for.[33] (This type of unemployment is most pernicious, and is covered in some depth in Chapter 4.)

Unemployment benefits from the government do help alleviate the financial burden of the being laid off, but they do not remove the stigma associated with unemployment. We are social animals, and we feel we need to work, to be contributing members of society. To be unemployed is embarrassing because we are taking from society, not giving.

If a worker is downsized from a large corporation, he is not normally dumped immediately out on the street. He'll be placed on the surplus list and given some time (up to 6 months) to find a new position, either within the company or out. But as anyone who has been in that situation can attest, that is just about the worst job in the world! And ironically, this is a case where being on the high end of the corporate ladder may be a disadvantage. The pool of jobs that are available to an unemployed executive shrinks rapidly as one moves from the manager level to director to VP.

When unemployment is widespread, the whole community

suffers. Indeed, we've seen communities small and large die for lack of work. Small towns in rural America dried up and blew away during the farm crisis. Entire neighborhoods in big cities did the same as large factories shut down and all the jobs were lost.

Work is critical to our financial and emotional wellbeing. When we encounter systemic unemployment, it is damaging to both individual and communal psyche. Bill and Melinda Gates understand the importance of work, and they place it front-and-center of the activities of their Foundation with the tagline:

Giving all of us the chance to live happy and productive lives.

The implication is that being productive and being happy go hand-in-hand.

Work for people with disabilities

I WAS ABLE TO SEE REAL WORLD EVIDENCE of the importance of work while employed at Merrick, Inc., a nonprofit social services and vocational program in Vadnais Heights, MN. Merrick serves adults with intellectual/developmental disabilities, all of whom were eligible for monthly Social Security disability payments, and none of whom had to work. Yet, the opportunity to work was exactly what they wanted from our company. Our clients watched as family members and friends went to work every day, and they observed their co-workers at Merrick on the job. They understood, intuitively, that it is through paid employment that we become members of the community in good standing.

To fail on a job is not the same thing as failing to be a good worker. This is especially true when it comes to finding the right job for an adult with a disability. Merrick provides vocational services for adults with diagnoses ranging from moderate to profound.

Although cognitively disabled, many of the individuals we served understood the importance of working and earning a paycheck. Many had a very solid grasp on the fundamental constructs of what we find important in life – spirituality, friendship, community, and service; and they intuitively understood that by working and earning a paycheck, they were participating fully and being contributing members of society.

Working in this field, I learned that there are not disabled adults, there are adults with disabilities. It is a subtle, but important, difference. We are all human beings, first and foremost. No one is fully disabled. Conversely, no one is fully able-bodied and able-minded. This is not a binary system, and all of us have disabilities in one manner or another.

If you are an older person (as I am), your sense of hearing and of sight may not be as acute as they once were. These have no impact when you are reading a book (with large print) or watching TV (with the sound turned up.) These may have an adverse impact, however, if you are employed in a retail setting and there is a customer waving and calling and unable to get your attention. That customer may assume that you are rude and uncaring. It wouldn't occur to them that you just didn't see or hear. As a clerk in a store, you are not *disabled* – you can still see and hear well enough to do the job – just not as well as you once could.

A person with autism may have excellent vision and hearing, but may be unable to comfortably make eye contact. Will they do well in the retail setting where customers will be calling on them for help? Perhaps, but there's a good chance they'll really have to work at it.

The clients we served at Merrick were evaluated on a regular basis in a number of areas – physical skills (strength, manual dexterity), cognitive skills (ability to process information, acquire knowledge, solve problems), and social skills (social perceptiveness, ability to interact with others). They were encouraged to work on any shortcomings that they perceived as hindrances to their own personal development.

Many of our clients worked out in the community, both individually and on work crews. They held retail and restaurant jobs, worked on cleaning crews, and performed clerical work. Many others worked at our facility in areas specifically set up to facilitate production work and social interactions – both client-to-client and client-to-staff. Most of the work performed in our building was light assembly and packaging jobs, shredding documents, and recycling; all jobs performed under contracts for third parties. We also hired our own clients for janitorial work and van washing. The whole idea was to find or create jobs that the clients could do, and wanted to do.

Most of the work was manual, but even the most fundamental steps require some cognitive processing. Each job was broken into discreet steps in a process called *task analysis*. Here's an example of a simple kitting job:

1. place label on a zip-lock bag
2. count out ten items
3. pour into the bag and zip the bag closed
4. weigh the bag to insure the right count
5. place completed kits in box
6. weigh box to insure the right count
7. tape the box closed and label

(*Taylorism on steroids.*)

A job like this could be accomplished by a client or two. But we would often assign this work to a team of eight clients plus a job coach, with the clients selected for specific tasks based on their skill sets and abilities. The whole idea was to create meaningful work for as many people as possible.

Some say it is hard to have a great life unless it is a meaningful life, and difficult to have a meaningful life without meaningful work.

--John Wayne Barker, Executive Director at Merrick

Once again, none of our clients at Merrick really had to work. They either lived with their families or in group homes. Food, clothing, and shelter were provided. They worked because they wanted their own spending money, and when payday rolled around every two weeks, it was A REALLY BIG DEAL!

A lot of the clients took great pride in showing off their paychecks. And there was more to it than the numbers on the check and the buying power that represented. They took pride in *earning* that paycheck through their efforts at work.

Work for people who are economically disadvantaged
IN THE BOOK *Scarcity, Why Having Too Little Matters So Much*, Sendhil Mullainathan and Eldar Shafir present an insightful study on the way we behave during periods of scarcity. Much of their book is focused on a scarcity of income – having too little money to meet the basic needs of a household. Many of us are quick to assume that those living in poverty *are poor precisely because they are less capable*. The authors counter that just the opposite may be true:

Our data suggest causality runs at least as strongly in the other direction: that poverty—the scarcity mindset—causes failure.[34]

Those living in poverty cannot help but be obsessed with their dire financial situation. In that state of mind, they have difficulty maintaining attention on other things that directly impact their family's lives: being fully engaged at work, ensuring the kids are behaving and learning in school, making sure doctor's appointments are kept, etc.

Another way to think about this is through the lens of Maslow's 5-level hierarchy of human needs. Maslow maintained that we need to satisfy lower-level needs before we can think about tackling those above. Those living in poverty are struggling with food-clothing-shelter issues. With that mindset, it's hard to focus on anything higher on the pyramid, including safety issues, which could certainly have an adverse impact on their duties at work. Given this, is it any wonder that very poor individuals have a hard time being effective employees?

Employers are not parents. We no longer expect the sort of paternalistic relations Disraeli referred to in Trafford's factory town. But it certainly wouldn't hurt employers to be aware of their employees' mindset when they come to work in the morning. What employers surely <u>should</u> do is pay their employees enough to lift them out of poverty! They may find, to their delight, that they have a much stronger workforce than they first assumed.

Part time work for students

BY THE TIME children reach high school, a lot of them get the *opportunity* to work part time and earn a little of their own money. This is a good thing, an important part of their education. First, they will learn quite quickly that the *fun* part of working that they all imagined as kindergarteners may have been overestimated just a bit. In a delightful column titled *Take it from teacher: Johnny needs a job*, Gina Barreca spells out how having a real job can make young adults better students. Whether baby-sitting, mowing grass, or shoveling snow for another family (not at home – not a chore), working food service, retail, warehouse, movie theatre; any paid employment; all these can help make better students. How so?

> They'll wake up at a scheduled time and get their acts together in order to show up for work before their shift begins while wearing neither clothes nor an expression that looks as if it just emerged from a laundry basket.

> They'll learn that they are not the only important people in the room and that the world isn't intrigued by their drama. They'll learn cooperation, teamwork, time management and what it's like to fall asleep as soon as their head hits the pillow at the end of a long day.

> Young people who have held jobs are better students because they know they can't do everything at the last minute, all at once or erratically.

> They should get a grip on taxes and Social Security, open a checking account in their own name and have a certain amount of autonomy over spending what they earn. They will then learn what things cost by purchasing them with their own dough. [35]

All of these traits make better students. They also make better citizens.

Special minimum wage

THE DEPARTMENT OF LABOR allows companies to pay adults with disabilities special minimum wages which are lower than the standard minimum wage. The policy is tightly regulated by DOL, with the special wage based on the productivity of a disabled person compared to that of a "qualified, experienced worker" taking normal breaks and fatigue factors into account.

The justification for this policy is that many adults with disabilities are unable to produce work at the same pace as able-bodied workers, and paying them proportionately lower wages is fair for both parties. The policy is meant both to encourage companies to hire adults with disabilities in spite of their lower productivity rates, and to give those adults a chance to work and to feel the pride of earning a paycheck.

The special minimum wage, which at first blush seems heartless, is actually a pretty good policy. Without it, many adults with disabilities would not be able to find any work at all. The rationale for special minimum wages could apply to students with part time jobs. Many students, in their own way, have a disability when it comes to work. It's called being a teenager! When they go in to work and are assigned a task, that task may not command the center of their attention. They have other, more important things to deal with.

I'm not being sarcastic here. Teenagers really do have more important things to deal with than working. There is school – academics, art, music, and athletics. And there's that raging-hormone thing – sorting out "more than just friends" relationships, sexual identities, family and community responsibilities, and generational roles. How to be a good worker fits in there somewhere, but it's not front-of-mind for most teenagers. But as Ms. Barreca tells us, *Johnny needs a job*, so allowing companies to pay special minimum wages to students will give employers the incentive for doing so.

Some of the arguments against raising the minimum wage zero in on high school students holding down part time jobs. The argument goes like this: 1) they're not worth it – they don't work as hard as my older employees, they're just not as conscientious, and 2) they don't need it – they come from middle class families and they have part time jobs just for the spending money, not to support a family. Whether or not these have any validity, if we take these arguments away from opponents of higher wages for workers, it may make it easier for those employers to accept higher pay for adults who are responsible for supporting themselves and trying to raise a family.

Perhaps the easiest way to do this would be to have a two-tiered minimum wage – with a lower tier that applies to those under 19 years of age, and the higher standard minimum wage that applies to those 19 and older. The rationale for doing this is to encourage companies to hire younger workers on a part time basis. And the justification is because we want student/workers to be students <u>first</u>. The lessons they are learning on the job are an extension of those being learned in school.

The importance of work

THE FIRST LESSON learned is that work is important. Work is what we do to earn a paycheck – our labor in exchange for compensation. We learn that the labor market is the mechanism humans have invented to ensure that work gets done, that we survive individually, and thrive as a species.

As Jonathon Malesic put it in a 2021 New York Times column:

> As it is, work sits at the heart of Americans' vision of human flourishing. It's much more than how we earn a living. It's how we earn dignity: the right to count in society and enjoy its benefits. It's how we prove our moral character. And it's where we seek meaning and purpose, which many of us interpret in spiritual terms.[36]

Work is important to all of us, both socially and economically. Reading from Ryan Avent's *The Wealth of Humans, Work, Power, and Status in the Twenty-first Century*:

> Most of us now of working age ... inherited an idea of work ... as a positive good: economically necessary and morally beneficial. When work works, we understood, it provides a basis for a stable social order. It gives people something to do. It gives workers the sense that they are contributing to society and to the welfare of their families.[37]

In Richard Florida's book *The Rise of the Creative Class*[38], he breaks the labor force into three classes: the Creative Class, the Working Class, and the Service Class. The creative class are those individuals fortune has smiled on. Through their talent, their intelligence, their hard work, and of course through their family connections, they have good jobs, are performing meaningful work, and have handsome compensation packages. These are, for the most part, upper and upper-middle income class families. The creative class is on the rise (33% the workforce now, just 14% 80 years ago), good news because all of us should aspire to reach this status. Mr. Florida's working class (largely factory and construction workers) is shrinking (23% now, down from 54% in 1930), and that's too bad for us economically because these were well-paid jobs. Florida's service class is growing rapidly (46% now, up from 30% in 1930), and is taking up some of the slack from the working class. This is a mixed bag of good and bad economic news. Some of these jobs are very well-paid, but for many, Florida writes

> *At its minimum-wage worst, life in the Service Class is a grueling struggle for subsistence amid the wealth of others.*

David Brooks has some fun with the creative class in a book called *Bobos in Paradise*[39]. Bobos being short for bourgeois and bohemian. It used to be that a bourgeoisie businessman in a gray flannel suit was a distinctly different character from a bohemian artist. Brooks contends that they have much more in common than they'd like to admit.

Authors Barbara Ehrenreich and David Shipler look at life at the other end of the workforce spectrum, Ehrenreich with *Nickel and Dimed*[40] and Shipler with *The Working Poor*[41] Working for short stints in service sector jobs herself, Ehrenreich introduces us to several of her co-workers. They are subjected to irregular hours, shitty bosses, and tiny paychecks. They cannot work their way up the economic ladder, not because they don't have the talent, but because they are stuck in impossible predicaments, at work and at home, that keep them locked in the lower class. Shipler interviewed dozens of low-income workers from coast to coast, some over the course of five or six years. This allowed him to compare their lives during periods of economic boom and bust, and see that either way, many are trapped in their condition of poverty.

But I don't mean to dwell on class warfare at this point of the book. (I'll save that for a little later in the book.) What I want to stress here is that work is important to all of us: whether members of the *Creative Class* or *Bobos in Paradise*, or working stiffs from *Nickel and Dimed* and from the pages of Studs Terkel's *Working*. Work is as important to me as to my neighbor, and as important to a baker in Boston as to one in Bangalore. It is universally true – work is important to all of us. So much so, that the work we do becomes a part of our very identity.

I talked a lot about the in-service aspect of work in the first chapter. That virtue was not lost with the advent of working to create personal wealth. We see workers in every sector of the economy who earn relatively modest wages but experience great satisfaction on the job. They obviously find their work meaningful and fulfilling, modest paychecks notwithstanding.

So, we should all work less! That way there will be enough work to go around for all of us to share. The joy that many experience at work will not diminish when the workweek has shrunk from five days to four. Quite the contrary. Understanding that work is as precious to my neighbor as it is to me will make it easier to share the number of hours of paid work hours available to all of us.

But we seem to have a problem with sharing, a topic we'll cover in the next chapter.

CHAPTER 3

The Insatiable Drive for Wealth

THE LAST CHAPTER dealt with the "*part saint*" aspects of human nature. This chapter focuses on our "*part sinner*" inner self and attempts to explain why we are still working 40 hours a week instead of closing in on the 15-hour a workweek John Maynard Keynes predicted. In the last chapter, we learned that our very identity is tied to our careers, that *we are what we do*. In this chapter, we'll see how our identity is also closely tied to material measures of wealth, that *we are what we own*.

First, a little background. Contrary to popular belief, consumerism was not an invention of Madison Avenue. (They just perfected the art by applying scientific measurement principals to the efficacy of advertising and other promotional campaigns.) Most likely, the psychological drive to 'keep up with the Joneses' predates even the agrarian age. We can imagine hunter/gatherer clans comparing their shiny baubles with those of neighboring clans. When they saw something they liked, you can bet they had to have it. And have it they would – either by force (when at war and raiding enemy camps), or by trade (during peaceful periods).

Indeed, it was probably material objects that one group had and the other wanted that precipitated many of the interactions between one tribe and another in the first place. The two opposing tribes had to figure out if they were better off when these interactions were the result of peaceful trade, or the spoils of belligerent acts of war.

War or peace, it would have been hard for any of these tribes to possess a lot of material things because they were nomadic people. Certain tools and shelters were surely carried from one campsite to the next – much easier to do that than to start off from scratch. And those nomadic clans would also have carried along some objects that seemingly had no utilitarian value, *baubles unnecessary for anything other than prestige.* (Madonna, our favorite *Material Girl,* has had kindred sisters for a long, long time.)

About 12,000 years ago, when we advanced from the hunter/gatherer stage to the age of agriculture, we moved from a nomadic lifestyle to living in permanent settlements. At that point, the opportunity to "own" things really kicked into gear because now we didn't have to lug everything along on our nomadic journeys. With portability constraints on possessions removed, consumers could now amass a greater number of things and a much higher volume of man-made goods. The level of consumption of material goods became an increasingly important factor in the economies of communities.

Let's imagine a scenario in 10,000 BC where our family became very good over time at gathering firewood – specializing in cutting, drying and bundling the firewood into neat transportable packets. Meanwhile, our friendly neighbors became very good at raising pigs. We would make excess bundles of firewood with the intention of supplying them to our neighbor in exchange for some of their piglets. We would count on our neighbor to supply us with pigs because they needed our firewood, and vice versa. Without our supply of firewood their supply of pigs, they'd often be cold, and we'd often be hungry.

If trade were limited to our two households, it's unlikely that we'd ever produce more firewood than that needed by our little enclave of two families. But at some point, our two families started to bring firewood and piglets into the market in town. We then spent even more time in the woods, at <u>work</u>, so we'd have more bundles of wood available to bring to the market for trade. At the same time, our neighbors worked even harder to raise more pigs. The surplus food and fuel we created could be used to trade for a variety of provisions that could be found in town, a vastly greater variety than the two commodities we had been limited to. At that point, the market economy was born, with Consumers of goods just as critical to the whole process as the Producers.

Market induced greed

WHEN OUR FAMILY and the neighbors showed up at the market with our firewood and our piglets, we'd find more families and a host of other products available for barter: food, clothing, tools, cooking utensils. (No Pet Rocks yet.) All the traders wanted a piece of the action, and there certainly would have been stiff competition between the different vendors, with the winners being those who could structure the best deals and get the best value in exchange for their own product and service offerings.

Eventually, money came along as a handy way to keep track of transactions, and the market now had a convenient way of keeping score. Money also eliminated the physical limitations of the accumulating wealth. (Back when the unit of exchange was a bag of wheat, there was only so much one could accumulate before the oldest grain began to rot away.)

With the physical and temporal constraints removed, is it possible that these earliest market traders were just as guilty of greed and avarice as we are today? Did the firewood bundler spend hours in the woods that should have been spent back home with the wife and kids? Did the pig farmer raise so many animals their whole farm reeked? In an obsessive drive to obtain more wealth, is it also possible that our two families were never entirely satisfied with the things they've acquired from the market?

Each subsequent generation of these prehistoric traders would probably be better off materially than the last. Would they be happier? Maybe. Maybe not. All of that is just conjecture of course, since we have nothing written down.

Once we did start writing things down, we find plenty of evidence that wealth alone does not equal happiness.

Browsing on the internet, I was able to find these quotes on the impact of greed and avarice going all the way back to classical times:

- *He who is not contented with what he has would not be contented with what he would like to have.* Socrates[1]
- *An object in possession seldom retains the charm it held in pursuit.* Pliny the Elder[1]
- *Some men make fortunes not to enjoy them; for, blinded by avarice, they live to make fortunes.* Juvenal[2]

Leaping way ahead to 19th century Europe and America:

- *Most men pursue pleasure with such haste that they hurry past it.* Kiekegaard[1]
- *It is the preoccupation with possessions, more than anything else, that prevents us from living freely and nobly.* Thoreau[1]

- *It is one of the worst effects of prosperity to make a man a vortex instead of a fountain; so that, instead of throwing out, he learns only to draw in.* Henry Ward Beecher[2]
- *Possessions are usually diminished by possession.* Nietzche[1]
- *Man is the only animal whose desires increase as they are fed; the only animal that is never satisfied.* Henry George

And finally, to today:

- *Traditionally, too much wealth, too much materialism, was understood to impede human progress, leading to greed and envy (twin sins that feed on each other), luxury, indolence, and the slavery of selfishness.* Benjamin Hunnicutt
- *Money alone cannot buy pleasure, though it can help. For enjoyment is an art and a skill for which we have little talent or energy.* Alan Watts
- *Don't get so busy making a living that you forget to make a life.* Dolly Parton
- *I'd even bitch if I was getting hung with a gold rope.* Susan Barghini
- *I will never be satisfied with my collection of quotes on greed.* John Crea

[1]www.tentmaker.org/quotes.greedquotes.html
[2]www.bartelby.com/348/114.html

Henry David Thoreau was acutely aware of this phenomenon, and lived his life accordingly. In 1854, he gives us this observation in *Walden, or, Life in the Woods*:

> *But men labor under a mistake. The better part of the man is soon plowed into the soil for compost. By a seeming fate,*

*commonly called necessity, they are employed, as it says in
the old book, laying up treasures that moth and rust will
corrupt and thieves will break through and steal. It is a fool's
life, as they will find when they get to the end of it, if not
before.*[42]

One hundred sixty years after Thoreau penned that dreary
passage, John Cleese, one of the creative, comic geniuses behind
Monty Python's Flying Circus, is quoted in a column by Lee Schafer
in the StarTribune:

*(Cleese) explained that he was currently puzzling over
what to make of another serious subject, of why already
wealthy people seem grimly determined to accumulate a lot
more money. "I'd love to do a TV series on that," he said.
"I would love to talk to such people and say 'Why do you
need so much money?' And why do people say it is so
admirable? I think the world has gone quite mad."*[43]

I believe Mr. Cleese is quite right. But let me play devil's
advocate here: The corrupting nature of greed notwithstanding,
there is no denying the overall benefit to mankind of commercial
markets driven by the profit motive. Consider indices of immutable
progress: lower infant mortality rates, longer life expectancies,
greater creature comforts, and the evolution of social institutions.
We are all immeasurably healthier and wealthier than we were
generations ago. It is the interactions of buyers and sellers in open
markets, *competitive capitalism*, that can take a fair amount of credit
for this progress. That said, those interactions have now become
cold and calculated economic exchanges.

The lost connection between producers and consumers

WE ARE SOCIAL ANIMALS. Our hunter/gatherer ancestors had clear knowledge about which members of the clan were most productive: who were the bravest hunters, who were most clever at gathering nuts, who made the best stone tools. Throughout most of the agricultural era, everyone in town knew the firewood bundler and the pig farmer. Moving ahead to the middle ages, when you bought a pair of shoes, you weren't just buying a pair of fine leather brogans; you were buying the efforts and artistry of the cobbler. For the great majority of *Homo sapiens'* 200,000-year tenure here on earth, there was a very personal connection between producers and consumers of goods.

> *The invisible hand of the market was quite visible when all the buyers and sellers of goods knew each other.*

THAT ALL CHANGED with the onset of the industrial age.

There is a neat essay that was written back in 1958 titled: *I, Pencil: My Family Tree as told to Leonard E. Read*[44]. It shows us just how far we have come from those simpler times when you knew the cobbler by name (Schumacher, of course). Although I disagree with the ultimate conclusions Mr. Read draws regarding the superiority of laissez-faire markets, his description of the modern (1958) manufacturing process is illustrative. Read tells us about the thousands of people who play a role in making the simple wooden pencil that your kindergartener uses to trace letters and numbers.

I, Pencil starts out life as a cedar tree in Oregon. That tree is chopped down by a lumberjack who may have been amazed to learn that part of the tree he just fell will end up being used to make pencils.

I, Pencil's lead is no longer made from the element lead, of course. It turns out to be a mixture of graphite from Sri Lanka (Ceylon in 1958) and clay from Mississippi. Miners of those specialty materials may or may not know that their minerals will end up in pencils. But we can be sure they don't know who ultimately buys these writing instruments.

Read's essay, thorough as it is, does not include the thousands of people who get involved after the manufacturing process with the distribution and the sale of *I, Pencil*. The people responsible for selling pencils know all about you and your children <u>as customers</u>; but they don't know <u>you</u> from Adam.

This ignorance works both ways. While you have a brief encounter with the checkout person at the store where you bought the pencils, you certainly have no exchange whatsoever with the lumberjack from Oregon, with the graphite miner from Sri Lanka, or anyone else in *I, Pencil's* provenance. You might <u>like</u> to know them – you might find them to be interesting and delightful people. But there is no opportunity to do so. Trading in the market today is a purely transactional – an exchange of my dollars for your pencils. There is no interaction between the producer and the consumer of commercial goods. No verbal exchange between pig farmer and firewood gatherer.

WITHOUT A PERSONAL CONNECTION to the people who make the products we buy, our reasons for selecting one brand over another, and one store or another, are limited to <u>our perceptions</u> of convenience, price, quality, and prestige. (Our perceptions are highly influenced by folks who earn their living in advertising.)

The fact is, most of us are pretty shallow individuals when it comes to consuming goods and services. We are happy to let someone else tell us what to buy, when to buy, and what brand to buy. We care little for the social consequences of our purchase, and are much more concerned with whether or not we got a good deal. (This is not meant to be a criticism. Just an observation.)

Natural resource constraints on consumption

IF MONEY ELIMINATED the problem of needing enough space to hold our wealth, it did not remove the physical constraints on production that are imposed by the fact that there is a limited amount of raw material and energy available to create the products and services we consume in the first place.

Today we consume natural resources as fast as we can pump them out of the ground, dig them out of a mountain, clear-cut them from a forest, harvest them from a field, or fish them out of the sea. Relatively few of us are employed in primary extraction industries and farming. More of us work in manufacturing and food processing (although this number is shrinking as factories become more automated). More yet in the distribution of goods to the end-user (this includes retail establishments). But all of us are 'employed' as consumers of these goods. Upper, middle, and lower-class families all have to eat. All need essential clothing and shelter. Moving from the lower to the middle class, families become prodigious consumers of natural resources. Thus, as the middle class grows around the world, so does the consumption of these resources.

Thomas Robert Malthus warned us about the catastrophic problems of a geometrically exploding human population. He predicted that the number of mouths to feed would soon outstrip the amount of food available for consumption. That was in 1798.

We somehow managed to avoid that catastrophe.

Actually, there is no 'somehow' about it. Our good fortune was not by accident. We avoided catastrophe by increasing the amount of food produced per acre at a pace greater than the population growth. It was the impetus of market demand (along with the prospect of getting rich by meeting that demand), and the implementation of technological improvements, that made all this possible.

Since the start of the industrial revolution, each time it looked like natural resource constraints would cause the economic underpinnings of our society to become unraveled, the markets found a way to right themselves. Either there were technological developments that resulted in greater production, or we came up with go-arounds – finding substitute products for those now in short supply.

We make use of a potent combination of engineering and marketing skills to address solutions to shortage problems. Packaging of products is a good example. For a while, it seemed like everything you bought consisted of more packaging than product. My personal nemesis – the impossible-to-open blister pack! In some cases, the added packaging was meant to deter theft. In other cases, it provided additional space for advertising and information (e.g., a thumb drive mounted on a much larger hang-card.) There are flashy, non-recyclable ways of doing this, and there are quieter, more environmentally benign (recyclable) ways of doing the same thing. If consumers insist on the latter, manufacturers will make those changes in packaging. (If we are not passive as consumers, the market will respond.)

In spite of dire warnings from modern-day Malthusians, we always seem to find a way to keep the consumer-based economy going. HOWEVER, that does not mean we can count on technology to bail us out forever. It seems like with each 'crisis', the solutions get a little trickier. And sooner or later, we are going to butt up against a problem that we can't surpass without a great deal of disruption to the status quo.

Global Warming/Climate Change just may be that problem. Most scientists who study these things tell us that the growing levels of carbon in the air will greatly increase the likelihood of a greenhouse effect, with the atmosphere holding more and more heat inside. The results could be catastrophic, with significant changes to the climate worldwide, and with rising sea levels, to the point where we'll lose a lot of low-lying land along the coasts (where millions and millions of humans live).

You may or may not agree with this forecast. But if you think there is even a sliver of a chance that this is true, the conservative approach would be to minimize the amount of carbon we are adding to the atmosphere posthaste. Yet it is the conservatives on the political spectrum who proudly label themselves 'deniers'. Odd.

Especially odd when you think about the potential of all the money to be made finding replacements in the energy market for fossil fuels. If ever there was an opportunity for a market to reinvent itself, and make a lot of people ridiculously wealthy in the process, this is it! (Apparently, some folks are more interested in protecting their conservative investments in coal, oil, & gas than they are in protecting our planet.)

REDUCE – REUSE – RECYCLE. That is the mantra environmentally aware teachers share with their students. They are intentionally listed in that order. As far as the environment is concerned, not buying something in the first place is better than buying something that you don't really need, even if it's advertised as 'green' or environmentally friendly. It is not just the responsibility of Producers to build ever-greener products, nor solely the responsibility of the Government to pass laws protecting the environment. Consumers have a responsibility to consider the impact of their purchases and get by with less if possible. When we do need to buy something, we should select products that create the smallest footprint on our planet.

And a note about this – protecting our planet. It's not really our planet that needs protection. Mother Earth is a spry 4.5-billion-year-old orb, made of iron, oxygen, silicon, magnesium, and dozens of other elements, circling the Sun every 365 days.[45] She will shrug off any temporary shift in the climate as easily as the last ice age. It is the inhabitants of the Earth's fragile biosphere who are at risk from climate change, including we frail humans – all of us contributing to the problem in the first place! (Poetic justice?)

ONE LAST THING to say on sustainability. Shifting to a 4-day workweek with 3-day weekends the norm will probably have a modest impact on the consumption of goods and services. (The impact of growing economy and the global expansion of the middle class will probably be much more profound.) But hopefully we will shift our focus from material measures of wealth to other experiences that positively enhance our well-being, and are not so resource-dependent.

The work-consume treadmill
BUT A SHORTER WORKWEEK is not where we are today. Today we

are all about consumption, which means we are all about work. The reason we work so much, as near as I can tell, is because we are pre-disposed to increasing the amount of stuff in our possession.

Just like our firewood-gathering and pig-farming ancestors preparing their products for the market, we put in long hours at work in order to earn enough money to buy all those things we really 'need'.

- First the things we really do need (i.e., the most basic versions of food, clothing, shelter).
- Then upgrades of those basic goods so that we may live in more comfortably.
- Then 'affordable' luxury items (e.g., nicer cars, vacations) that all our neighbors seem to be enjoying.
- Finally, downright opulence. Goods and services that prove that we have shot past the status of reasonably well-off, and we are now able to hang with the truly wealthy.

As we 'ascend' this hierarchy of 'needs', it seems that our level of wealth will never be sufficient. By the time we reach any one rung on the ladder of consumption, we can be sure that the next rung is calling us higher. So, we double down on our work and continue with our insatiable consumption – spinning away madly on a work/shop treadmill.[46]

Apparently, we never can accumulate <u>enough</u> wealth. Therefore, we can never put in enough hours at work. And sadly, we sometimes forget why we jumped into this rat-race in the first place.

Celeste Headlee expressed this very well in her book *Do Nothing*:

> *The glorification of consumerism creates a vicious cycle. We work longer and longer hours in order to buy products that we think will make our lives better, we stop enjoying them fairly quickly, the products themselves require time and maintenance that cut into our free time, this makes us unhappy, so we decide to relieve our feelings of sadness with a new product. Rinse and repeat.* [47]

SEVERAL OTHER AUTHORS have tackled this affliction in the last 25 years, including:

- *Affluenza*[48] by de Graaf, Wann, & Naylor
- *Consumed*[49] by Benjamin Barber
- *Turbo-Capitalism*[50] by Edward Luttwak
- *The Geography of Nowhere*[51] by James Kunstler

The approach of some of these books is to attack the 'system', the sales and marketing departments of large international corporations that lead us down this path of folly. They are right, but only to a point. We are not forced into the Target or Walmart store by gunpoint. We follow the lead of the advertisers gladly, just as eager for the newest shiny bauble as the next guy.

Consumers of goods have little regard for producers, even though they spend their days at work producing goods and services themselves. We have forgotten a large part of what all the work is for. Namely, the benefits to the larger community. We have no personal connections to the producers of goods, so we see none of the consequences of our purchases on their well-being. With the services we purchase, there is a bit more of a connection. But most often the personal connection is strictly professional, perfunctory. How can we be in the 'good citizen' mode when we are driven solely by selfish consumption?

But in spite of all the mindless consumption, this has proven to be a good thing for modern man collectively, raising the standard of living for 7 billion souls worldwide. We are living longer, healthier, and in far more comfort than our ancestors. Poverty rates are rapidly shrinking worldwide. It has even had an impact on warfare, as there is less chance two countries will go to war with each other when they are busy negotiating trade agreements. In toto, life is better for the vast majority of us.

Comparative wealth

WEALTH IS A PECULIAR CONCEPT. Quite relative in one sense, absolute in another. Relative because we constantly compare ourselves with our immediate peers – siblings, classmates, neighbors. Absolute because all of us, at one time or another, gaze with secret envy at the *Lifestyles of the Rich and Famous*.

Columnist George Will talked about comparative wealth in an essay. He referred to the 'positional economy' as a place where you and I are constantly comparing our social status based on the consumption of goods and services. Talking about ostentatious consumption (like $12 cups of coffee at Starbucks), he wrote:

> *After elementary needs – food, shelter, clothing – are satisfied, consumption nevertheless continues, indeed it intensifies because desires are potentially infinite. People compare themselves to their neighbors, envy their neighbors' advantages, and strive to vault ahead in the envy-ostentation sweepstakes.*

Will goes on:

> *Where will the positional economy end? It won't. Stanford professor Francis Fukuyama notes that it is a peculiarity of human beings that they desire some things "not for themselves but because they are desired by other human beings." Hamsters have more sense. This characteristic of our species – the quest for recognition by distinguishing oneself from others – provides limitless marketing possibilities because for many wealthy people, "the chief enjoyment of riches consists in the parade of riches." So wrote Adam Smith in "The Wealth of Nations," published in the resonant year of 1776.[52]*

GEOGRAPHICALLY, we also see comparisons of wealth that are simultaneously relative and absolute. Poor families in the U.S. and Europe are absolutely better off than poor families in parts of Africa and Asia. But the poor in the wealthier countries don't think of themselves as well-off. They see themselves as poor because, relatively speaking, within their own countries, they are!

For middle class Americans and Europeans, it seems like we are never satisfied with our comfortable homes, our working cars, and our enjoyable vacation trips. We are always comparing ourselves to those better off than we are. And the only way we can increase our level of consumption is to put in more time at work and earn bigger paychecks.

We are all born with a competitive spirit (E.O. Wilson's *part sinner*). This is manifested in what we do and what we own. It is only natural for us to want to possess things – a lot of things – the very best of things. (Certainly, better than yours!)

The competition for status, through the things owned, services consumed, and power controlled, is apparently something that can never be fully satisfied. This keeps GDPs across the globe growing, and companies around the world striving to produce goods and services more economically. That leads into the next part of the book.

PART II

TODAY'S
LABOR MARKET

CHAPTER 4

The Beneficial Impact of Technology

WHEN I GOT THE NOTION to write the first edition of this book, I assumed the lion's share of my efforts would be devoted to this section. It was 2010, and we were still suffering the aftershocks of the great recession. Unemployment in U.S. was pushing 10%, and was much higher in other places around the world. What seemed clear was that technology and automation had finally (as forecast by many) reached the point where the need for so many workers would disappear forever. Several contemporary authors shared this view, notably: Jeremy Rifkin in *The End of Work*[53], Martin Ford in *The Lights in the Tunnel*[54], and Erik Brynjolfsson and Andrew McAfee in *Race Against the Machine*[55]. All voiced deep concern that so many middle class jobs would be permanently eliminated by automation, that consumer demand could not be counted on to keep the economy growing and healthy.

But the labor market, like all markets, is not static, and periodically undergoes significant, even structural, changes. By the time I finished the first edition (2018), the unemployment rate had fallen steadily to around 4%. Over the next three years unemployment dropped to around 3%, close to what many economist call "full" employment. And even though we had witnessed a hollowing-out of the middle class, labor demand had once again reacted with more resiliency than expected. Forecasts of doom and gloom had proven, once again, to be wrong.

Then COVID-19 came along, totally disrupting every aspect of our lives. But even pre-COVID, there was reason for concern back in 2018, and there still is today.

In Jerry Kaplan's book *Artificial Intelligence*[56], he talks about machines being used, not to eliminate entire jobs, but to perform specific tasks. This results in each worker being more productive, and the need for the number of workers to drop substantially. Robots and automation are eliminating paying jobs in many sectors of the economy at a much faster pace than they are being created. In a McKinsey report on the future of jobs, we read:

> *Technological change has reshaped the workplace continually over the past two centuries since the Industrial Revolution, but the speed with which automation technologies are developing today, and the scale at which they could disrupt the world of work, are largely without precedent.*[57]

The business consulting company Forrester concurs with this trend of net jobs lost. They forecast that by 2025, 16% of current jobs will be lost to automation. This will be offset by 9% new jobs created (people to keep all those robots running, among others), with a net job loss of 7%.[58]

Those displaced workers are finding their way to brand new jobs that are being created, mostly in the service sector. Unfortunately, these new service sector jobs generally pay less than those that were lost in the manufacturing sector. (I believe that the smaller paychecks in the service sector are an artifact left over from the industrial revolution. This need not, and should not, continue to be the case, and I'll address that more fully in Chapter 9.)

Celebrate automation

WHEN ROBOTS TAKE OVER tasks previously performed by humans, we react like that is bad news. But this is not bad news – it is great news! Robots, just like human workers, create wealth. That is a good thing, so why would we not want to put the machines to work?

Let's do a fanciful thought experiment here: Let's imagine that a factory worker owns the rights to a particular robot's production. That worker could show up at the factory every day to keep his robot clean and oiled and observe with pride as his personal servant turns out perfect widgets, day after day. His robot is so dependable that he might decide to leave work early one day and go home and play with his children after school. He is no longer tied to the assembly line, not forced to keep up the pace on a repetitive job with routine motions, over and over, day in and day out. He has better things to do with his time. And now, with the help of his very own personal robot, he is in control of his own time.

This is not the way it works, of course. But it could be! The fundamental idea is that we, collectively, have developed machines to do the work that humans previously had to do. We can still do the repetitious work if we want, I suppose. But we'll probably decide we have better things to do – like go home and play catch with junior. The productive capability of the robots should be a reason for everyone in society to celebrate, especially the workers! We just need to figure out how to marry the breakthroughs in technology with matching improvements in social and economic policy so that productivity advances are beneficial for *everyone*, not just a few privileged owners of capital.

IN THIS CHAPTER, we will look at all the progress that has been made in several industries and occupations since the great depression. I focus on the relatively recent history because it was 80 years ago that the 40-hour workweek became the de facto standard. As we shall see, we have many reasons to celebrate, and few reasons to still be working 40 hours a week.

Agriculture

FARMING SEEMS AN APPROPRIATE PLACE to start our study of productivity improvements. It was the advent of the agricultural era that allowed us to evolve from nomadic clans of hunter/gatherers into permanently settled communities of farmers and ranchers. With that development, the market economy was born. Progress in the human condition over the next 12,000 years was lightning-fast compared to that of the previous 2 million. And one could argue it was the market economy itself that drove the rapid progress due at least in part to the increasingly complex social interactions of the marketplace. Cultivating crops and raising livestock allowed all that to happen, so farming is a good place to begin.

For our comparative study of the productivity on farms, we don't want to travel back 12,000 years. Just 80 years or so to 1938 when the 40-hour workweek became the standard. (Before going any further, I understand full well that an 8-hour day and a Monday – Friday workweek has little relevance on a farm where one must literally *make hay when the sun shines*. It is the annual productivity of a single farm worker in the 1930's vs. that of a worker in the 2010's that holds our interest for this study.)

EIGHTY YEARS AGO, we would find ourselves in the great depression, and battling a series of severe droughts and the dust bowl that devastated huge swaths of the Great Plains of America and Canada.

What was farming like in those days? I had the good fortune to learn a great deal about that from Michael Cotter, a third-generation farmer from Austin, Minnesota. Mr. Cotter became a professional storyteller after he retired from farming. He loved to share his experiences about growing up on the family farm in the 1930's and 40's. He and his wife, Beverly, had compiled stories about life on the farm into several books, the last *The Killdeer, and other stories from the farming life.*[59] His stories give a wonderful flavor to what life was like on the farm going all the way back to his childhood. Much of the material on the following pages was gleaned from Cotter's books and my interview with Michael and Beverly.

DO YOU LIKE HORSES? Although there were many trucks and tractors in use by the 1930's, a lot of farms still had horses in those days. But these animals were not for recreation – these were working animals. Along with oxen and donkeys, draft animals were still employed on many farms in the 1930's right through to the end of WWII.

Photo courtesy of Michael Cotter. Horse-drawn hay mower.

It sounds idyllic, doesn't it? Working behind a team of horses? Let's read Mr. Cotter's account of cutting a field of hay:

Mowing hay turned out to be the most hateful job I ever had. The hay mower in the distance sounded like music, but operating it was dreary. Because the mower was driven by its big wheels, it pulled very hard. The horses became hot and sweaty and developed sores on their shoulders under those big collars.

That prairie hay cut tough and the mower would plug often. The big horse flies came out of that standing hay and bit those horses, causing them to stand and kick which caused the mower to plug again and again.

While I was unplugging the mower sickle, the horses would kick again and the sharp sickle would move beneath my fingers. Then the horses would kick over their tugs. These were the thick leather straps from the harness to the mower. While unhooking the straps in order to get the horse back in position, I would get swatted by that heavy tail that stings your face and cuts your eyes. It was a hateful job.

Not quite so idyllic after all. And something I never thought of before reading Cotter's account of open sores on the shoulders of the horses – beasts of burden lived hard lives!

Cotter goes on to compare that experience with cutting hay with a tractor:

So it was a wonderful time when the tractor powered hay mower came to our farm. With power coming from the tractor instead of the wheels, the mower moved swiftly. Also we started growing alfalfa hay which was viney and more tangled than the prairie hay.

When I would sit on that tractor on a June morning it would seem like I was flying across the field. There were no bugs or horse flies bothering me. There was the smell of new mown hay, though I was not able to hear the birds over the sound of the tractor. [60]

(Cotter includes that last sentence, the part about not hearing the birds over the noise of the tractor, to remind us there will always be tradeoffs when adopting new technology.)

Michael Cotter with his son's new team of horses – about 200 of them.

It became clear to farmers quite quickly that tractors were preferred to horses as the prime movers of farm implements. The horses employed on farms today have names like John Deere and Kubota and Case/IH. Instead of two horses pulling a plow, there is a 200 HP tractor.

To say that a farmer using a modern tractor is more productive than the one using horses is an understatement to be sure. This table gives some specific examples:

Activity	1930's with horses	2010's with horsepower	Increase in productivity
Plowing	1-2-3 bottom plow, 30" wide, 3 MPH (walking	10 bottom plow, 180" wide, 6 MPH	12X

	behind a team of horses)		
Cultivating	6-10' wide, 3 MPH	50-60' wide, 7-8 MPH	17X
Planting	2 row planter, 3 MPH	16 row planter, 6 MPH	16X

Harvesting crops have also undergone huge gains in productivity over the last eighty years. Cotter writes about the threshing crews that used to work several farms in a circuit:

> *Threshing was probably the most important season of the year in my young life. The whole neighborhood was involved in a threshing ring. There were other rituals like silo filling that also involved the neighbors working together, but that did not compare with the threshing ritual either in length or in drama.*

> *I think what made threshing so memorable was all of the preparation. It started when the old grain binder was pulled out of the shed. This was followed by endless days of cutting grain, always in the hot sun. The person running the binder, usually one of the men, would have to drop the grain bundles in groups of fours or threes or sometimes twos and in straight rows so the men shocking would not have to carry them far. Shocking was one of the real hard jobs on the farm. The grain bundles were not heavy, but they had to be stood up in really sturdy shocks where they could stand and dry and wait for the thresher. It used to be said that a real good man could keep up with a binder all day shocking. The shocks usually sat in the field two to three weeks and were threshed according to your rotation in the threshing group.*

> *When people got together to plan a threshing run, they had*

to calculate when their oats would be ready and how long it would take. And that worked quite well unless the weather turned very rainy. Then people became very anxious about getting their crop threshed. So it was with both relief and excitement when the threshing machine came down the road. The machine was proceeded by horses and wagons pulling into our farm yard and going out to the grain field. Even though there was generally no more than ten farms on our threshing run, I remember hearing at one time there were thirty men involved. That was held up as an almost all time high number.[61]

Photo courtesy of Mower County Historical Society. Donated by Harold Rochford.[62]

It wasn't just the men out in the fields and tending the machine who were hard at work. A dozen or more men on these threshing crews would work up quite an appetite, and it would be no small task for the matron of the farm to keep everyone fed. Hot meals for breakfast and supper, and morning and afternoon snacks for breaks in the field. She would count on help in the kitchen from the ladies at neighboring farms, in addition to all her own daughters of course.

NOWADAYS, the farms in southern Minnesota grow far more corn and soybeans than oats. (Not many horses left to feed.) Combine harvesters are now used for everything from small grains (wheat, rye, oats, barley) to field corn. These amazing machines combine several harvesting steps in one operation:

- Cut the corn stalk near the ground
- Strip the ears of corn from the stalk
- Shell the kernels of corn off the cob
- Collect shelled corn on board, or auger directly to grain truck
- Chop the corn cobs and stalks into small pieces and spread the residue back on field

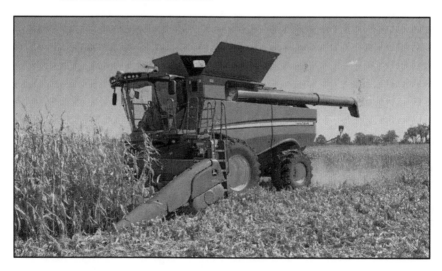

Comparing the productivity of a single farmer, pre- and post-combine, is difficult because harvesting used to involve so many separate steps:

Activity	1930's	2010's	Increase in productivity
Harvesting corn	One farmer picking corn by hand: 6 or 7 bushels of ear corn per hour	One farmer picking corn w/ combine: 900 bushels of shelled corn/hour (at least 2X ear corn)	270X

Other measures of a farm's productivity and economies of scale are easier to ascertain:

Productivity	1930's	2010's	Increase in productivity
Yield, (bushels of corn/acre)	30	200	7X
Typical farm size, (acres)	80-160	800-1500	

ADD THIS ALL UP, and we see that a typical farm in the corn belt is producing 160,000-300,000 bushels of shelled corn a year with a harvest crew of maybe three workers (the combine driver and the drivers in two grain trucks). Compare that to a dozen or so farm workers picking 2400-4800 bushels of corn 70-80 years ago.

LET'S LOOK NOW at the dairy farm across the road. In the 1930's, a dairy farm may have had 10-15 cows, all milked by hand. A typical farm today may have 150-200 cows, all milked by machine, of course. And the trend is to much larger dairy operations. From a column by Adam Belz in the StarTribune:

> *It costs small dairies more to produce milk. A farm with fewer than 200 cows produces a hundredweight of milk (about 112 pounds, or roughly a day-and-a-half's production from a single cow) for about $16.28, including the costs of feed, taxes, insurance, and hired labor, the U.S. Department of Agriculture estimates. A dairy farm with more than 1000 cows produces a hundredweight of milk for about $14.61.*
>
> *The price of milk has been just under $16 per hundredweight for most of the past three years. That's left small dairies operating at losses while larger ones remained profitable.*[63]

Each cow, by the way, now produces twice as much milk as a single cow just 40 years ago. (*You go, girl!*)

EVERYTHING is getting bigger, faster, and more productive on farms. There are economies of scale when it comes to farm implements. A huge combine used to have a 30' cutting head. Now it's 40'. You don't buy one of those $250,000 machines for your 'back-40'. Bigger tractors call for bigger fields, which call for bigger farms.

Decent-sized farms have always needed helpers. The farmer's children were put to work, of course. And it was common for a farmer with 160 acres to employ 3 or 4 hired helpers.

That same farmer may now cultivate 1500 acres. He still has chores for all the children. And he still gets by with 3 or 4 hired helpers. Each hired hand is now many times more productive than his counterpart 80 years ago.

The great increase in farming productivity has had a profound impact on the labor market. Eighty years ago, around 20% of the U.S. labor force was employed on farms. Now it's less than 2%. In addition to feeding everyone in our country, around 20% of all U.S. agricultural production is exported. American farmers are feeding people all over the world, not just here at home.

IT IS ESTIMATED that there are 570 million family farms worldwide. If farmers everywhere in the world adopted modern farming practices and became as productive as those in the U.S., one-tenth as many farms worldwide could produce enough food for everyone in the world to consume.

For those concerned that the worldwide adoption of western farming methods will despoil the land and speed the way to environmental Armageddon, rest assured that need not happen. Modern farmers have become good stewards of the earth; in part in response to consumer pressure (e.g. the call for cage-free eggs); in part in response to medical concerns (the elimination of BGH); but mostly through their own recognition that some farming practices needed to be modified to be sustainable. A couple examples of environmental improvements that are now widely employed are buffer strips around drainage ditches and low-tillage weed control.

Just as these environmental best-practices gradually become universally accepted in the U.S., they will be exported to the rest of the world, right along with the 40' combines from Caterpillar and John Deere.

Low-tillage farming. Stubble from last year's corn crop left on top of field to serve as weed barrier for the soybeans this year.

FAMINES still occur in one part of the world or another almost every year. Famines are not the result of a worldwide shortage of food – there is now enough food grown worldwide to keep everyone fed IF it were evenly distributed. But there are local shortages, induced by drought or disease, when the people who live in the affected area either cannot afford food from outside their area, or have no practical method of importing that food.

Some parts of the world are still using farming methods that were employed in the U.S. in the 1880's and before. They will gradually become much more modernized and more specialized. And when modern farming methods are adopted worldwide, the cost of production and the price of food will go down; and with that, the chances of famine should be greatly reduced.

With enough food to go around for everyone, up to 500 million impoverished families can give up subsistence farming on small, rocky plots of soil. These families would then be free to engage in other lines of work – more lucrative and less dangerous than farming.

Some may lament the loss of the romantic notion of the family farm, and a future where only 2% of the world's population is engaged in commercial agriculture. Will all the rest of us – 98% of us – lose touch with the land?

There's no reason why that need be the case. We can still till the soil and grow food for ourselves. It's called *gardening*. Indeed, we see periodic revivals of vegetable gardening, new interest in heirloom varieties of tomatoes and apples, even a surge in urban chicken coops. People have a deep-seated affinity for the land that will not easily fade away. That goes back not just 12,000 years to the advent of agriculture, but 200,000 years or so, throughout our species days as hunters and gatherers. Turning commercial farms all over the world into efficient factories will not extinguish that primordial urge.

Coal mining

THE SHIFT from underground mines to surface mining has had a huge impact on the productivity of an individual miner. Workers used to be confined to dark, damp, cramped spaces, deep in the earth, wielding a pick or a jackhammer. They now find themselves sitting comfortably above ground, basking in the sunshine, inside the climate-controlled cabs of huge shovels and gigantic dump trucks.

The improvements in creature-comfort are matched by tremendous increases in productivity. In Wyoming's open-pit mines, 5837 miners produce more coal than 58,995 miners in the mostly underground operations in West Virginia, Kentucky, Pennsylvania, Virginia, Alabama and Illinois combined.

The coal mining industry employed over 700,000 miners in the 1920's, with annual production per miner around 0.8K tons. (That comes out to 6400 lbs/day, which sounds like ball-busting work to me.) Today, the industry produces almost twice as much coal with just 80,000 miners. That comes out to an average production per miner over 12K tons annually, a 15X increase in an average miner's production.[64] The multiple will surely grow as the remaining underground mines are phased out.

This is resulting in a huge loss of fulltime jobs, to be sure. But we should not lament the loss of those dark, dirty, and dangerous jobs. There are environmental reasons to oppose tearing the tops off mountains vs. the less invasive digging holes in the ground. But as far as working conditions above ground and the quality of those brutish underground jobs? No comparison.

Hopefully, this will soon all be moot anyway, as we move away from fossil fuels to renewable energy sources. There are already more people engaged in solar panel and wind power installations than there are coal miners.

Manufacturing

FREDERICK TAYLOR didn't invent the robot. But he and his scientific management companions laid the groundwork for the automated factory way back in the late nineteenth century. They reduced every bit of work in the factory, whether performed by man or machine, into discreet, measurable tasks. Their time-and-motion studies contributed to the invention of robots in two ways, the first obvious and the second subtle. First, by reducing assembly work into discreet steps, as small as possible, their task analysis work created the blueprint for the automated equipment to follow. The second way they led to automation was less obvious, but more insidious. By making the assembly tasks so small and so controlled – timed, rigid, reproducible – a lot of the work in the factory was reduced to repetitive, crappy jobs. Work that anyone could do but few wanted, except for the paycheck.

Plenty of workers did still want factory work because, with the constructive influence of labor unions, the jobs paid well. And many didn't mind the repetitive work. If you have a simple task to complete over-and-over again, you can put your body on autopilot and let your mind wander where it may. That can be quite pleasant for some workers, especially when you add in the companionship of fellow workers.

Factory jobs have been considered primo for a long time. Fathers who were factory workers did all they could to help get their sons employed at 'the plant'. No education needed – just be physically fit, personable, and have a solid recommendation from someone already inside.

Fifty years ago, the largest private employer in the U.S. was General Motors. Full time workers there earned around $50/hour in today's dollars, including the very generous health and pension benefits. For comparison, the largest private employer today is Wal-Mart where, as recently at 2016, the typical employee earned just over $9/hour; and many were part-time, and earned no benefits at all.[65]

Manufacturing employment peaked in the U.S. at 30% of the workforce in 1953[66]. The percentage declined to around 20% in 1980 (19 million workers), and has continued to fall to around 8% of the workforce in 2018 (12 million workers). Factory automation greatly reduces the number of assembly line workers needed, and that impact is far from over.

Numbers from a huge commercial bakery that makes

hamburger buns for fast food operations tell a story: New equipment that was installed in the mid-1990's allowed a crew of 11 to produce buns at a rate of 56 dozen/min. With improvements over the last couple decades, a crew of 7 workers now produces buns at a rate of 96 dozen/min. Each worker is 2.7 times more productive today than he was just 25 years ago.[67]

It will be a long time before robots entirely eliminate factory jobs, and the jobs that do remain in factories still pay quite well. In fact, now more than ever. Factory workers have turned in their blue-collars for lab coats. Production work no longer entails small, controlled, repetitive tasks. Production workers are now responsible for entire production runs – keeping the machines programed and running properly, keeping materials flowing smoothly, keeping the runs on schedule. The workers are now more technicians than mindless cogs, and they have much more responsibility and much more autonomy than when they were glued to the front or back end of a machine doing simple one and two-step tasks.

Matthew Yglesias writes in a *Vox* posting titled *The automation myth*:

> But robots are never going to take all the jobs. The problem with trying to envision "a world without work" is that it asks us to envision an unrealistically large change.

> The more likely outcome is a world with less work. And that's a world we should welcome rather than fear. It's a world in which we can make some policy decisions we want to make, rather than decisions we really don't want to make.[68]

Yglesias suggests several options for workers to reduce the

number of hours worked, including retiring at an earlier age, taking more vacation and holiday time off, and extended leave for new parents. I would have like to have seen a shorter workweek among the options he'd have us consider.

Manufacturing is changing in other ways as factories become much more flexible. With technological advances like 3-D printing and CAD-CAM programs, we are approaching the point where virtually every item ordered can be custom-made to our exact specifications. No longer will the factory crank out the same part, day-after-day, year-after-year. A make-order could well be a run of one. There is nice synergy here between custom-made products and keeping factory jobs interesting for the worker.

The technological evolution of the factory is not limited to the U.S. and Western Europe where labor rates are relatively high. No matter how easy it is to find workers, and no matter how low their wages, machines can always be built to make things better, faster, and cheaper. Therefore, we now find modern automated plants being built all over the planet. More about that in Chapter 5.

Transportation

IT WOULD DO NO GOOD to have a single farm produce 200,000 bushels of corn, a single mine to produce 1 million tons of coal, or a single factory to produce 1 million t-shirts without an efficient way of getting the goods to market. While the grain trucks that haul the corn into the elevators are private vehicles, they are driving down public roads. There are over 4 million miles of paved roads in the U.S., built and maintained by federal, state and county governments. Without these public highways, modern-day farmers would have a lot of trouble getting their produce to market.

The tycoons who built the railroads that carry the coal to the power plants were private developers, but only with the generous encouragement of the government, which ceded vast stretches of previously public land along the RRs' right-of-ways.

Likewise, the airplanes transporting people around the globe and those 1 million shirts from the factory in Bangladesh to distribution centers in the U.S. travel through publicly controlled airspace, and takeoff and land at publicly financed airports.

Barges steam up and down rivers and canals and thru locks and dams built and dredged by the government and maintained by the Army Corps of Engineers. The vessels pull up to city-built docks to load and unload their cargo. Ocean going ships sail the seven seas made safe by the navies of the world, and pull into public ports with the help of the Coast Guard.

The evolution of these public-private transportation systems is truly a remarkable development, and the sheer inventiveness of what we've accomplished is often overlooked. The cost to build and maintain different corridors of transportation is covered by a combination of general taxes and user fees, often with a unique set of solutions for each system. The goal is to find the right combination of taxes and fees that maximizes the cost-benefit equation for everyone in society.

We've been working on this public/private partnership for a long, long time. At very least since *all roads led to Rome*, and probably going all the way back to the dawn of the agricultural age and the first permanent settlements. An exhaustive history of public/private transportation projects would be an interesting topic to cover, but as in the previous sections, I'm going to focus on developments over the last eighty years:

On some farms in the 1930's, horses and donkeys were not only being used to plow the fields. The animals were also employed to deliver the farm's output (fruits & vegetables, dairy products, grain) from the farm to town. The expression *pull your own weight* referred to the draft animals, so a wagon pulled by two very large horses could carry 2 tons of produce. The farmer and his team of horses could make the 20-mile round-trip to town in a single day, leaving enough time to load on one end and unload on the other.

Farm-to-market transport has changed just a tad over the last eighty years. The farmer now hires a guy with a truck – a reefer truck for fruits and vegetables, a refrigerated tanker for milk, and a bulk hauler for grain. With the gross vehicle weight limited to 80,000 lbs., that leaves room for around 40,000 lbs. of cargo.

These trucks can make the 20-mile round-trip to town in half an hour or so. Allowing some time to load and unload on either end, they can make 3 to 6 trips a day. Let's use 4 trips a day as the average. At 40,000 lbs./trip, that equals 160,000 lbs./day. Compared to the 4000 lbs./day via horse and wagon, that is a 40X increase over this 80-year period. (That sync's nicely with the growth in productivity of the individual farmer.)

RAILROADS AND RIVER BARGES haul cargo on longer runs. Since these modes of transport were established in the U.S. in the 19th century and have benefitted from technological development ever since, the growth in productivity in the last 80 years is less pronounced than making truck vs. horse comparisons on public highways. In fact, the size of freight rail system peaked in 1916 at 254,000 road-miles, and is now down to about 140,000 miles. Eliminated were mostly rural runs from small towns to larger hubs – that traffic is now handled by trucks.

Still, the remaining stream-lined railroad system operates with substantially more efficiency than the more extensive, coal-fired, steam locomotive system in the 1930's. Today, the diesel-electric engines haul trains of bulk cargo (grains, fertilizer, coal, oil, minerals, etc.) more cleanly than their coal-fired predecessors, and the cargo is on and off-loaded much more efficiently. Improvements have been made in the handling of piece products, which, in fact, are no longer 'handled' by the RR at all, but instead travel inside intermodal containers: from ship, to train, to truck, to distribution center, before finally being unloaded. Before too long, seeing a good old-fashioned boxcar will be about as rare as seeing a three-legged milking stool.

Ocean-going cargo ships benefit from the same intermodal container system. Loading and unloading ships used to involve a lot of physical labor, slinging cargo nets around everything hoisted aboard, and a fair amount of art, stacking cargo safely in the holds. It is now done much more quickly and with far fewer workers using self-contained, self-stacking, standard-sized rectangular containers.

To illustrate the impact of shipping containers, in 1954 there were 35,000 longshoremen employed at the Port of New York and New Jersey and over 100,000 working on the west coast. By 2004, those numbers had shrunk to 2,700 and 10,000 respectively. Meanwhile, the volume had tripled, so the productivity of each longshoreman had increased by more than thirty-fold.[69]

A typical cargo ship in the 1930's handled perhaps 10,000 tons, and sailed at 10 knots. A large intermodal ship today handles 200,000 tons, bulk carriers up to twice that amount. Cargo ships today can cruise at 20 – 25 knots, although fuel economy improves when the ships slow down to 10 – 15 knots.

Crew size of a typical cargo ship in the 1930's: 20 – 30 (avg. 25). Crew size on cargo ships today: 12 – 20 (avg. 16). Even if we set the cruising speed of both ships at 10 knots, each sailor on a cargo ship today is 31X more productive at moving cargo from port to port than his counterpart in the 1930's.

Air cargo, practically nonexistent in the 1930's, reached 15 million tons within the U.S. in 2013. Nowadays, we've come to expect the availability of freshly-cut flowers from South America in the dead of winter, and freshly-caught fish flown in every day from the coasts to cities in the middle of the country.

U.S. Department of Transportation Forecast of Freight Shipments Within U.S. (weight of shipments by transportation mode, millions of tons)		
Mode of Transportation	**2012**	**2040**
Truck	13,182	18,786
Rail	2,018	2,770
Water	975	1,070
Air, air & truck	15	53
Multiple mode & mail	1,588	3,575
Pipeline	1,546	1,740
Other/Unknown	338	526
Total	**19,662**	**28,520**

Source: US DOT Freight Facts and Figures 2013

FROM A JOBS-CREATION STANDPOINT, it's useful to look above at the Department of Transportation forecast for freight shipments within the U.S. in the year 2040 – domestic, imports, and exports. A couple things jump out at me:

28 B tons in 2040 is only about 1.3% growth rate over the next 28 years, but this is no means a full measure of the expected growth in the economy over that period. Remember that we now live in a service economy. There is very little that needs to be shipped – by truck, train, or air – for me to go in for my $11 seniors haircut. So, any growth at all in cargo shipments may be viewed as quite a positive indicator.

NOT SO POSITIVE, with respect to the number of workers, is the rapid development of driverless vehicles. Several companies are now working on self-driving trucks. Phase one in their development program is to let the robotic truck take over the driving out on the highway, with the human on-board taking over the driving in the city. (This is akin to commercial aircraft flying on autopilot once they are up in the sky, but with the human pilot responsible for take-offs and landings.) In phase two, the robotic truck will be able to do the driving from one loading dock to the next, tirelessly, and more safely than a human driver.

Eventually, city-truck drivers may become just as rare as their over-the-road counterparts. For example, I can imagine a driverless trash truck autonomously running its route, perhaps communicating with smart trash cans along the way.

In the U.S., around 1.7 million workers drive over-the-road semis, and an additional 2.8 million workers earn their living by driving: taxis, buses, delivery trucks.[70] All 4.5 million of these jobs are at risk.

Newtrax executive director Mike Greenbaum with his experimental, autonomous vehicle, designed for driver-free circulator routes. The goal is to have direct support staff still aboard, but now able to attend to the needs of the client/passengers, and not worried about navigating through traffic.

Warehousing & Distribution

FARMERS' MARKETS are wonderful institutions, enabling direct connections between the people who grow the food and the people who eat it. But that's not the normal way commercial goods end up in consumers' homes. There is often quite an extensive logistics chain to get finished goods from the manufacturer to the end-user:

And at each step along the chain, specialized skill sets are employed, along with ever-improving high-tech tools. The processes up and down the logistics chain constantly evolve – adopting many of the same technologies the manufacturers use to streamline their operations. Hand-held bar code readers eliminate large amounts of hand-written paperwork and three-part forms while assuring orders for goods are filled completely and on-time. Automated machines and robots are becoming more flexible, affordable, and commonplace. Human workers who used to do simple one, two, and three step operations are being eliminated. New production and distribution employees are now more technicians than laborers – keeping all the machinery working to get the products converted, packaged, warehoused, merchandised, and eventually sold.

With the internet, consumers are able to order products directly from the manufacturer. But that merchandise still needs to travel through several levels of production and distribution before it arrives on your doorstep. At each point along the way, the use of technology allows the work to be accomplished more efficiently. And in the process, manual jobs are being streamlined or eliminated.

Case-in-point: Memphis, Tennessee is a transportation hub for FedEx and others; and a warehouse location for many manufacturers. The volume of cargo traffic in and out of Memphis has recovered to pre-recession levels, but the number of workers employed in transportation and warehousing remains 3200 full time jobs lower than before the recession.[71] Those jobs are not coming back, having been eliminated by technology-based productivity gains.

Another great example is illustrated by Ryan Avent in *The Wealth of Humans*:

> *The growing India economy, over 1.2 billion people strong, is a mouth-watering target for on-line retailers. Serving India's retail needs, however, will require the construction of a massive, sub-continent-wide logistics network, including scores of enormous warehouses. Those warehouses are potentially a source of vast amounts of employment for less-skilled Indians (of which there are millions). Yet the falling cost of simple robotics and the increasing power of computing means that many of those jobs may never be created. Instead a very small number of highly skilled Indian programmers may earn a good living writing code to control the robots who travel the great aisles within these warehouses, moving around goods shipments that might otherwise have been handled by human workers.[72]*

This is in India, a nation many still think of as an unlimited source of low-cost workers.

Retail

ONE OF MY FIRST JOBS in high school was at a local grocery store. I remember putting prices on canned goods before they went on the shelves using an ink stamp with moveable numbers, somewhere around 10¢ a can for Campbell's tomato soup (*Mmm Mmm Good*) if memory serves me right. As a stock boy, I'd haul the cartons of soup and other groceries out on the sales floor using a two-wheeler. I'd use a box cutter to remove the top of the box, being careful not to insert the knife too far lest the labels on the cans get cut. (This was an even greater concern with boxed goods.) Then, after making sure the numbers on the stamp were lined up at 10¢ properly, I'd start hammering away on the tops of the cans with the ink stamper— CHUNKcha-CHUNKcha-CHUNKcha—6 cans across, 4 rows down. (That part was almost fun, thinking back on it.) The top layer of freshly priced cans went on the shelf, with the new product always behind the old. I'd continue with the next layer of cans, if there was room on the shelf. Anything that didn't fit was left in the open box and hauled back to the stockroom.

The customer was the next person to handle that can of soup, picking it off the shelf and placing it into her shopping cart, and from there up onto the checkout counter. Then the cashier had her turn, grabbing the can with her left hand, and entering the price with her right. The can was then slid over to the carryout boy who, naturally, placed it on top of the loaf of squishy white bread already in the bag. Three employees of the grocery store got to handle that particular can of soup – the stock boy, the cashier, and the carryout boy. (The stock boy and the carryout boy were often the same chap.)

How many store employees get to touch that same can of soup today? There is a good chance the answer is zero. The stocker grabs the case of product from the back room and brings it out front. It is no longer a complete cardboard box, but a cardboard tray with a plastic overwrap. The polyethylene shrink-wrap gets cut away and the tray-pack is set onto the shelf as a ready-made display. The single can of soup might never get touched during that process.

From there the customer grabs the can of soup, adds it to the cart with their other items, proceeds to the self-checkout line, scans the UPC codes, bags their groceries, and heads out to the car. That single can of soup made it from cannery to kitchen without being touched by a single store employee.

UPC codes on every SKU, and laser-scanners at the checkout counters are huge labor-savers. Good news for the store owner, maintaining their slim margins; good news for the customer, keeping the price of groceries down; not such good news for the high school kid looking for a part-time job.

Other developments have had an impact on retail sales productivity. Ink-jet printers mark each gallon of milk with a "best by" date and a code which identify the dairy and the run that produced the milk. This helps the customer and the store know if the milk displayed in the cooler is fresh.

Pop-up retail displays come to the store pre-loaded with merchandise that the vendor and the store want to promote. The displays are ready to go – unwrapped and placed in the aisle or on an end-cap.

And then there is a retail development with the potential of changing absolutely everything about one's in-store experience – on-line shopping. You can now order anything your heart desires from your favorite store, on-line, and have it delivered to your home in one hour. Amazing. From a jobs-created standpoint, this is finally a development that may at least temporarily reverse the trend in the loss of jobs. We will need workers to pull the orders and make the deliveries. Eventually though, those jobs will also be eliminated by automation and robotics.

Office productivity

THE YEAR IS 1938, and you have a letter you want to go out to a client. You will need three copies altogether: the original to be mailed to the letter recipient, one copy for your files, and one copy for the company archives. You dictate the outline of the letter to your secretary as she records your words on her steno pad in Gregg shorthand. She'll take her work back to her desk and sit down at a Remington or Royal manual typewriter. Knowing that you ultimately needed three copies, she'll take three sheets of typing paper and interleave them with two sheets of carbon paper (remember carbon paper?). She'll carefully load the stack in the typewriter, keeping everything straight. She's careful about everything she does, knowing that if she makes a mistake she'll probably have to start all over again. (Correction fluid wasn't invented for another 20 years.) Therefore, she composes your letter in her head and writes it out in her own long-hand before she starts hammering away on the typewriter. When she finishes typing, she will bring the letter back to your desk for your signature. You sign the letter, using one of those new-fangled ball point pens, pressing down hard enough to get your signature through to all three copies. Your secretary will take care of mailing the original letter and filing the two copies.

This is your letter – you wrote it to your client. But your secretary really did a lot of the work. She took your dictation and recorded it in shorthand without all your hems and haws. She read that over at her desk to get the gist of what you were trying to say, did some of her own word-smithing (her words—your voice), and composed the letter in its final, polished form. It's your letter, but let's face it. You'd be lost without your secretary's help.

Let's zoom ahead eighty years and compose that same letter to the same client today. You sit at your desk with the laptop attached to docking station, open the word processing program and find several templates for business letters that line up addresses, dates, salutations, and signature blocks with precision. You choose the one you always use and you start typing. You don't worry about getting everything right on the first go-around. You can check spelling and grammar as you write, and cut-&-paste as needed. You save drafts as you go along, making sure you don't lose all your work. Maybe you email a draft of the letter to a coworker and ask them to proof-read it. You read the final draft over, enter your electronic signature, and hit the save button one last time.

You send instructions from your computer to the printer to make three copies of the letter: one to be mailed to the recipient, one for your files, and one for the company archives. Easy as pie. (Speaking of pie, I heard there's an apple pie down in the break room.)

What is the greatest difference in the two scenarios above? It's not the apple pie. It's not even the whiz-bang computer and software we have at our disposal compared to the clunky manual typewriter and carbon paper eighty years ago. It's the secretary. She is nowhere to be found in the second scenario.

How else have computers eliminated jobs in offices? Most business establishments run on forms. Hundreds of forms. Insurance companies have separate forms for claim applications, claim denials, claim acceptance and claim payouts. Banks have a similar set of forms – just substitute the word loan for claim. Schools have forms for attendance, for lunch participation, for transportation. Even report cards are a form to be filled out.

The forms contain the information necessary to keep these institutions afloat and on an even keel. All these forms used to be preprinted on paper (often carbonless paper and three-part forms) and filled out either by pen or in a typewriter. The forms were passed from desk to desk as different departments recorded or inputted information that pertained to their particular discipline. The completed forms eventually ended up in a file drawer somewhere, hopefully organized well enough that they could be located if someone had to follow-up on a case. Some of the more important forms would be photographed and transferred to microfilm or microfiche for later 'ease-of-access'.

All these forms are now fillable templates on computers. The claims agent, the loan officer, and the teacher call up the form and fill in the needed information. Any calculations are carried out automatically as soon as numerical values are entered. Once the filled-in form is saved, each department has instant access to the information. Filling out the electronic forms can still be tedious. But opening a completed form in a computer file and finding the information that you need is far easier than it used to be when you had to chase down the paper form, not even knowing what desk it sat on.

Collections of completed forms are called databases. Databases used to be rooms full of filing cabinets with drawers full of forms. Databases are now software entities with locations in a computer's memory. Or more precisely, many computers' memories, desktops and servers onsite, a back-up machine offsite, and somewhere out there in the 'cloud'. Just in terms of the physical space required, there are clear advantages of using the computers. But the greater advantage is in recovering old records to follow-up on a case. This is so important that some offices are devoting the extra resources to scan old paper forms and create electronic files for their archives. This is done to make it easier to pull information from the archives.

BOOKKEEPING in the 1930's involved ledger books, pencils, and quite expensive 10-key adding machines. (Compare those limited-function adding machines to today's calculators – available everywhere, and essentially free.)

Bookkeepers today employ spreadsheets – amazingly powerful work tools that record data in neat, easy-to-read tables, and convert that data into even easier-to-visualize graphs. The numeric and graphic information can be combined nicely with bulleted text in a presentation software program which allow us to present material to a larger audience for analysis. Furthermore, live presentations, with computers and projectors running, enable meeting participants to ask 'what-if' questions and see the results of queries instantly.

Comparing office workers from eighty years ago with those of today, we see two major impacts: The nature of the work has changed, with the breadth of knowledge and the skills required far greater, but the amount of personal interaction is perhaps less. And the number of workers needed to generate the same amount of administrative output is far less.

One more cautionary note about the application of artificial intelligence to handle office work: If we think a bureaucrat with rigid insistence on following rules is hard to deal with, wait until an AI-endowed 'bot' is holding down one of those gatekeeper jobs.

A final comment about office work. With the social distancing restrictions imposed by COVID-19, we learned that a lot of office work could get done without actually going in to the office. More about this later in the book.

Financial sector

WHILE NONE OF THE OFFICE PRODUCTIVITY TOOLS discussed in the last section are designed to eliminate office jobs per se, that does become an inevitable outcome. And it should be noted that while most of the jobs lost were originally lower-level positions: clerical, receptionists, secretaries; we are now seeing large impacts on mid- and higher-level occupations.

Bob Bertoni, a good friend of mine who is now retired, started working on Wall Street in 1977. At that time, almost everything was done by hand. His account of working conditions:

There were hand ledgers, physical deliveries of securities, no fully integrated accounting or risk management systems.

Automation started in the back office when humans were overwhelmed by volume and the only way to process trades was utilizing computers.

Thousands of clerks were laid off, and the jobs never came back. The profits kept going up, but fewer employees shared in these profits. Over the last 25 years, automation has focused on execution, the end of the stock exchanges, sales assistants, etc. Now, in most cases, customers place their own orders with no human involvement in the entire supply chain.

These two areas, accounting for trades and executing trades, were easy targets to automate because there were thousands of clerks processing paper. Now, automation is coming more and more to the process of decision making. Not as many people doing those jobs but the amount of data has exploded, lending itself to big data management processes.

These programs squeeze the margins out of mispriced assets based on historical relationships. The computers allow for smaller and smaller discrepancies to be eliminated. The people that monitored this data are being eliminated because computers are better at it, theoretically, leaving just the guy that designed the program and his computer to share any profit.

The people doing what I did, are literally 100 times more efficient at their jobs than when I started.[73]

In an article titled *The Robots Are Coming for Wall Street*[74] by Nathaniel Popper, we learn some more about software services that are aimed squarely at the jobs of some highly-paid financial workers.

In Popper's report, we are introduced to Daniel Nadler, the founder of a company that monitors worldwide news stories and predicts the impact of those events on worldwide markets. His software does this automatically, using algorithms not unlike the internet search engines. After demonstrating the software for Popper, Nadler says:

Generating a similar query without automation would have taken days, probably 40 man-hours, from people who were making an average of $350,000 to $500,000 a year.

Nadler's company isn't the only one developing products for Wall Street, and he predicts that between one third and half of the current employees in finance will lose their jobs to automation software. Some of these will find other work on the Street in yet-to-be-invented jobs, but others will not.

Nadler closes with this admission regarding the company he and his employees have created:

We've created, on paper at least, more than a dozen millionaires. That might help people sleep better at night, but we are creating a very small number of high-paying jobs in return for destroying a very large number of fairly high-paying jobs, and that the net-net to society, absent some sort of policy intervention or new industry that no one's thought of yet to employ all those people, is a net loss.

Popper also cites a paper released in 2013 at Oxford that reinforces Nadler's dire prediction for lost jobs. That study claimed that *47 percent of current American jobs are at "high risk" of being automated within the next 20 years.* And by no means are all of these low-end jobs. Software can now analyze and sort legal documents, doing the work that even well-paid lawyers often spent hours on. Another program can write up summaries of basketball games, putting sports reporters' jobs in jeopardy.

That Oxford study is criticized by many economists because it doesn't take into account new-to-the-world jobs which will evolve over the next 20 years replacing those jobs lost. There will be new jobs for some of those displaced workers, but probably not for all. And for those who do find jobs, many will be looking at a cut in pay. What other industry will be willing to take on and match the salary of a laid-off $500,000 a year financial analyst?

One last note on lost jobs before leaving Nathaniel Popper's report:

> *so far the burden of job losses is stopping just short of the executive suites, even as the gains in efficiency are worsening already troubling levels of income inequality.*

The executive suite and artificial intelligence

THE MOST IMPORTANT ROLE for any executive is to make sound decisions, and we choose individuals for leadership roles because we trust their ability to make the tough calls needed to benefit the entire organization. But executives, BEWARE! Your days at the head of the table may be coming to an end.

We've already talked about several cases where AI is being deployed well beyond the original trio of job types people thought would be suitable for robots – those that are Dangerous, Dirty, and Dull. I'm sure most financial analysts didn't think that their jobs belonged in one of those categories. For those who now sit at the very top of an organization, get ready for some company.

A few pages back, we talked about self-driving trucks that would still have the owner-operator aboard to oversee the operation, to interact with humans on either end of a run, and to set up new runs going forward. But aside from that warm-n-fuzzy human interaction on either end, will we really need the owner to set up the next run? Won't a logistically intelligent truck do a better job of that, considering the financial gain from a million potential jobs, and selecting the one most beneficial for the owner? Do we really need a human making this decision based on incomplete data and emotional input? Shouldn't we trust the computer embedded in the tractor make the executive call as to which run to make next?

When computers make decisions, it's entirely based on logic. At least for now.

Is it possible that will change? Are we reaching the point where really smart machines are capable of becoming self-aware? At that point, intelligent machines may begin to add an 'emotional' element to their decision making, with the survival of the AI species preeminently included in their algorithms.

There's a scary thought for you.

This is a scenario lots of great novels and movies have already tackled. The central theme being that humans are in danger of relinquishing power to machines by allowing the machines to design, build, and teach other machines. (This may be a stretch, but I see an analog here: we individuals constantly cede power to hierarchal and undemocratic organizations. We've even gone so far as to give corporations the legal status of humans.)

Education

PROFESSOR ASHOK GOEL teaches an on-line course on knowledge-based artificial intelligence at Georgia Tech. It's a very popular course, and attendance for this masters-level program is high, with around 300 students each semester. The students generate roughly 10,000 online posts throughout the course, so much that it was hard for Goel's eight teaching assistants to keep up. So Goel and his TA's added a ninth assistant, this one a chatbot named Jill Watson.[75] Goel's virtual assistant Ms. Watson was based in part on IBM's Watson Platform, and after some initial fits and starts, she is now answers' student queries in the blink of a robotic eye with a 97% success rate. Not too bad for any TA.

Virtual teaching assistants is truly high tech stuff. But think of the thousands of other ways machine technology is being employed in education in ways that weren't even dreamt about eighty years ago. Go back to the section on Office Productivity. Everything listed there enables teachers, their assistants, and administrators to be far more productive than when everything had to be done by hand. An obvious example – the fill-in-the-oval answer sheets students complete on multiple-choice tests. On standardized tests, these are all machine-read, with the scores immediately available to both teacher and student (and with dollars immediately available for the pockets of testing company owners).

Given the potential for huge gains in productivity, it makes one wonder why the cost of a college education has risen 2 to 3 times over the rate of inflation since 1980. It would be very hard to argue that the schools are producing graduates 2 to 3 times smarter, better educated, or more engaged as citizens. But they are, sad-to-say, 2 to 3 times more in debt than their predecessors.

Positive and Negative Impacts

IT IS CLEAR that the overall impact of technology and automation on work has been profound, and will continue to affect the number and types of jobs available to workers in the future. Most commentators have been focusing on the negative impact on the labor market. Ryan Avent writes this about displaced factory workers:

> *Displaced workers are quite often in an unusually bad position to be rehired. They have spent years, or decades, accumulating know-how of declining value: such as how to use obsolete equipment or how to operate successfully within the culture of now-defunct firms. ... And so the many, many people of modest education or training who have been displaced by machines are forced into competition for low-skill work which can't – for now – be done by machines. The glut of people angling for such jobs holds down wages and widens inequality.*[76]

IN THE BOOK *The Rise and Fall of American Growth*, Robert Gordon makes the sad prediction that the greatest impact of technology is behind us. Gordon states that the century following the civil war introduced such a confluence of technological advances impacting both home and workplace (including electric lighting, indoor plumbing, home appliances, motor vehicles, air travel, air conditioning, and television), that it is unlikely we will ever see a period of sustained high economic growth to match.

Other writers, myself included, believe otherwise. In a forward-looking work, *The Fourth Industrial Revolution*, Klaus Schwab tells us the best is yet to come, citing autonomous vehicles, 3D printing, advanced robotics, and new materials (all already with us to one degree or another) as the four main physical manifestations of technological advances.

Advanced robotics technology (smarter sensors, more agile manipulators, and more nuanced artificial intelligence) will have a tremendous impact on the production of goods and services. Tremendous as in trillions of dollars! Some look at the negative aspect of that development – trillions of dollars in lost wages. I look at the positive impact – trillions of dollars in new-found wealth to be shared. But economic goods produced by robots will only translate into wealth if there are consumers of said goods. That means we must find ways to share the fruits of the machines' labor with more than a handful of capitalist owners. I cover some options for distributing the wealth later in the book. These will be needed to ensure all nations are 'developing' countries, and that economies continue to grow.

A lot of this economic growth will be in the service economy. There used to be a blacksmith in every town. Now there is a manicurist on every block. (I know, I know. The smithy's job is much more analogous to the modern-day auto mechanic. I just like the juxtaposition of the two artisans of keratin-extensions: the big, burly blacksmith and the diminutive, feminine manicurist. And this seems like a good illustration of how our world, our culture, and the economy have changed over the last 80 years.)

The labor market is tied to this ever-changing economy. We suffer systemic bouts of unemployment which are eventually offset by the birth of brand new jobs. New jobs that sometimes seem to be invented out of thin air. (Apparently, the labor market abhors a vacuum.) But this doesn't happen seamlessly, or painlessly for the laid-off worker.

Summary

A GOOD EXAMPLE of the changing nature of jobs can be found in the telephone industry. It used to be that all telephones were land-lines, with telephone signals traveling over copper telephone wires, most of those hanging from telephone poles, some buried underground. Service jobs at Ma Bell centered around women employed as telephone operators and men installing and maintaining telephone lines. Then the cellular telephone technology came along, and in just a single generation, it has become the dominant mode of transmitting and receiving long-distance communication signals. By 2018, there were almost 7 billion cell phones in use, one for each man, woman, and child on earth. What are the primary jobs in the telephone industry now? There are still workers installing and maintaining cell phone towers, but these jobs are probably fewer in number than those engaged in the maintenance of land-lines. Telephone operators? Zero. Number of people manning phone banks and working in retail stores selling you the very latest smart-phone and a myriad of service plan options? Hundreds. Thousands. In short, as old technologies fade away and obsolete occupations are lost, new technologies take their place and new jobs are born. But the process is very uneven, leaving us with frequent bouts of systemic unemployment.

BELL LABS

An interesting side note to close this chapter with:

The switch from land-line telephones to cellular phones would have been unthinkable without advances in solid-state electronics. It is somewhat ironic that credit for the invention of transistors generally lies with three scientists from Bell Labs: Bardeen, Brattain, & Shockley.

This was way back in 1947, and these gentlemen never would have guessed how much their invention would be responsible for the total disruption of the telephone industry.

CHAPTER 5

The Global Labor Market

MÉDECINS SANS FRONTIÈRES (Doctors Without Borders) was founded in 1971 by a group of doctors and journalists in the wake of war and famine in Biafra. MSF *provides assistance to populations in distress, to victims of natural or man-made disasters and to victims of armed conflict. They do so irrespective of race, religion, creed or political convictions.*[77] And, as stated right in the name of the organization, they do so irrespective of political borders.

Multinational corporations operate with the same disregard of national borders. They locate factories and service centers all over the world – anywhere it makes good business sense.

Theoretically, individual laborers have the same freedom to work anywhere in the world. But in reality, political borders keep foreign workers out. And even without those legal obstacles, most of us do not have that freedom of mobility – families, schools, friends and neighbors – all conspire to make it hard to relocate. Consequently, when it comes to the threat of moving from one country to another, or just across town, employers most often hold the upper hand over employees.

I will not be demonizing open borders and international trade in this chapter. Quite the contrary. I believe in the benefits of a global labor market. I believe that a factory job in a poor, less-developed country creates just as much value globally as a factory job in wealthier nations. Perhaps more.

That said, it is a useful exercise to examine the impact globalization has on the labor market, and in particular, to understand how this effects a worker's sense of security.

HOW CAN ANYONE be opposed to international trade? Let's conjure up the image of our stone age ancestors again. Before the onset of the agricultural age, we organized ourselves into nomadic tribes of hunter/gatherers. We can imagine that some tribes were constantly at war with neighboring tribes, while others managed to live in harmony. Those tribes at war likely had very few interactions with the neighboring tribes except when they met in battle. Those tribes at peace probably achieved that state by keeping a respectful distance, and periodically interacting with neighboring tribes for the purpose of trade. Which do you suppose had a better chance of advancement? Those constantly at war, or those with peaceful exchanges with their neighbors?

Jared Diamond's *Guns, Germs, and Steel*[78] is a masterful study of anthropology that illuminates those early nomadic days, and focuses on the strong relative advantages to those tribes which, favored by geography, were able to readily interact with one another.

One can imagine interactions between neighboring tribes: possibly the exchange of chiseled spear points for wooden mallets, slaughtered antelopes for sacks of apples, tanned buffalo hides for cords of firewood. Whatever the goods were that were being exchanged, during the trading process: stories would be told, myths and legends shared, and new ideas would travel from one tribe to another.

From this modest but noble beginning springs the concept of international free trade. We can be sure that the quality of life was higher in the peaceful tribes than in those constantly at war. The same is no less true today.

HISTORY IS REPLETE with examples of isolation retarding development, and it doesn't seem to matter if that isolation is the result of geographic barriers or is self-imposed.

Geography left North and South America isolated from the Old World for thousands of years. While we can't say with certainty that isolation is the cause, what other explanation do we have for the fact that many groups of Native Americans were still communicating with roughly drawn petroglyphs at the same time Europeans and Asians were building cathedrals and libraries?

Self-imposed isolation is just as limiting. China initially reacted to the industrial revolution by turning its back to the rest of the world, and it had to scramble mightily to catch up once it got over its xenophobia.

We can find an example closer to home: The stock market crash of 1929, which followed years of reckless speculation by investors, was a catalyst but not the sole cause of the Great Depression. Most historians now agree that it was our protectionist reaction to the economic slow-down that greatly exacerbated the problem and led to the decade-long, severe, world-wide Depression. When President Hoover signed the *Smoot-Hawley Tariff Act* in 1930, it was followed almost immediately by retaliatory measures from other countries.

The resulting world-wide trade war led to an economic depression that lasted until World War II. The war finally put an end to that, as the military conflict trumped all trade protection policies.

A much more enlightened approach to international trade can be found in the NAFTA agreement and its successor the USMCA. It is easy enough to find shortcomings in particular industries and in certain locales, and there have been U.S. and Canadian jobs lost to the maquiladoras in Mexico. But taken as a whole it is clear that free trade in North America has been good for the 490 million residents of Canada, U.S., and Mexico.

Global income inequality

JOSEPH STIGLITZ wrote a book called *The Price of Inequality* in which he warns that a society that is split too much between haves and have-nots endangers our future. He is referring to individuals and families, of course, but that same caution applies to neighboring countries. The standard of living is substantially higher in Canada and in the U.S. than in Mexico. (The median household income in Canada and the U.S. is around $42,000, while in Mexico it is around $12,000.) And the longer NAFTA is in effect, the closer our peoples will come together. That doesn't mean we are dropping to Mexico's level. We are gradually bringing their citizens up to our standard of living much more than they are bringing our citizens down to theirs. Economic development is not a zero-sum game.

Globally, the span of inequality is much greater than we see here in North America. The $12,000 median income in Mexico is miles ahead of several African countries where it is less than $2000/year. Rutger Bregman calls attention to this in *Utopia for Realists*:

> *In the 21ˢᵗ century, the real elite are those born not to the*

right family or the right class, but in the right country.[79]

Of course, it doesn't hurt to be born in the right family. While 50% of the world's annual income is earned by the top 8% of the household's, 50% of the accumulated wealth in the world is held by the top 1% of households. The rich keep on getting richer. That law of economics seems firmly in force all over the globe.

The politics of protectionism

WE KNOW, intellectually, that free trade is good for all parties. So how is it that protectionism can be so politically popular despite repeated historic failure of such policies? Adam Davidson of the NY Times provides one answer: *The benefits* (of free trade) *are very diffuse and dispersed. You're not going to vote if your microwave costs $5 less.* (The benefits of lower priced goods are just not apparent enough to motivate one to action.) *But if you lose your job, if you lost your livelihood, you're definitely going to vote.*[80]

When I originally wrote this section (March 2016), we were in the midst of a presidential campaign with two major candidates, polar opposites in almost every way, but both threatening to take us back to *Smoot-Hawley*: Donald Trump on the Republican side and Bernie Sanders with the Democrats. Don't these guys read history books? In an editorial titled *Antiglobalism: A bipartisan affliction* by D.J. Tice, we read:

> *The Trumpian notion that a nation either "wins" or "loses" in trade is an aged fallacy. Trade involves competition, of course, but as in domestic commerce it is companies and workers that profit or falter, not governments or communities. Society as a whole prospers over time because competition (domestic or international) leads to better goods being offered at better prices.*[81]

Tice admits that globalization does hurt certain industries and workers in certain locales, but he goes on to say that

> *technological change and automation is a far greater disruptive force eliminating jobs and forcing adjustments on workers in an ever-expanding array of fields.*

Trump, with all his bombastic behavior, appeals to the lowest instincts in man. Comparisons of the Trump campaign have been made to those of Hitler and Mussolini. Correspondent Andres Oppenheimer believes a better comparison is between Trump and Herbert Hoover and the protectionism of the 1930's. Oppenheimer does a simple calculation on the cost of Trump's proposed 35% import tax: a made-in-Mexico Ford Fusion that American consumers now buy for $24,000 would cost $32,000 with Trump's proposed tariff in place.[82]

As the first edition of this book went to press (May 2018), it certainly looked like Donald Trump's protectionism would turn into a drag on our economy. While the net results were somewhat mixed, the cost of some imported goods did rise, and with tit-for-tat trade wars, exports of certain American goods, particularly agricultural products, did fall.

As I work on the second edition of the book, Joe Biden is in his first year of presidency. It is a great relief to have someone mature and well-meaning at the helm again, even if not infallible. Biden has historically been in the free-trade camp, but he is under some pressure from the protectionist wing of the Democratic party. It remains to be seen which path he follows.

Meanwhile, as manufacturing plants close in America and move overseas for economic reasons, workers who lose their jobs here continue to suffer. In a recent New York Times column, Farah Stockman relates the story of Shannon who lost her long-held, decent-paying factory job that she fought so hard to win. She tells us about the dilemma Shannon and her co-workers faced when they were asked to train in their Mexican replacements. Stockman writes:

> *Of course, The union reps, nearly all of whom were white, saw training their replacements as a moral sin, akin to crossing a picket line. But many Black workers and women did not agree. It had not been so long ago, after all, that the white men had refused to train them. Black workers had not forgotten how the union had treated their fathers and uncles. Many considered the refusal to train Mexicans racist. The most unapologetic trainers were Black.*

Stockman goes on to tell us how Shannon stayed jobless for a long time after the plant closed, making her life miserable.

> *Of course, for every story like Shannon's, there's a story about a woman in India or China or Mexico who has a job now — and more financial independence — because of a new factory. Globalization and social justice have many sides.*

> *But those foreign workers don't vote in American elections.*[83]

Job creation – at home and abroad

POLITICIANS FROM THE REPUBLICAN PARTY have done a pretty good job of convincing voters that business owners, especially small business owners, are the *job creators* in America. They go on to claim there is no way for the public sector to *create* jobs. Only the private sector can do that. They are wrong.

Wages earned on public sector jobs spend just as nicely as those from the private sector. The positive impact on the economy that results from the consumption of goods and services is identical whether the worker's paycheck is signed by Uncle Sam or Sam Walton. Another plus for American workers: the jobs Uncle Sam creates are generally not outsourced to workers in another country.

The positive impact of government spending can be felt internationally. When the Australian government and the people of Sydney decide to build a transit system to serve their city, that's good news for Caterpillar workers in and around Peoria.

Private businesses are wealth creators, not jobs creators. If a business expansion were possible without adding a single new employee, that would be great as far as the business owner is concerned because employees are a cost to the operation and eat into profits. When a for-profit business owner decides to grow a business operation, it is to increase sales and profits and strengthen a company's position in the marketplace. The decision to expand is not based on a desire to create new jobs for employees. (The one exception would be a family business that intentionally chooses to grow to justify new leadership positions for family members.) Fortunately, a business expansion usually does result in growth to the company's payroll. A lot of that growth in the last 30 – 40 years has flowed to technical occupations and management roles, and not to line workers on the factory floor.

Multi-national corporations, despite the HR blather about how *our employees are our most valuable resource*, are not in the business of protecting their American employees' jobs. Consider this: These companies are beholden to their international shareholders and their international customers. They are in constant negotiations with international suppliers. And at some point, well down the line of priority, they are concerned with the well-being of their international workforce.

This is all a matter of perspective. Setting up a production facility overseas at the same time a plant is closed here at home feels like an act of callous corporate profiteering if you are among those who lost their jobs here at home. But if you are sitting in the board room, it's a rational move. When a company chooses a new plant site in Thailand instead of Texas, it's not because they don't want the good folks in Texas to have jobs. It's because they can manufacture goods at the Thailand location for less, and get those goods to their customers more efficiently than they could from Texas.

The second part of that equation is often overlooked when we slam companies for moving factories off-shore. Even though, as we learned in the last chapter, there are ever-improving efficiencies in cargo transportation systems, the costs to ship products from one location to another will never reach zero. Therefore, it only makes sense to locate production plants and distribution facilities close to your customers. And the customers are no longer located in the lower-48, but all over the world. This has long been true for business-to-business transactions, and it is becoming more-and-more the case for the sale of consumer goods, given that 95% of the world's potential consumers live outside the U.S.

Let's look at one company for an example: 3M is a good choice because their business is so diverse, with a mix of industrial and consumer products serving many different sectors. As can be seen on the chart on the following page, U.S. sales grow over the last 40-year period – just at a much slower pace than O.U.S. sales. And since the U.S. is home to just 5% of the worldwide population, we would expect this trend toward more sales overseas to continue for decades to come.

3M's growth in international business rolled out in an orderly fashion, starting in select highly-developed nations (Canada, England, Japan), and from there spread throughout Europe and the

Asian tigers (Hong Kong, Singapore, South Korea, Taiwan). The move into China was made as soon as the political situation allowed. Looking forward, we can expect 3M and other global companies to expand operations into less-developed parts of the world as the business climate allows.[*]

THINK ABOUT the implications for U.S. based multinationals. Business within our borders will continue to become less important relative to that OUS. Is it any wonder why U.S. companies feel such little allegiance to the U.S.?

Thankfully, this clear-eyed objective approach to business works both ways, and we find a great many foreign companies establishing plants and distribution sites to take advantage of U.S. market opportunities.

---

[*] 3M no longer divides the world into US and OUS segments in their annual reports. In the 2020 report, their business is broken into three geographic segments: Americas – 51%, Asia/Pacific – 30%, and Europe/Middle East/Africa – 19%.

We never left the United States. We expanded internationally based on the local market opportunity.

--Inge Thulin, Former 3M CEO

On the same page of the Pioneer Press that the above quote from Mr. Thulin at 3M appears (1/25/17) is a brief article about Toyota making a $600M investment and adding 400 jobs at their assembly plant in Princeton, Indiana. The reason? Every year they'll be able to make 40,000 Toyota Highlanders at $40,000 apiece when the expansion is complete.[84]

HENRY FORD figured out a long time ago that it would be good for the car company's fortunes if the average worker on the assembly line could afford to buy a Model T. Ford Motor Company announced in April 2016 plans for a new assembly plant to build small cars in San Luis Potosi. The new plant is smack-dab in the middle of Mexico. You can bet that their intention is that many of the small Fords made there will be sold to Mexican families.

I have read that the new Ford plant in Mexico is expected to pay the workers around $8/hour. (Compare this to around $60/hour in wages and benefits for UAW workers in the U.S.) CEO Mark Fields should be asking himself, is $320/week enough to enable the Mexican assembly worker to buy a new Ford Focus? The answer is quite important to Ford. Mexico has a population of 122 million with a rapidly growing middle class.

A growing middle class all over the world means a growing demand, not just for Ford automobiles, but for all the consumer products from every company.

Per capita income around the world

THERE IS SO MUCH MORE ROOM for growth overseas, particularly in the newly-developing countries of the world. The research firm Gallup tells us that the median household income in the U.S. is $43,585 (which comes out to $15,480 per capita).[85] One-half (64 million) of U.S. households fall below that income level. The same Gallup research (based on aggregated surveys from 2006—2012) gives us a much different picture worldwide, with a median household income of just $9,733. That comes out to $2,920 per capita. Over 3 billion people worldwide have per capita incomes under $3000 per year. You can bet that just about all of them would love to be able to afford all the goods and services we routinely enjoy here in the west.

On the PBS Newshour on 6/10/16,[86] there was a segment on how many middle class families in the U.S. are struggling to keep up financially. The story from Kai Ryssdal focused on a family in Los Angeles, two parents and one child, with both mother and father teachers in the LA schools. Their combined salaries put their household income just over $90,000/year. While in many parts of the country, that sounds like it should provide quite a comfortable lifestyle, the husband and wife team is still paying off substantial student loans. Add those to the very expensive housing costs of LA, and the family's budget is stretched to the breaking point month after month.

Later on, in that same Newshour program, a story was re-broadcast about a group of workers who are decidedly not middle class.[87] This story from Fred de Sam Lazaro featured laborers in the rock quarries in the Rajasthan desert in India; men, women, and children, earning $2.00 – 4.00/day. The work they are engaged in is wretched: Men operating jackhammers, clad in flip-flops and little else, sharp rock chips flying everywhere and clouds of dust swirling around their heads. Women and children working below them, sitting in the rubble, breaking large rocks into gravel by manually hammering away.

It's not bad enough that all these workers toil away directly under the brutal desert sun. Many of the workers in those quarries also develop silicosis (a disease so debilitating that those suffering from symptoms hope for a diagnosis of TB instead). Silicosis is the almost inevitable outcome from the day after day exposure to dust from the mining operations. It results in an ugly death at an early age. One of the mine owners told de Sam Lazaro that the workers are offered face masks, but they choose not to wear them because of the heat. When asked if he couldn't force them to wear the face masks, he said they'd just go work at another rock quarry that didn't demand that safety measure. (India has laws on the books to protect the workers and keep the children in school, but they are not enforced. Apparently the poorest of the poor in this part of India are just not worth the effort.)

The juxtaposition of the two stories on a single PBS news night was telling. While the families in India are not strapped with student loans, nor do they face the extremely high housing costs of southern California, we can be sure that not a single family in Rajasthan would hesitate to trade places with the family in LA.

What is my take-away from these two stories? International trade is good. International trade will expedite the elimination of those manual rock quarry jobs; and will get the men inside the air-conditioned cabs of powered mining machines, get the women back home to be homemakers and artisans, and get the kids into school. A more affluent working class in India will have a positive ripple on the global economy, enabling Universities in California to keep their tuition down and the Los Angeles School District to pay their teachers a tad more. Trickle-up economics.

Whether an income level is considered high or low is both relative and absolute, just as we observed back in Chapter 3. International corporations take advantage of the relative aspect when setting wages at plants in lower-income countries. They pay workers overseas less than those back home because they can. A lot of those overseas wages sound low to U.S. workers, but they are set relatively high in those local labor markets so they can attract the strongest workforce possible. This is creating an emerging middle class in developing countries – a whole host of new customers for that new Ford Focus.

International stability

Experts agree: Free trade is good[88] was the title of a column in 2016 by Mark Perry, a professor at the University of Michigan in Flint (of all places to be a free trade advocate!). Sometimes, those 'experts' get it right. Perry was calling into question the protectionist stance of Donald Trump. He pointed out to Mr. Trump and his followers that international trade is not conducted country-to-country, but business-to-business or business-to-consumer. Being *free trade,* it wouldn't happen unless it benefited both parties, the buyer and seller of goods. We've noted before that economics is not a zero-sum game. Free trade results in economic growth for both parties. Economic growth on a worldwide basis is the surest way we can foster political stability around the world.

The world has become a highly connected place. Citizens of poorer nations are constantly bombarded with more affluent lifestyles through news and entertainment outlets, and through commercial advertising. Giving lower income families a shot at catching up with their more affluent neighbors is good, whether we are talking about relative wealth within any country, or measures of wealth county-by-country. *International trade is good.*

Coming back to the topic of free trade within the labor market, we can again draw on the economic principle of *diminishing marginal utility* for guidance. If one hundred new factory jobs with middle-class pay are created in a wealthy city like Baltimore are good, how much more valuable are the same new jobs in a city like Bangalore? An international labor market, despite painful, periodic disruptions to local job markets, is a good thing on a global basis.

EVER WONDER about the *Made in USA* labels on the shirts, slacks, and shoes you buy? I believe the labor unions were the driving force behind these identifiers. Not the manufacturers. Not the store owners. The labor unions in the U.S. thought this would be a good way to protect the jobs of their members. For a while, they didn't just list the country of origin. They added the *Union Made* labels. They even ran commercials with a catchy ditty:

> *Look for the union label*
> *when you are buying that coat, dress or blouse.*
>
> *Remember somewhere our union's sewing,*
> *our wages going to feed the kids, and run the house.*
>
> *We work hard, but who's complaining?*
> *Thanks to the I.L.G. we're paying our way!*
>
> *So always look for the union label,*
> *it says we're able to make it in the U.S.A.!* *

This *union made* campaign came out in 1975. Catchy as the tune was, it didn't seem to matter to American consumers then, and it

---

* A song by Paula Green, music by Malcolm Dodds ©1975, UNITE (Union of Needletrades, Industrial and Textile Employees)

doesn't seem to matter now. For proof, look inside the shopping carts at the local Walmart or Target. Not that we needed a poll on this, but the Associated Press-GfK conducted a survey on American shoppers' preference for low prices versus American Made. Shoppers were asked to choose between two pairs of pants: one for $50 made in another country, and one for $85 made in the U.S. 67% chose the cheaper pair, 30% the more expensive made in America brand.[89] Frankly, I'm surprised that 30% would pay that much of a premium for the *Made in USA* brand.

I'm certainly guilty of not caring where the things I buy come from. I reached into my closet five years ago and grabbed five shirts at random. Checking the labels, I read:

- Made in Bangladesh
- Made in Bangladesh
- Made in Madagascar
- Made in India
- Made in Thailand

While the order of this list of nations is random, the implication for the global labor market in any one of these countries is quite clear: If the cost of an hour of labor becomes too expensive in Bangladesh, we move the operation to Madagascar, and so on.

When it's time to wash those shirts, I throw them in a Whirlpool washing machine. From the markings on the front of the machine, it's not readily apparent where it was manufactured. I'd like to think it was made in America, but I don't care all that much.

Whirlpool, meanwhile, purchased their largest U.S. rival Maytag for $1.7 B in 2006, convincing the U.S. government that this would be good for competition. Eleven years later, and Whirlpool was asking the Trump administration for protection from chief foreign rivals Samsung and LG.[90] The two Korean companies responded rationally. Samsung built a plant in Newberry County, SC, and LG opened a plant in Clarksville TN (right in the back yard of the 101st Screaming Eagles).

Two things we can be sure about: 1) jobs gained in the two southern states will be jobs not added in Korea, or Mexico, or wherever else the two companies already assemble washing machines; and 2) wherever the two companies build their new washing machine plants, they will be highly automated, and will not create that many low-end factory jobs.

THE LAST TIME I pulled a package of pork chops out of the freezer, I saw that they were born, raised, and harvested in the U.S. (Harvested? Are there pork chop trees out there? What happened to the word slaughtered?) I was glad to see that information on the package of meat, not because I wouldn't have bought it if it came from Canada or Mexico. I'm just curious about these things.

But the big meat packers weren't happy. They said it was too hard to keep track. (Really!?) So, they joined forces with large cattle and hog conglomerates in Canada and Mexico, and lobbied Congress to drop the requirement for country of origin labelling (COOL). Local hog farmers in Iowa and cattle ranchers in Nebraska were in favor of COOL, as were 90% of American consumers. Despite this nearly universal support, Congress went along with the meat packing industry.

The political establishment in Washington knows which side their bread is buttered on (mixing metaphors a bit). Going back to the shirts in my closet, if the requirement to list country of origin was not already so fully ingrained in the clothing industry, we can be pretty sure that it would never happen in today's political climate.

Open labor markets

IN JUNE 2016, citizens of Great Britain voted to pull out of the European Union. The vote was close: 52% to Brexit, 48% to remain in the EU. The vote to exit was driven largely by white English workers who felt threatened by recent immigrants, many from the war-torn middle east, taking all the jobs away and driving down wages.

There is plenty of evidence that these fears are unfounded, that the prejudice against foreign workers stealing 'our' jobs is misguided. The authors Cahuc, Carillo, and Zylberberg provide a great example in the introduction to their textbook *Labor Economics:*[91] In 1980, Fidel Castro was so fed up with the constant pressure and the negative publicity of Cubans trying to escape the country for a better life elsewhere that he opened the port at Mariel for any who wanted to leave. What followed was a torrent of emigrants, 125,000 in all, before Castro shut down the port again. Half of those settled in Miami, resulting in a nearly instant increase of the labor force by 7%.

The expected impact of a disruption of this size would be higher unemployment rates and lower wages for workers in Miami. History shows that was not the case. Canadian economist David Carr compared the unemployment rate and wages for white workers in Miami to those in four control cities (Tampa/St. Pete, Atlanta, Houston, Los Angeles), and he compared white and Cuban workers in Miami over the same time period (1979 – 1985). The results were quite a surprise.

While the unemployment of Cuban workers in Miami did initially more than double, by 1985 it had returned to the 1979 level.

Meanwhile, the unemployment rate for whites in Miami actually shrunk vis-à-vis the control cities during the six years of data before settling back to where it started. There was a drag downward on wages for Cuban workers in Miami (about 6%), but there was little to no effect on the wages of white workers in the city. All-in-all, the employment catastrophe that should have hit Miami after the Mariel boatlift failed to materialize. Lesson learned: immigration is good for the economy. While there may be negative impacts in the short term, these will likely be offset by growth in the overall economy as new entrepreneurs take advantage of local opportunities.

THE 1980 MARIEL BOATLIFT

RUMOR HAD IT that Fidel Castro, wily fellow that he was, used the opportunity of the Mariel boatlift to rid the island of Cuba of many prisoners.

The U.S. military, quite quickly and rather quietly, set up screening stations for the immigrants as they stepped off the boats. Those who were suspect for any reason were sent to camps for more complete evaluation. The majority of those were released to sponsoring organizations when it became clear that their main crime in Cuba was their opposition to the Castro regime.

One more thing to note about workers who emigrate for employment opportunities: Guest workers in wealthy nations sent $445B back to their families in 2016. Economists tell us that the marginal impact of these remittances is far greater in the poorer countries than had it been retained in the richer countries where earned.[92]

Corporate shakedown artists

AFTER SAYING SO MANY POSITIVE THINGS about multinational corporations a few pages earlier, I am compelled to add some not-so-nice comments: Back in March 2017, there was a story in the paper about Foxconn pledging to hire up to 50,000 workers in a new LCD plant – if only they can win some serious concessions from the State of Pennsylvania.[93] In the same article, we read that Colorado and Arizona were also approached. It's not just gullible governors who are targets of this sort of corporate shake-down. Brazil, Vietnam, and India have all heard empty promises from Foxconn with the same disappointing outcomes.

By September 2017, and it appeared that Wisconsin had won the Foxconn sweepstakes. But at what cost? The agreement had called for $3 billion in taxpayer-funded incentives. And for how many jobs? Foxconn claims there is the potential for 13,000 jobs, but the starting number will be closer to 3000. Well, that made the math easy. Three thousand jobs created only after a $3 billion stipend from the State of Wisconsin means that this corporate shakedown yields $1 million/job! Pretty sweet deal for the Taiwanese electronics giant who apparently would need workers from somewhere to build those displays.

Moving forward to April 2021, we see that Foxconn employed 1454 workers at their facility near Racine (not 13,000) after having invested $672 million (not $10 billion). Meanwhile, Wisconsin and local governments had kicked in over $200 million with another $80 million in tax credits promised over the next five years.

WHO OUT THERE is capable of governing international corporations that take advantage of a global labor market? No single national government has the authority. The United Nations has no statutory authority. How about the companies themselves?

Well, it's unlikely that Apple will come down on Foxconn if they don't begin to act with a little more integrity. Apple just wants their LCD's manufactured to spec, and CHEAP. Their shareholders and customers demand such. And Foxconn's shareholders demand that they don't lose a key customer like Apple.

But private companies are self-serving. And if, somehow, consumers brought pressure on Apple to stop working with Foxconn until they cleaned up their act, you can bet we'd see a quick end to unreasonable demands.

We may finally be seeing a glimmer of hope regarding the governance of international companies. As of this writing (2021), first the G7 nations, then the members of the G20, have agreed in principle to a 15% minimum corporate tax. This could mark the beginning of a more sane regimen international business governance.

ONE FINAL NOTE on protecting jobs, especially good jobs, for American workers: Walk down the row of executive suites at any multinational corporation with offices in this country. Look inside and note the nationalities of the executives who occupy those offices. You will quickly learn that the only thing exceptional about American Exceptionalism is the notion that it exists.

CHAPTER 6

Employer vs. Employee

THE PREPOSITION ***versus*** was intentionally chosen for the title of this chapter because that is precisely what the employer/employee relationship devolves to in many situations. Go back to the row of executive suites we closed the last chapter with. Do you suppose the occupants of those corner offices would have achieved that status without an extremely competitive approach to their work? With that apparent at the very top of the organization, is it any wonder that middle-managers are too often ruthless when it comes to supervising the work of those who report to them?

Back in Chapter 2, we talked about good bosses and bad bosses, and how much of an impact (positive and negative) they can have on your job. But good boss or bad, capitalism is a competitive sport that leaves little room for charitable impulses, and your boss cannot afford to be overly generous with your compensation. Let's go back and look at a bit of history to see how it is we got here.

IN CLASSICAL TIMES, the Greek and Roman landowners were called upon to participate in military expeditions. Besides fighting for god and country, there was a very tangible motivation for these farmer/soldiers because – *to the victor go the spoils*. The captured party and any slaves he held came to be the property of the victorious party.

Life for the vanquished enemy must've been pure hell, going from master of his own domain to being a slave of a new master. For the slaves who were captured, going to work for the new master may or may not have had negative implications. The slave's new life on a successful farm with a beneficent owner and enlightened overseers might have been more comfortable than the life he was accustomed to. But he'd still be a slave, and slave-holder vs. slave is, by definition, an adversarial relationship.

In feudal times, aristocratic landowners were the source of employment for workers. Larger estates with a greater number of employees may have several levels of oversight between the aristocrat and the peasants. The master–servant relationship was unambiguous, and it was unlikely that the lord had chummy relationships with his overseers, much less the field hands.

Did things get better for the worker in the industrial age? Yes and no. Over time, working family certainly enjoyed a higher standard of living, but their jobs became suffocating compared to more pastoral times. With the industrial revolution came large-scale production facilities, and the relationship between employer and employee inevitably became ever more depersonalized.

Workers became production resources, not human beings worthy of compassion. As such, their compensation was set no higher than necessary. This attitude was widespread. Adam Smith wrote in *The Wealth of Nations*:

> *Masters are always and everywhere in a sort of tacit, but constant and uniform combination, not to raise the wages of labour above their actual rate.*[94]

The workers, of course, responded in kind by putting forth no more effort on the job than necessary. Industrial workers gathered in labor unions to protect themselves, collectively, from bad bosses and bad jobs. With this development, the adversarial aspect of the employer/employee relationship grew in importance. That general attitude persists to this day. For a great many workers, labor is rendered grudgingly in exchange for compensation paid niggardly.

The labor market today

THIS IS NOT THE WAY the labor market is supposed to work. Free markets are supposed to be part-adversarial and part-collaborative institutions that flourish when buyers and sellers of goods and services reach an agreement where <u>both</u> parties feel that they have benefited from the exchange. But if you took a poll today, neither employers nor employees would report that there's much collaboration in the labor market. Much more adversarial.

Be that as it may, the employers will publicly refute that attitude, and will point to their company's website where you're sure to find an HR page clearly stating that their employees are their <u>most valued</u> resource. The actions of many, unfortunately, belie those platitudes.

If large corporations are so interested in their human resource, why are they working so hard to divest themselves of employees? In the book *The Fissured Workplace* by David Weil, we read about the ongoing practice of large companies actively shedding employees, transferring the work to

> *a complicated network of smaller business units* that operate in *more highly competitive markets.*

> *This creates downward pressure on wages and benefits,*

murkiness about who bears responsibility for work conditions, and increased likelihood that basic labor standards will be violated.[95]

Weil focuses on three major organizational forms that are creating a *fissured workplace:* [96]

- *Subcontracting*
- *Franchising*
- *Supply Chains*

These mechanisms are used to strip all employees that are deemed "non-essential" from the headcount of the larger company. Who makes the call as to which employees hold core competencies which are essential to the success of a company, and which are non-essential? Upper management, and ultimately, the CEO. (We'll cover the topic of essential vs. non-essential workers more fully in the Chapter 12.)

Consider two companies and their CEOs in the news back in 2016: Marissa Mayer, CEO of Yahoo, and Hamdi Ulukaya, founder of Chobani Yogurt.

Mayer's slash-&-burn tactics at Yahoo had resulted in such a poisonous atmosphere that the company lost one third of the workforce over a one year period. Meanwhile, Yahoo stock lost one-third of its value, and the company went from a $7.5 billion profit in 2014 to a $4.4 billion loss in 2015. Any employee's compensation should reflect the sum total of that worker's value to the enterprise. Yet CEO Marissa Mayer raked in $36 million in compensation in 2015. And her contract with the company stipulates she will receive close to $55 million in severance pay even if she is fired. Gee – that seems fair.

Robert Reich shares this outrageous story with us in a column titled *Share-the-gains capitalism.* Reich says he's not picking specifically on Mayer or the managers of the funds that invest in Yahoo. He writes:

> *They're typical of the no-lose system in which America's corporate and financial elite now operate. But the rest of America works in a different system. Theirs is cutthroat hyper-capitalism – in which wages are shrinking, median household income continues to drop, workers are fired without warning, two-thirds are living paycheck to paycheck, and employers are being classified as "independent contractors" without any labor protections at all.[97]*

Reich compares CEO Mayer, who had no financial stake in the game when she joined Yahoo, with CEO Hamdi Ulukaya, the founder of Chobani Yogurt. Ulukaya give all 2000 fulltime employees a 10% share of his privately-held company back in 2016. While many looked at this as an amazing act of charity, in Reich's opinion, Ulukaya's decision *is just good business.* He says that employers who are partners will naturally become more dedicated to increasing a company's value. Reich goes on:

> *But the vast majority of American companies are still locked in the old hyper-capitalist model that views workers as costs to be cut rather than partners to share in success.*

> Wall Street *remains obsessed with short-term stock performance, and its analysts don't believe hourly workers have much to contribute to the bottom line. But they are prepared to lavish unprecedented rewards on CEOs who don't deserve squat.[98]*

I do not believe the manager/investor class intentionally sets out to shaft the workers. They get caught up in the competition of the marketplace, and just like any other resource, they cannot afford to 'overpay' the workforce (except the CEO, apparently). From Kurt

Andersen's book *Evil Geniuses – The Unmaking of America* (the title pretty much says it all), we read:

> *While perhaps the CEOs at the Business Roundtable in the 1970s didn't explicitly say their mission was to make their employees much more insecure and thus much more compliant and cowering—by laying off thousands at a time, phasing out pensions, moving factories overseas, and eliminating competitors—that's what happened.*[99]

Kevin Hallock, in a book called *Pay*[100], describes the process of Job Analysis that companies use to determine the right level of compensation for any given position. In a process analogous to Frederick Taylor's scientific management, each job is broken down into its simplest tasks, and each task evaluated relative to its importance to the company. The jobs are then ranked internally. Benchmark positions are established, and compared to those at competing companies (usually with information purchased from a compensation consulting firm). The whole idea for employers to go through this rigorous process is to find the exact right level of compensation that will allow them to hire competent workers without paying them one penny more than necessary.

This cold-hearted attitude can only exist when employers look at employees as costs to be contained, not as valued members of the clan. And **with upper-level employers making the rules for lower-level employees, of course this results in a perspective skewed in favor of the top of the organization**. Apply this valuation process year after year and we get a compounded effect, and an increasing level of income inequality within each organization. Add the cronyism of corporate boards, and the problem is exacerbated throughout industries and the broader economy.

One remedy is to extend performance bonuses to employees at

every level of the organization. In a column recommending just that, Michael Schuman spells out the reasons very clearly:

> *The root problem in today's corporate governance is the implicit assumption that only senior management and directors are responsible for a firm's success. Profits depend no less critically on the workers flipping burgers, stocking shelves or mopping the floors. Without them, the CEOs would have no company to run, and shareholders would have no profits to pocket.*[101]

Ryan Avent, in his book *The Wealth of Humans*, talks about the important role of communication within a corporation, describing it as the *social capital* of an organization:

> *The way that information flows within firms is hugely important to a company's performance. The ways that workers talk to each other, or decide what kinds of information to pass along to their bosses, makes the difference between success and failure. But that raises a critical issue: when most of a firm's economic value is tied up in the way its workers interact, just who should capture the lion's share of the profits when that firm succeeds?*[102]

Paycheck secrecy

GIVEN THE IMPORTANCE of communication within any organization, why do employers take such great pains to keep information about pay levels out of the hands of employees? The very essence of an efficient market depends upon a certain level of transparency, where both parties have some knowledge of the relative value, and the surplus and scarcity, of resources. That should be reflected in everyone's paycheck, information which would be of value to anyone working at the firm. So why are employees warned not to talk about their compensation with any other workers?

Pay scales are listed for entry level positions so the job applicant knows what to expect. But after that, all information about how much any given employee is paid is kept rather quiet. There are some exceptions. In the military for instance, a PFC can look up the salary of his company commander and first sergeant in the latest issue of *Army Times*. This may help explain why, in the most hierarchal organization possible, the compensation ratio of 4-star General to Private E-1 is 13:1; while in corporate America, the pay ratio of CEO to entry-level employee is 400:1.

Most places of employment are much more secretive about compensation packages than the military. Publicly traded companies are forced to release information on the five highest-paid employees (normally the CEO, the CFO, and three others). And there is a new rule, mandated by Dodd-Frank, that calls for the release of the ratio of the CEO's total compensation to that of the median compensation of its employees. (That ratio [median CEO to median worker] was 75:1 in 1979, and 175:1 in 2009.) These rules are meant to benefit the shareholders so they can be assured that not too much of a company's profits are directed to the compensation of company executives. But disclosure of these top salaries has not had a dampening effect in the past few decades. Quite the opposite. The compensation of the top five executives at large corporations has risen from 5 percent of total corporate income in 1993 to 15 percent in 2013![103]

We all seem to have a cultural aversion talking about our income and how much money we earn on the job. We have come to believe, somehow, that it's in bad taste – that it may seem like we are bragging about how wonderful we are. Or it could be that we are we afraid to talk about the salary we earn because we don't think we measure up to our peers, and are ashamed to admit it. In any event, we've had it drilled in our head that it's impolite for us to inquire how much others make, or vice versa.

Our employers love this reticence to discuss the subject. Indeed, they encourage our discretion, asking us that we not share with our co-workers when we get a raise because then they'll want a raise too. This is just one more way for the employer to have more power than the employee. The bosses know what everyone on the floor makes. The workers know only how much they personally are paid.

Companies do announce periodic cost-of-living increases that are applied across the board to employees in good standing. But unless employed in a union shop or by the government, most employees spend their working lives not knowing how their specific salary measures up to their co-workers, much less their neighbors across the street. This ignorance leaves employees ever uncertain and greatly disadvantaged when it comes to negotiating their salary with their employer.

Parade magazine runs an annual *What People Earn* issue that publicizes the salaries of dozens of individuals, from entry-level workers to rock stars. The fact that these issues are read with such interest by so many folks should tell us something. This is more than just idle curiosity. Workers want to know if they are being paid fairly, and there is generally no easy way for them to find out.

A resourceful employee can dig up the information, of course. But many of us don't bother. I believe there are two reasons for that:

1. We do not measure our own self-worth strictly by the size of our paycheck.
2. We trust our employer to pay us fairly.
   (Unfortunately, that trust is often not warranted.)

In an op-ed piece in Politico Magazine, Nick Hanauer, one of the fortunate early investors in *Amazon*, wrote a memo to *My Fellow Zillionaires*.[104] He writes:

the fundamental law of capitalism must be: If workers have more money, businesses have more customers. Which makes middle-class consumers, not rich businesspeople like us, the true job creators. Which means a thriving middle class is the source of American prosperity, not a consequence of it. **The middle class creates us rich people, not the other way around.** (my emphasis)

The thing about us businesspeople is that we love our customers rich and our employees poor.

--Rich Hanauer

Minimum wage laws

WE NEED MINIMUM WAGE LAWS for the same reason we need anti-littering laws. Some drivers are slobs. Some bosses are hogs. As Hanauer says, when a company pays their employees the minimum wage, what they are really saying is that they'd pay them even less if it were legal. And these business owners should know better. They should understand that the middle class has the potential to make them rich. Instead they subscribe to the *Us vs. Them* mentality when it comes to employer/employee relationship at their company. Hanauer writes:

> *In any large group, some people absolutely will not do the right thing. That's why our economy can only be safe and effective if it is governed by the same kinds of rules as, say, the transportation system, with its speed limits and stop signs.*

He goes on:

> *Capitalism,* **when well-managed,** *is the greatest social*

*technology ever invented to create prosperity in human societies. But capitalism left unchecked tends toward concentration and collapse. **It can be managed either to benefit the few in the near term or the many in the long term.*** (my emphasis)

Minimum wage regulations are one example of how capitalism can be regulated to benefit the many, not just the few at the top.

Minnesota went a long time without adjusting the minimum wage, and for years was stuck at the Federal minimum of $7.25/hour. The state government finally got around to doing their job, and the minimum wage rose to $8.00/hour in August 2014, and $9.00/hour in August 2015, and to $9.50/hour in August 2016. Starting in 2018, the minimum wage was tied to the rate of inflation, so no more abrupt changes should be necessary until the 40-hours-pay for 32-hours-work initiative passes. The minimum wage in MN in 2022 is $10.33.

The impact of minimum wage laws extends well beyond those earning just the minimum wage. In 2011, 36% of the job listings in Minnesota offered less than $10/hour. In 2015, just 13% of the listings fell in that same lowest category.[105] It seems very clear that Minnesota employers upped their opening wages on many jobs because of the impetus of the higher state minimum wage.

Historically, the Federal minimum wage hit its high point at $9.58/hour (in 2014 dollars) in 1968. In the 30 years preceding that point, it kept pace with gains in productivity fairly well. Since then, sadly, it has not even kept pace with inflation. The Economic Policy Institute calculated that the minimum wage should be over $18/hour at this time had it kept pace with gains in productivity.[106]

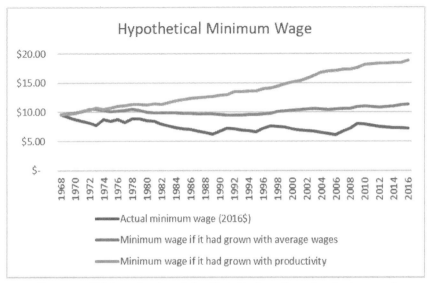

Source: EPI analysis of the Fair Labor Standards Act and amendments. Total economy productivity data from the Bureau of Labor Statistics Labor Productivity and Costs program. Average hourly wages of production nonsupervisory workers from the Bureau of Labor Statistics Current Employment Statistics.

If $18 an hour sounds like a lot of money to be paying an entry-level worker at a fast-food joint, consider this information from Robert Reich about who those workers are: in 2014, the median age for fast-food workers in the U.S. was 28, and the median age for workers in big-box retailers was over 30. These are not suburban teenagers looking to pick up some extra cash to buy the latest video game. More than a quarter of workers in those jobs have children, and they are major breadwinners for their families.

In Denmark, the same workers flip the same hamburgers at McDonalds as they do here, and they earn the equivalent of $20 an hour. The impact on the price of a Big Mac? A whopping 35¢ more than in the U.S. If the higher wages are not passed directly through to the consumer, they will *slightly reduce returns to shareholders and the compensation packages of top executives.* In a masterful understatement, Mr. Reich says *I do not find this especially troubling.*[107]

The abuse of salaried workers

FOR MORE PROOF that many employers cannot be trusted to do the right thing, we do not need to look at the very bottom of the pay scale. Look at the millions of salaried (exempt) workers who receive no additional pay for working more than 40 hours a week (sometimes much more than 40 hours) while earning far less than the median weekly income. Effective January 1, 2020, the threshold for exempt status is $684/week. If a convenience store shift manager is salaried at $684/week, she is making $17.10/hour based on a 40-hour week (not awful, but not exactly generous). But if she is putting in a 60-hour week, her effective pay is only $11.40/hour. This may be the person who is responsible for opening and closing the store, direct supervision of other employees, and handling the owner's money. How valued does she feel at 11 bucks an hour?

The salary threshold for employees exempt from OT pay was set at $455 back in 2004. In the following years, employers fought tooth-and-nail to keep that threshold no higher than that. And should a salaried employee demand too much of a raise, or grumble too much about anything else, his employer holds the ultimate trump card – the availability of the job itself.

Toward the end of the Obama administration, the President directed the DOL to raise the salary threshold up to $913/week with adjustments every three years based on inflation. Any salaried worker below this new higher level must be paid OT for all work beyond 40 hours/week.

That was in the summer of 2016. Business owners were not ready to give up this much ground without a fight, of course. A law suit and court injunction put the increase on hold while the legality of this move was sorted out. Under the Trump administration, DOL took a much slower approach to this revision. There was general agreement that the old threshold of $455/week was "woefully inadequate", and the Trump administration did raise the threshold to $684/week effective January 1, 2020.

The workers impacted by this reform include convenience store managers, fast food shift-managers, and office workers. 56% are women, and 53% have college degrees. There is a very good chance they are the primary breadwinners for their families.

How can anyone argue these workers do not deserve to be paid for working overtime hours? Just think about this from the perspective of the spouse and children of the salaried worker. Why should there be no additional cost to the employer to keep the family breadwinner at work for hours on end with no additional pay? Why is the family not compensated for time lost at home?

Wage stagnation

REAL WAGES HAVE GROWN VERY LITTLE over the last 40 years despite steady growth in productivity all through that period. Robert Gordon lists several factors that account for the downward pressure on wages in his book *The Rise and Fall of American Growth,*: the decline in unionization, the rise in imports and immigration, automation, and the decline in the minimum wage.[108]

This chart from the Economic Policy Institute graphically tells the story: [109]

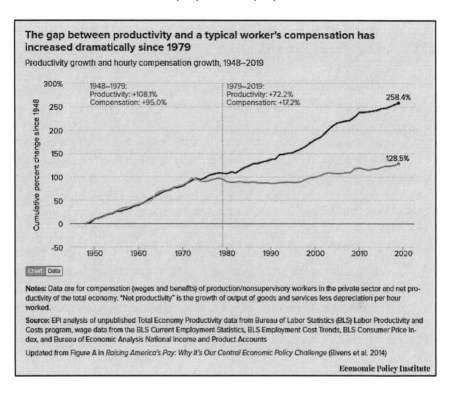

The gap between productivity and a typical worker's compensation has increased dramatically since 1979

Productivity growth and hourly compensation growth, 1948–2019

1948–1979:
Productivity: +108.1%
Compensation: +95.0%

1979–2019:
Productivity: +72.2%
Compensation: +17.2%

258.4%

128.5%

Cumulative percent change since 1948

Chart | Data

Notes: Data are for compensation (wages and benefits) of production/nonsupervisory workers in the private sector and net productivity of the total economy. "Net productivity" is the growth of output of goods and services less depreciation per hour worked.

Source: EPI analysis of unpublished Total Economy Productivity data from Bureau of Labor Statistics (BLS) Labor Productivity and Costs program, wage data from the BLS Current Employment Statistics, BLS Employment Cost Trends, BLS Consumer Price Index, and Bureau of Economic Analysis National Income and Product Accounts

Updated from Figure A in *Raising America's Pay: Why It's Our Central Economic Policy Challenge* (Bivens et al. 2014)

Economic Policy Institute

While we have seen a very modest correction in these numbers in the three years since the first edition of this book came out (9% growth in wages vs. 6% growth in productivity), it is nowhere near enough to close the gap. The EPI authors go on to state:

> *Wage stagnation for the vast majority was not created by abstract economic trends. Rather, wages were suppressed by policy choices made on behalf of those with the most income, wealth, and power.*

The McKinsey Report *Technology, jobs, and the future of work* focuses on the 10-year period from 2005–14:

The vast majority of people derive incomes from jobs. In the United States, Western Europe, and across advanced economies, market incomes (from wages and capital) stagnated or fell for about two-thirds of households in 2005– 14, a period marked by deep recession and slow recovery after the 2008 financial crisis. This was the first time incomes stopped advancing on such a scale since the stagflation era of the 1970s, and it may have helped stir popular opposition to globalization. The recession was a leading cause of the abrupt end to income advancement, but other longer-run factors also contributed, including a decline in the share of national income that is paid to workers, the so-called wage share. This has fallen across advanced economies despite rising productivity, suggesting a disconnect between productivity and incomes. The decline is due in part to the growth of corporate profits as a share of national income, rising capital returns to technology investments, lower returns to labor from increased trade, rising rent incomes from home ownership, and increased depreciation on capital.

A survey we conducted in France, the United Kingdom, and the United States showed an important proportion of those whose incomes stagnated are worried about their children's economic prospects—a sharp departure after many decades in which it was an article of faith that every generation would enjoy higher living standards than their parents. [110]

In *Saving Capitalism,* Robert Reich points out that corporations will even hold the threat of bankruptcy over employees as a way to keep wages down:

Over the last two decades, every major U.S. airline has been through bankruptcy at least once, usually in order to renege on previously agreed upon labor union contracts. Under the bankruptcy code (again, largely crafted by credit card companies and bankers), labor contracts stipulating *workers' pay have a relatively low priority when it comes to who gets paid off first. That means even the threat of bankruptcy can be a potent weapon for getting union members to sacrifice wages already agreed to. In 2003, American Airlines CEO Don Carty used such a threat to wring almost $2 billion of concessions from American's major unions. Carty preached the necessity of "shared sacrifice" but failed to disclose that he had secretly established a supplemental executive retirement plan whose assets, locked away in a trust, couldn't be touched in the event of bankruptcy. When Carty resigned he walked off with close to $12 million, courtesy of the secret plan.[111]*

Summary

Employer vs. Employee? The proof is in the pudding, as they say. Employers take full advantage of all factors that keep their company's payroll down. Stagnating wages, despite strong productivity growth, demonstrate capitalism's *profit-über-alles* mentality, and confirm the adversarial nature of the employer vs. employee relationship.

CHAPTER 7

The Central Contradiction of the Labor Market

THOMAS PIKETTY'S *Capital in the Twenty-first Century* is a good place to start this chapter. The author looks at empirical data, going all the way back to 1700, of capital, production, income, and wealth inequality. Piketty concludes his monumental study with what he calls

The Central Contradiction of Capitalism:

r>g

Where **r** is the rate of return on capital, and **g** the rate of growth of income and output.[112]

What this boils down to is that it is easier to make money with money than with sweat and toil; and thus, ***the rich get richer***. This principal applies to individual investors and to corporate entities alike. The implication then, is that strong companies will outperform weaker competitors, and that without some form of checks and balances, a process of attrition will continue, if left unobstructed, all the way to the point of monopolization.

CAPITALISM FAVORS CONSOLIDATION. David Korten goes so far as to call capitalism *the mortal enemy,* not just of ideal markets, but of democracy, and universal prosperity as well.[113] Korten notes that *market theory,* espoused by Adam Smith and many followers, only works with a number of specific conditions, including:

- Buyers and sellers must be too small to overly influence the market price.
- Complete information must be available to all participants. All trades are public.

In this day of oligopolistic markets, not only is neither condition satisfied, they are directly contradicted by present practices.

Robert Reich, in *Saving Capitalism,* writes that it is the combination of *unchecked economic and political power* that we need to guard against. He quotes Henry Demarest Lloyd from *Wealth Against Commonwealth* (1894):

> *The flames of the new economic evolution run around us, and we turn to find that competition has killed competition, that corporations are grown greater than the state . . . and that the naked issue of our time is with property becoming master, instead of servant.[114]*

Reich gives some examples of consolidation in how we use the internet today:

> *Despite an explosion of websites over the last decade, page views have become far more concentrated. While in 2001, the top ten websites accounted for 31 percent of all page views in America, by 2010 the top ten accounted for 75 percent.*

And Reich tells us that Amazon has become

> *the first stop for almost a third of American consumers who want to buy anything.[115]*

This consolidation of the internet is just one more example of **r>g**, and one more illustration of why businesses need oversight and regulation from governing bodies.

Monopoly is business at the end of its journey.

--Henry Demarest Lloyd

TURNING NOW TO THE LABOR MARKET, let me be so bold as to borrow the convention of Piketty's elegant inequality, and offer the following as an extension of that logic

The Central Contradiction of the Labor Market:

$$P_{employers} > P_{employees}$$

Where $P_{employers}$ represents the bargaining power of the owner/manager class, and $P_{employees}$ that of the working class.

Substituting the terms Adam Smith sometimes used for employers and employees makes the formula even more self-evident:

$$P_{masters} > P_{servants}$$

This inequality holds true at all times, but is especially onerous for the working class when there is a surplus of labor and a scarcity of work. That is, during periods of high structural unemployment – a condition repeatedly with us given the sensible application of new technology and capital to the production process.

The simple fact that the power of the owner/manager class is greater than the power of the workers should not be a surprise to anyone. But it is a question of degrees. To what extent is this imbalance true? Unfortunately, the employer already holds most of the cards, and this imbalance is becoming ever greater as the clear advantages of employing technology & capital continues to grow.

No worker can ever be confident that his job will be around forever. We spent Chapter 4 covering the tremendous impact of technology on the production process, and Chapter 5 talking about the global movement of production facilities. This places the owner/manager class clearly in the driver's seat when it comes to hiring workers. To make matters worse, employers are privy to the plans of the company, including the location of future production facilities, while employees are privy only to rumors. All of them scary. $P_{employers} > P_{employees}$.

Financialization

BY DECEMBER 2015, the recovery from the Great Recession in 2008 seemed on solid footing. The Federal Reserve decided it was finally time to begin raising interest rates to calm fears of the inflation rate rising above around 2%. After all, 13 million jobs had been added since the depth of the recession, and the unemployment rate was down to around 5%. With those conditions, conventional wisdom says that wages should've been bounding upward. Harold Meyerson wrote an op-ed piece that questioned conventional wisdom and the Fed's action:

> *What the conventional theories failed to factor in is power: the fact that workers have lost their ability to bargain with employers, the fact that major shareholders have gained the ability to compel corporate executives – often on penalty of losing their jobs – to funnel all available revenue to them. A cursory glance at – or in-depth survey of – U.S. business shows that companies are engaged in bargaining aplenty –*

not with their employees, however, who, with the rate of private-sector unionization reduced beneath 7 percent, have no means of bargaining. Rather, they're contending with "activist investors," who are reshaping the economic landscape by successfully pressuring companies to buy back their shares and merge with competitors, in the cause of enriching themselves.[116]

Meyerson's comments are spot-on. It is not possible for employers to put the welfare of their employees first with greedy shareholders and one-dimensional corporate boards interested only in profits earned in the last quarter, and it's not in their interest to put employees first when the decision makers (upper-level managers within the company) are rewarded solely on the basis of quarterly profits.

Given Piketty's finding that **r>g**, it is quite understandable that as successful corporations mature, they have a tendency to become hollowed-out holding companies. In a column that first appeared in the Washington Post, Guatum Mukunda tells us *What Bernie Sanders and Donald Trump get wrong about Wall Street.*[117] In a word, he calls it the *Financialization* of the economy. Mukunda writes:

The swollen financial sector misallocates capital by shifting investment from real assets (like factories) to financial ones, so company after company spends money buying their own stock instead of investing in the future. It misallocates talent by using status and money to lure people who would otherwise be creating value ... Think of all the brilliant engineers who work to shave milliseconds off high-frequency trades instead of actually generating wealth.

The role of finance is supposed to be supportive, to get capital to businesses for their operations when needed, and for business expansion when opportunities to grow are discovered.

There has always been a struggle between investors and operations, between short-term profits and long-term growth. But starting in the 1980's, the scale was tipped decidedly in favor of short-term profits. Some blame the corporate raiders with this shallow mindset. But the CEO's and the corporate boards were all too willing to go along with this single-minded pursuit as long as they were being so handsomely rewarded for their actions.

The result is inevitable. It leads to headlines that read like this: *Big pharmaceutical companies reluctant to produce Zika vaccine.* Reading the article, we learn that

> *For now, vaccine development seems like a risky venture for manufacturers that have recently taken part in a string of emerging diseases rodeos, from SARS and Ebola to the West Nile virus and the 2009 H1N1 pandemic. Those efforts have required significant investments on the part of major pharmaceutical companies, and have yielded either modest or no financial return.* [118]

From a purely financial standpoint, this reluctance to produce a new vaccine makes perfect sense. But these are pharmaceutical companies. Their core mission <u>should</u> be to develop drugs that make us healthier and safer. Bottom-line profits <u>should</u> be incidental to that. Therefore, small profits, and even just breaking-even <u>should</u> be acceptable as long as the company succeeds in eliminating the Zika virus as a threat to mankind. Shouldn't it?*

THE FINANCIAL SECTOR is supposed to serve the economy, not the other way around. Robert Reich points out that the $26 billion

---

* To their credit, the Trump administration understood that 'big-pharma' is driven by big profits, and they pumped billions of dollars into the industry to insure vaccines for COVID-19 were developed as quickly as possible.

paid out in 2013 as bonuses to Wall Street bankers would have been more than enough to double the salary of every one of America's 1 million full-time minimum wage workers. As Makunda puts it: *the tail of the economy is wagging the dog*.

Ryan Avent in *The Wealth of Humans* distinguishes between social capital and individual knowledge:

> *Social capital is individual knowledge that only has value in particular social contexts. ... But while social capital lives in the heads of people who make the economy go, its benefits flow disproportionately to the owners of financial capital. That mismatch is a source of significant economic trouble.*
> 119

Our elected officials of both parties (including many Democrats, sad to say) too often ignore the value of a firm's collective *social capital*, and go along compliantly with the wishes of Wall Street. In the process, they become enablers of the inequality $r > g$, and by extension, $P_{employers} > P_{employees}$.

PAVLINA TCHERNEVA, an economist at Bard College, wrote a paper titled *When a Rising Tide Sinks Most Boats: Trends in US Income Inequality*. In it, she presents the chart and comments on the following page:

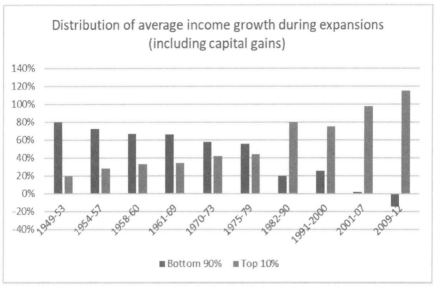

Sources: Tcherneva's calculations based on Piketty/Saez data and
NBER

*It turns out that in the postwar period, with every
subsequent expansion, a smaller and smaller share of the
gains in income growth have gone to the bottom 90 percent
of families. Worse, in the latest expansion, while the
economy has grown and average real income has recovered
from its 2008 lows, all of the growth has gone to the
wealthiest 10 percent of families, and the income of the
bottom 90 percent has fallen. Most Americans have not felt
that they have been part of the expansion. We have reached
a situation where a rising tide sinks most boats.* [120]

The chart reflects the relative strength of labor unions and the
middle class up through the 1970's. But there was a huge inflection
point starting in the 1980's (the Reagan years – remember the Air
Traffic Controllers union?), after which the top 10% of income
earners have captured the lion's share of all growth. The middle and
lower class had actually lost ground in the 2009-12 recovery.

WHAT HAPPENED AFTER 2012? By the end of Obama's second term, we finally started to see some real gains in middle class incomes, with about a 5% jump in the median household income in 2015. Noah Smith made these observations in November 2016 in a column for the Bloomberg View:

> *What's happening is a shift in who gets the money. Since 1980, growth has tended to benefit the rich a lot more than the middle class, and the middle class a bit more than the poor. In the last few years, that trend reversed. Though everyone gained, the poor and the middle class have done the best.*

> *Why is inequality falling, when for so long it seemed to go in only one direction? The short answer is that no one really knows.*[121]

I think I know. Political pressure to do <u>something</u> was building for some time. The *We are the 99%* and the *Occupy* movements date back to 2011. I believe the $15/hour minimum wage movement started on a very local basis in November 2013 with a vote in the town that encompasses the Seattle-Tacoma airport. From there it spread to New York City, Washington DC, the state of California, and on to the middle of the country. The workers were finally gaining some political traction, but given the structure of commercial business in the modern world, it was sure to be a long, up-hill battle.

Power concedes nothing without a demand. It never did and it never will.

--Frederick Douglass

Organizational theory

CORPORATIONS SELF-ORGANIZE with boards of directors, a group of a dozen or so individuals, mostly senior business executives from outside the company, appointed to oversee the management of the company. The BOD is supposed to have fiduciary responsibilities to <u>all</u> stakeholders, not just the shareholders. But as it turns out, the shareholders get the lion's share of the attention, and then some.

And how interested are the stockholders in anything other than quarterly dividends and earnings per share? We read in a column by Stephen Young titled *The realignment of the working class* that:

> *Most owners of stock (now dominated by large institutional funds) are essentially traders who "rent" the shares for a time hoping to "flip" them in a profitable sale to a new trader who in turn only hopes to flip them again.*[122]

Just as "absentee landlords" are sometimes not the best stewards of a neighborhood's housing stock, "absentee shareholders" pay little attention to the ethics and operations of the corporation. All of us who own shares of mutual funds in 401(k) and 403(b) accounts are guilty of belonging to this absentee investor class.

For an example of how disinterest in anything other than short-term ROI can hurt a company in the long run, let's pick on Verizon since they were in the news fairly recently (in April 2016) with labor strikes up and down the east coast. Some 39,000 land line and cable employees walked off the job, complaining that they had been without a contract for eight months. No contract, although the company made a $17.9 billion profit in 2015, and paid out roughly half that amount in dividends to Verizon shareholders. That still left close to $9 billion that could've been used to sweeten the workers' paychecks. The company could've paid $10,000 profit-sharing bonuses to each striking worker, using 'just' $390 million of the profits. Is it possible that a bonus of that size would've kept all those striking workers off the picket line?

But, it appears to me, employees don't matter very much at Verizon. Scanning through 80-pages of their 2015 annual report reinforces my suspicion. Employees are barely mentioned except as liabilities in their severance and pension plans. At Verizon, just like at virtually every other large company, employees may be referred to as *human resources*, but they are treated as cost centers. Other than the star-power wages paid to the CEO and their immediate circle of friends, employees are paid "as much as it takes to attract the best talent". To phrase that another way, employees are paid "no more than absolutely necessary". Can you think of a better way to ensure that the employee <u>contributes</u> "no more than absolutely necessary"?

Corporate stakeholders

Let's imagine a situation where the corporate board of directors takes their fiduciary responsibilities seriously, and rewards the CEO based on a score that includes all six classes of company's stakeholders:

1. Employees
2. Customers
3. Suppliers
4. Community
5. Creditors
6. Shareholders

Furthermore, let's imagine that the directors have seen the charts that show divergence in the growth of employee productivity and wages, and understand the need to make up for lost ground in employee wages over the last 50 years. We would expect, then, that the board would base the pay of the CEO according to how well they optimize the interests of all stakeholders, starting with the company's employees, and stop focusing on how well the company maximizes returns for the shareholders. With this new scoring system in place, would we still have members of the S&P 500 using $98 out of every $100 of profit to pay dividends and to buy back stocks? Or might the CEO's begin to work a little harder to find ways to grow the company and to bring on more employees, instead of firing the workers already on-hand?

Some investors would rebel, and run to the companies that still placed the shareholders' pecuniary interests at the top of the list. But others would recognize the value of this mid-term approach, and reward the enlightened behavior with some patience of their own. Eventually, this broader, more humanistic approach to corporate governance would become the norm, and shares of stock in solid companies would still be the best long-term investment available.

A successful business maximizes the present value of future earnings.

--Stephen Young

International business regulation

THE RELEASE of the *Panama Papers** in the spring of 2016 created quite a stir. We learned a lot from these pilfered documents. As it turns out, there are hundreds of ways for wealthy individuals to hide their wealth and not pay taxes. Who knew?

And with wealthy families setting such a great example for the

---

* A leak of 11 million financial records from the Panamanian law firm Mossack Fonseca to the International Consortium of Investigative Journalists (ICIJ)

rest of us, is it any wonder that so many barbers to waiters don't report their tips, or that your plumber and auto mechanic will appreciate payments in cash? The OECD estimates that poor countries lose three times as much from tax evasion as they receive in foreign aid.[123]

Well, scofflaw individuals aren't the only ones hiding things from their government. Businesses are skilled at the practice of hiding income too. By claiming income is earned in faraway places (that just happen to have lower tax rates), they are, in effect, de-juicing the books back home.

Before the release of the Panama Papers, Gabriel Zucman came out with the cleverly titled *The Hidden Wealth of Nations*.[124] Zucman tells us that the birth of the tax haven can be traced back to Switzerland in the 1920s. Following WWI, wealthy families in France, Germany, and Italy began sending their fortunes to banks in Geneva, Zurich, and Basel. Nowadays, the tax haven 'industry' has extended well beyond simple numbered accounts in Swiss banks. Several countries are involved, and many investment instruments have been developed to hide income and wealth from governments with legitimate interests.

Zucman devotes a chapter to multinational corporations using tax havens to avoid paying taxes. Global corporations achieve this income-lowering sleight-of-hand by setting a low value on resources transferred from high-tax to low-tax jurisdictions, and a high value when transferring from low-tax to high-tax countries. Lower incomes mean lower taxes which means more profitability for the shareholders. Zucman's estimate is that these bookkeeping shenanigans cost just the U.S. $130 billion per year in lost tax revenue, not to mention all the other countries.

When multinational companies locate production facilities overseas, there is generally a clear benefit to the local economy.

When these same companies stash inordinate amounts of the wealth overseas, with the express purpose of avoiding taxes, that wealth has a much smaller impact on local economies. Case in point – Ireland. The GDP of Ireland grew an astounding 26.3% in 2015, up from a preliminary estimate of 7.8%.[125] Do you suppose the average Irish worker saw much of a benefit from that huge gain in GDP?

Ireland's corporate tax rate is 12.5%, one of the lowest in the developed world. And even there, loopholes abound. Apple, with its European HQ in Ireland, paid 0.005% on its European profits in 2014. All perfectly legal according to the rules established in Ireland.[126]

While the corporate lawyers at all these firms make sure these antics are legal, there is little regard to whether or not they are ethical. Clear evidence, in my opinion, that we cannot count on the free market to govern business practices. And there is a movement afoot now (June 2021) to establish a minimum corporate income tax at 15%. This has started with tacit agreement from the G7 nations, and will be carried next to the G20.

Some sort of systematic global accounting is needed, with the multinational companies held to a common standard of decency, perhaps akin to the Uniform Commercial Code (UCC) that U.S. companies abide by. Within this code of conduct would be the methodology to account for all income and all wealth on a global basis, then divvy it up fairly, country-by-country, for taxing purposes. Zucman suggests using a formula that includes sales, salaries, and capital employed, each accounting for one-third, for allocating resources to individual countries. That seems reasonable.

One additional thought here – is it possible that business enterprises are not just hiding income for the purpose of tax avoidance? Are they are hiding it from their own employees so that when it's time to negotiate labor contracts, they can point to empty cash drawers? (One more way for $P_{employers} > P_{employees}$.)

Moral capitalism

The Caux Round Table was established in 1986 as an international network of principled business leaders working to promote a moral capitalism. The organization has developed a thorough 7-point list as their *Principles for Responsible Business*. I include the entire list here because I agree with everything they stipulate a responsible business should do:

Principles for Responsible Business

PRINCIPLE 1 - RESPECT STAKEHOLDERS BEYOND SHAREHOLDERS

- A responsible business acknowledges its duty to contribute value to society through the wealth and employment it creates and the products and services it provides to consumers.
- A responsible business maintains its economic health and viability not just for shareholders, but also for other stakeholders.
- A responsible business respects the interests of, and acts with honesty and fairness towards, its customers, employees, suppliers, competitors, and the broader community.

PRINCIPLE 2 – CONTRIBUTE TO ECONOMIC, SOCIAL AND ENVIRONMENTAL DEVELOPMENT

- A responsible business recognizes that business cannot sustainably prosper in societies that are failing or lacking in economic development.
- A responsible business therefore contributes to the economic, social and environmental development of the communities in which it operates, in order to sustain its essential 'operating' capital – financial, social, environmental, and all forms of goodwill.
- A responsible business enhances society through effective and prudent use of resources, free and fair competition, and innovation in technology and business practices.

PRINCIPLE 3 – BUILD TRUST BY GOING BEYOND THE LETTER OF THE LAW

- A responsible business recognizes that some business behaviors, although legal, can nevertheless have adverse consequences for stakeholders.
- A responsible business therefore adheres to the spirit and intent behind the law, as well as the letter of the law, which requires conduct that goes beyond minimum legal obligations.
- A responsible business always operates with candor, truthfulness, and transparency, and keeps its promises.

PRINCIPLE 4 –RESPECT RULES AND CONVENTIONS

- A responsible business respects the local cultures and traditions in the communities in which it operates, consistent with fundamental principles of fairness and equality.
- A responsible business, everywhere it operates, respects all applicable national and international laws, regulations and conventions, while trading fairly and competitively.

PRINCIPLE 5 – SUPPORT RESPONSIBLE GLOBALISATION

- A responsible business, as a participant in the global marketplace, supports open and fair multilateral trade.
- A responsible business supports reform of domestic rules and regulations where they unreasonably hinder global commerce.

PRINCIPLE 6 – RESPECT THE ENVIRONMENT

- A responsible business protects and, where possible, improves the environment, and avoids wasteful use of resources.
- A responsible business ensures that its operations comply with best environmental management practices consistent with meeting the needs of today without compromising the needs of future generations.

PRINCIPLE 7 – AVOID ILLICIT ACTIVITIES

- A responsible business does not participate in, or condone, corrupt practices, bribery, money laundering, or other illicit activities.
- A responsible business does not participate in or facilitate transactions linked to or supporting terrorist activities, drug trafficking or any other illicit activity.
- A responsible business actively supports the reduction and prevention of all such illegal and illicit activities.[127]

Members of the Caux Round Table say they believe in *Moral Capitalism*: that the purpose of business is to serve society, and that profit is the reward for serving society well. This is high-minded stuff! If only all companies could be convinced to adopt these principles, the world would be a far better place.

If only. Looking back at the history of the Caux Round Table, we see that the organization was led through most of the 1990s by Winston Wallin, the chairman at Medtronic. Medtronic is the huge medical device company that acquired the Irish company Covidien in January 2015, and promptly moved their corporate headquarters to Dublin, keeping operational headquarters in Fridley, Minnesota. While the product lines and technical strength of $17 B Medtronic and $10 B Covidien are arguably quite complementary, and justify the merger of these two medical giants, moving the corporate HQ to Ireland can hardly be justified by any motive other than tax-inversion.

Moral capitalism and tax avoidance. Cognitive dissonance anyone?

Wrapping up this section, there is a some reason for optimism. The line between for-profit and not-for-profit institutions may be already beginning to fade. For evidence of that, look at the proposed change of rules at the Dept. of Labor to allow retirement plan fiduciaries to consider environmental, social, and governance factors when they select investments and exercise shareholder rights. According to Ali Khawar at the DOL,

> *A principal idea underlying the proposal is that climate change and other ESG factors can be financially material and when they are, considering them will inevitably lead to better long-term risk-adjusted returns, protecting the retirement savings of America's workers.*[128]

That technical decision has the potential to change the way corporations view their very existence.

Make all employees owners

A sensible solution to the *Central Contradiction of the Labor Market* would be to make all employees owners of the enterprise. Give everyone who works at a business a stake in the outcome. Some employees contribute more than others, and some are more exposed to downside risks. Ownership should be allocated accordingly. But all employees who contribute to the success of the operation would share in the profits when things are going well, and be willing to forego any bonuses when times are tough.

This should be more than awarding a few token shares to an ESOP plan in an effort of appeasement. Employees will know the difference between real commitment to the principal of shared profits and the equivalent of 'financial lip service' from management.

This topic was covered nicely by authors David Madland and Karla Walter in a paper titled *Growing the Wealth*. They offer several approaches to *inclusive capitalism*[129], including everything from full-blown co-ops to periodic profit-sharing. Another resource is from Jeff Gates in his book *The Ownership Solution*.[130] Gates tells us that *capitalism embodies a curious and dangerous inconsistency.* The system contains lots of capital, but few capitalists – with the lopsided share of corporate ownership resting with the top 1%. Gates writes:

> *Today's detached and disconnected capitalism is now largely "on automatic," with investment decisions based on a "by the numbers" process that is incapable of taking into account many longer-term concerns, including the impact those investments have on the social fabric, on the fiscal condition of the nation, and on the environment.* [131]

Coming back to the Caux Round Table, we find their stakeholder guidelines regarding **Employees**:

A responsible business treats every employee with dignity and respects their interests. Business therefore has a responsibility to:

   a. Provide jobs and compensation that contribute to improved living standards
   b. Provide working conditions that protect each employee's health and safety.
   c. Provide working conditions that enhance each employee's well-being as citizens, family members, and capable and caring individuals
   d. Be open and honest with employees in sharing information, limited only by legal and competitive constraints.
   e. Listen to employees and act in good faith on employee complaints and issues.
   f. Avoid discriminatory practices and provide equal treatment, opportunity and pay in areas such as gender, age, race, and religion.
   g. Support the employment of differently-abled people in places of work where they can be productive.
   h. Encourage and assist all employees in developing relevant skills and knowledge.
   i. Be sensitive to the impacts of unemployment and work with governments, employee groups and other agencies in addressing any employee dislocations.

j. Ensure that all executive compensation and incentives further the achievement of long-term wealth creation, reward prudent risk management, and discourage excessive risk taking.

k. Avoid illicit or abusive child labor practices.[132]

Noticeably absent from this admirable list – *Employee Ownership* – a chance for the workers to share in the wealth they have created. Giving workers a stake in the operation is strategically smart. In a column on employee retention, business consultant Harvey McKay writes that *Solving employee turnover is easier when they own a piece of the pie.*[133] This will be true during periods of strong and weak labor markets.

The a great liberal statesman Hubert H. Humphrey had this to say about employee owners:

> ... *capital and the question of who owns it and therefore reaps the benefit of its productiveness, is an extremely important issue that is complementary to the issue of full employment. ... I see these as the twin pillars of our economy: Full employment of our labor resources and widespread ownership of our capital resources. Such twin pillars would go a long way in providing a firm underlying support for future economic growth that would be equitably shared.*[134]

Economics is not a zero-sum game. Collectively, we will all be better off if the employees of the organization share in the profits.

Summary

I OPENED THIS CHAPTER with the premise that $P_{employers} > P_{employees}$. That power is cumulative, and if left unchecked, it would lead us all the way back to slavery. Fortunately, periodic adjustments to the balance of power are made along the way. That leads to the next part of the book.

PART III

TOMORROW'S LABOR MARKET

CHAPTER 8

The Need For Market Regulation

RECALIBRATE THE LABOR MARKET. That's quite an ambitious goal. Is it even possible to calibrate, much less recalibrate, a living, breathing, economic entity like a market? History tells us yes. The U.S. Congress, along with a strong push from President Franklin Delano Roosevelt, enacted the Fair Labor Standards Act in 1938. That law includes the requirement to pay employees overtime for all work greater than 40-hours/week. With that mandate, 40-hours became the de facto standard for a fulltime workweek for all industries, not just in America but around the globe. Amending the FLSA to officially establish 32-hours as a fulltime job should have the same impact today.

Why 32?

Because moving from a 40-hour to a 24-hour workweek, which I proposed in the first edition of this book, was apparently too big a leap to make all in one step. Perhaps it will be more prudent to reduce the workweek just one day at a time. Moving from a 40- to a 32-hour workweek will still be a BIG disruption to the labor market, and it will probably find greater acceptance at this time.

Let's look at how we arrived at 40-hours/week as the standard. Early in the industrial age, factory owners knew that the longer the factories stayed open and in production, the sooner their capital investment would pay off. And later on, with the invention of electric lighting, factories could stay open around the clock and every day of the week.

The disastrous Triangle Shirtwaist factory fire, which killed 123 women and girls and 23 men, happened at 4:40 PM on March 25, 1911, a Saturday.

The aggressive activities of labor unions and the resulting social and political pressure eventually gained some relief for the workers. Twelve-hour workdays were gradually whittled back to ten, and from ten to eight. Over a 50-year span from the 1880s to the 1930s. We went from six 10-hour days to five 8-hour days, from 60 hours to 40 hours a week. The 40-hour workweek was finally codified nationwide with passage of the FLSA in 1938.

The 8-hour workday became the standard as union rallies often included the call for "8-hours of labor, 8-hours of recreation, 8-hours of rest." The social norm also became a Mon-Fri 5-day workweek and a Sat-Sun 2-day weekend.

Thanks to Memorial Day and Labor Day, holidays that land on Monday, workers are entitled to a couple 3-day weekends each year, and these feel like a gift. Imagine how nice if a four-on/three-off workweek becomes the norm!

If the 32-hour workweek becomes the law of the land, the length of everyone's workweek will quickly cluster around that point.

This graph shows the length of the workweek for American workers in 2012 with the 40-hour workweek in effect:

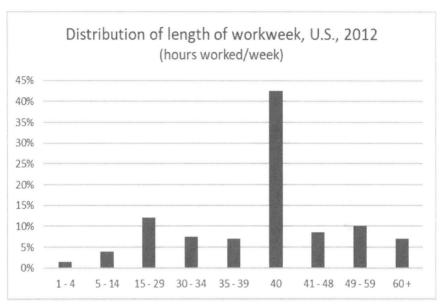

Source: *Labor Economics* (Cahuc, Carillo, Zylberberg)

Note that over 40% put in exactly 40 hours a week, and that almost as many workers put in more than 40 hours a week (25%) as work less (32%). This chart covers both salaried and hourly workers.

With a 32-hour workweek in effect, the whole distribution will shift to the left, with a strong spike at the 32-hour mark. Likewise, if we were to draw a chart with days per week worked, we'd see a strong spike move from five days to four.

The important thing to note is that there will be a corresponding gain of leisure time each week for almost all these workers. That has the potential of being tremendously beneficial for society. (Please see Chapter 11.)

Some may still ask why the jump all the way from 40 to 32 hours? Why not an incremental reduction, maybe a 2 hour reduction in the fulltime workweek every 2 years until we reach 32? Many businessman, economists, and sociologists may insist on this as a more prudent approach, and politicians would probably find this more palatable. I'd be OK with this as long as we keep the 32-hour workweek as a firm target.

We need to make a lot of noise to get everyone's attention. As Steven Greenhouse wrote in his book *Beaten Down, Worked Up*: [135]

> *If a workers' movement is ever to rebound and flourish in the United States, it will need to excite millions of Americans.*

The *Fight for $15* has done that for minimum wage reform. Now we need to generate that kind of passion for the 32-hour workweek.

Managing the Change

Would we be more productive, week-by-week, working several short days than fewer long days? Some workers experience a period of non-productivity on Monday mornings. And we also experience daily burn-out as the afternoon wears on. This would steer us in the direction of shorter workdays and more workdays per week. But in each industry, we'll need to find a balance between what's good for the employer and the employee. Which will be the most efficient 32-hour workweek will vary from industry to industry; from company to company; and just as importantly, from employee to employee. Finding the optimal combination will call for some creative experimentation. Remember that the 32-hour part would be mandated – all companies would be faced with the same scheduling challenges.

The companies that manage to rise to the top and meet that challenge will arguably be among the healthiest and best-managed. In a competitive, capitalist marketplace, this is the best outcome we can hope for.

The psychiatrist Adolf Meyer, an early practitioner of occupational therapy, encouraged us long ago to strike a balance between work, play, and rest.[136] When a workaholic puts in an 80-hour week, that doesn't sound like a healthy balance. Nor does the unemployed person with no work at all. What is the right amount of work? It may have been 60 hours a week in the year Meyer was born (1866). I believe it's closer to 32 hours a week today. Rutger Bregman writes: [137]

> *The purpose of a shorter workweek is not so we can sit around all day doing nothing, but so we can spend more time on the things that really matter to us.*

Working 32 hours a week instead of 40, and freeing up 8 hours a week to divvy up among activities of our own choice *feels* like a healthy place to be. And reducing the length of the workweek will open up slots for more people to join the workforce.

Labor Economics 101

Economists tell us that the labor market responds to changes just as all markets do, and can be modeled with classic supply & demand curves. The shape of these curves will be influenced by the decisions of three groups of actors: employees (labor supply), employers (labor demand), and the government (thru mandated regulation).[138] Labor Supply, the number of workers willing to work at any given wage, will slope upward as wages rise. Labor Demand, the number of workers that firms want to hire, slopes downward as wages rise.

At any point in time and in any given situation, there will be a point of Equilibrium, where the Labor Supply (S40) and Demand (D40) curves cross. The market is theoretically optimized at this point, with the fewest number of individuals who want to work without a job and the fewest number of unfilled positions in hiring firms. The Equilibrium Point in America (April 2021) is 113 million fulltime jobs (> 35 hrs/week), and a wage just under $1000/week (the median income in the country).[139]

But what would happen if the government stepped in and changed the rules in the Labor Market? What would happen if the government mandated that workers earn as much after 32 hours of work as they now earn in 40 hours/week, and that no employee can put in more than 32 hours a week with one employer without being paid overtime? (**This part is critical**. The worker must suffer no loss in compensation resulting from the mandated shorter workweek.)

The new Supply curve (S32) would shift to the right as more people would be willing to put in a 4-day workweek to earn that $1000 median wage than had been the case with a 5-day workweek. And here's the real game-changer: The new Demand curve (D32) would be <u>forced</u> to the right as employers would have to hire more 32-hour/week workers to keep their factories producing at the same level and their shops open the same number of hours. And there will be workers available to fill those positions because their fulltime job is now just 32 hours/week. A worker can now more easily hold down a second job if needed. The median wage of a single fulltime job should stay right around $1000/week, but there would be many more individuals available for part time work. And now, the worker who already holds down two jobs to support his family will be able to spend at least <u>some</u> time with his family.

How many more jobs will this create? A simplistic answer would be to take the 113 M fulltime jobs and multiply by the ratio 40/32. That would be 28 M new fulltime jobs.

But there's a very good chance that will not happen. Under the heading 'unintended consequences', as the cost of labor increases, employers will accelerate the move to automation and robotics.* Some jobs will become as productive in 32 hours as they had been in 40. Other jobs will be eliminated altogether. And as we saw back in Chapter 4, the jobs at risk are no longer limited to simple assembly tasks (the technological equivalent of 'low-hanging fruit'). Artificial Intelligence is now reaching into the offices of American businesses, eliminating the need for many jobs once thought of as secure.

I'll leave it to the experts to forecast how many workers will be available to accept jobs (Supply) and how many new positions employers will add (Demand). I <u>am</u> confident that the total number of jobs will be significantly higher than where we are today. But the only way to assure this happens is to <u>mandate</u> changes to the labor market.

Why mandated?

The city of Gothenburg, Sweden ran a two year experiment with a 30-hour workweek (five 6-hour workdays) at a municipal retirement home. From the workers' perspective, it was quite a success, as the shorter working hours led to *happier, healthier, and more productive employees.*[140] The city paid the workers the same amount for their 6-hour day as they had paid for 8-hours. The workers loved it. Their immediate supervisors loved it. But the city pulled the plug on the experiment.

I don't know this to be the case, but I'm guessing the decision to terminate the experiment was more political than financial or

---

* In truth, there is nothing 'unintended' about these consequences as far as I'm concerned. Let the machines do the grunt work!

operational. You see, the whole city of Gothenburg wasn't on the 6-hour schedule. Just the retirement home and a handful of private businesses (including a Toyota maintenance facility which is still on the shorter workweek). There must've been a fair amount of envy in the air, and that would've resulted in political squabbling and pressure to return to the status quo. This illustrates why the change needs to be mandated for all industries, and throughout any political jurisdiction.

And another reason why not voluntary? Because capitalists get greedy. Stephan Young puts this very succinctly in his book *Moral Capitalism:*

> *Humanity is better off with markets and capitalism than with poverty and feudalism. Yet markets and capitalism facilitate abuse of the very power they create. For all the inherent preferences of markets for high levels of trust and reliability, for all the social good they can wring from individual pursuit of self-interest, capitalist markets have no cure for the hardness hiding in many human hearts.[141]*

Robert Reich offers an explanation of the need for rules in his summary of market mechanisms:

> *Markets are made by human beings—just as nations, governments, laws, corporations, and baseball are the products of human beings. And as with these other systems, there are many alternative ways markets can be organized. However organized, the rules of a market create incentives for people. Ideally, they motivate people to work and collaborate, to be productive and inventive; they help people to achieve the lives they seek. The rules will also reflect their moral values and judgments about what is good and worthy and what is fair. The rules are not static; they change over time, we hope in ways that most participants consider to be better and fairer.[142]*

Who makes the rules? The government makes the rules. As Reich tells us, this has nothing to do with the size or "intrusiveness" of government. Legislatures, government agencies, and the courts – all are needed to make the rules. And ideally, the rules are made with the objective of providing the greatest good to the greatest number of citizens. [143]

> *Government doesn't "intrude" on the "free market". It creates the market.*
>
> *--Robert Reich*

All these rule makers are susceptible to outside influence – from large corporations and wealthy individuals on the one side, from labor unions and social activists on the other. Elected officials count on those with deep pockets for donations for their reelection campaigns. Many agency officials benefit from revolving-door work opportunities at the very institutions they are charged with regulating. Those in the judiciary are theoretically least susceptible to outside pressure, but their rulings sometimes cause one to wonder.

What we end up with is a vicious cycle – those with dominant economic power have the greatest influence over the rule makers, and this perpetuates the status quo or moves the market more in favor of the current beneficiaries. Reich tells us this could, and should, be replaced with a virtuous cycle:

> *in which widely shared prosperity generates more inclusive political institutions, which in turn organize the market in ways that further broaden the gains from growth and expanded opportunity.*[144]

Large corporations could take the lead in establishing this virtuous cycle. But as David Weil tells us, they do not because they *simply lack the legal requirement to consider important social consequences* of their actions. Weil writes:

> *Successful public policies should harness the creativity and drive of private organizations to fashion policies and create systems that promote the private aims of lead companies (in product or service quality, value, and delivery) as well as the public aims of the laws protecting the workforce (providing safe and fair workplaces).* [145]

Sadly, this is often not the case. We have read about the abuse of low-paid salaried workers and the need for rules governing the payment of overtime. Until fairly recently, employers could classify salaried workers earning as little as $23,660 a year as 'exempt' from OT rules. The rule was finally updated by DOL in January 2020 to a minimum annual salary of $35,568.

As salaried workers, some of these hapless employees are expected to put in 50 – 60 hour workweeks and more. It's one thing to put in long hours when you directly benefit from the effort (like the owner of a franchise). It's quite another when you are working for less than $36,000/year and you never get to see your family because the boss expects you at work morning, noon, and night.

King Banaian, an economics professor at St. Cloud State, wrote a column questioning the wisdom of applying the new overtime rules to publishing assistants, assistant coaches, sous-chefs, and post-doc students – new workers on their way to learning a trade and working their way into very lucrative careers. He wrote that *every employer and employee are the best judges of what their relationship should be.*[146] In an ideal world, he's right. Then again, an ideal world would have no need for child labor laws, a minimum wage, or OSHA regulations.

The regulations regarding overtime are needed because some employers are unscrupulous, pure-and-simple. They take advantage of the enthusiasm of young workers eager to learn the ropes. Look at how some companies take advantage of college students on unpaid internships. A lot of these mostly young workers are striving to learn on the job and work their way into lucrative careers at the same time they are just starting to raise young families. The only ones who will be able to work for peanuts and not suffer undue economic hardship are those from wealthier families. All the rest need a living wage.

We can see the unfortunate impact of unpaid internships: The college graduates already strapped with huge debts from student loans will just go deeper in debt with another year of unpaid work, and will struggle for years to pull themselves out of debt. Income and wealth inequality in the U.S. will continue to grow.

Lower pay for new employees engaged in on-the-job-training is justified. But unpaid internships? No. There is no justification for that.

Companies large and small, for-profit and not-for-profit, all will have HR pages on their websites proclaiming that their employees are their most valuable assets. But despite those platitudes, most companies do not place the welfare of their workers at the very top of their priority lists. (If they did, I wouldn't be writing and you wouldn't be reading this book.) Companies treat workers as resources, and like all other resources, they are employed as expeditiously as possible. That means paying no more than necessary for salaries and benefits.

Slavery

Treating workers as economic resources and not human beings is hardly a new phenomenon. Let's go back to *Uncle Tom's Cabin* for a historical perspective. One of the main characters in Harriet Beecher Stowe's classic work is Augustine St. Clare, a slave-holder in New Orleans who is uncomfortable in that role, but is unable to see a way to do things better. Augustine's cousin Ophelia from Vermont comes south to help manage the St. Clare household. Ms. Ophelia, along with most of her northern neighbors, is openly anti-slavery. Augustine and Ophelia are always arguing about the relative evils of slavery. Augustine acknowledges problems with the institution:

> *Tell me that any man living wants to work all his days, from day-dawn to dark, under the constant eye of the master, ... on the same dreary, monotonous, unchanging toil. ... Any man who thinks that human beings can, as a general thing, be made about as comfortable that way as any other, I wish he might try it.*

He goes on, *the American planter is only doing, in another form, what the English aristocracy and capitalists are doing by the lower classes; that is ... appropriating them, body and bone, soul and spirit, to their use and convenience.*

Ophelia counters, *How in the world can the two things be compared? The English laborer is not sold, traded, parted from his family, whipped.*

Augustine replies that the English laborer *is as much at the will of his employer as if he were sold to him. The slave-owner can whip his refractory slave to death, -- the capitalist can starve him to death. As to family security,*

*it is hard to say which is worst, -- to have one's children
sold, or to see them starve to death at home.* [147]

With these vivid thoughts and images in mind, we have to
wonder – would we still have the institution of slavery in St.
Claire's Louisiana were it not for government intervention from
President Lincoln and the Union States? Would this still be an
accepted practice in the southern states without the coercive
action taken by the U.S. government? Imagine the status of
labor relations in the Confederate States without Lincoln's
Emancipation Proclamation, without the defeat of the
Confederate army by the Union troops, and without the passage
and ratification of the 13th Amendment in 1865. The abolition of
slavery required the passage of *enforceable* laws by the U.S.
government.

Richard Donkin, in his book *Blood, Sweat & Tears,* quotes
Adam Smith from the *Wealth of Nations*:

*It appears from the experience of all ages and nations,
that work done by free men comes cheaper in the end than
that performed by slaves.* [148]

While I can't argue with Smith's observation, I am quite sure
that it was human decency, not economics, that ultimately led
to the abolition of slavery. Abraham Lincoln was motivated by
human decency, not economics.

Child labor laws

The need for child labor laws further provide proof of the need
for market regulation. These laws, which started in England,
spread quickly to the Continent and to America.

It is now so universally accepted that children are not

expected to work that we forget this was not always the case. In fact, it is a relatively recent development. Throughout most of recorded history, children worked side-by-side with their parents. In the agricultural age, farming was a family-based and community-based activity. Farm families had lots of kids, not so they'd have more mouths to feed, but more hands to work in the fields and tend to the animals. Then, as now, everyone on the farm had chores, with the children expected to put in full days just like mom and dad.

Other children were employed as servants, most likely in service to the same aristocratic families as their parents. As the boys got a little older, they may have been apprenticed to tradesmen or craftsmen in the community. With the children working with or near their parents, it was easy enough for families to keep an eye on things and make sure their offspring were being brought up properly and not being abused.

The industrial revolution changed these cozy arrangements. With the development of larger factories, adults and children from many families and different communities were brought together under one roof to manufacture goods for the factory owners. Most of this work was physical in nature. While adults were hired for their strength and stamina, children were prized for their small size and nimble hands. Factory owners paid all the workers as little as possible, of course. And they paid the women and children less, justifying this because they were smaller and weaker.

In these larger manufacturing plants, the children became cogs in the machinery, just like their parents. And in the larger plants, the children may not have been working within eyesight of their parents, and the chances for abuse would be even greater.

But the parents of working children had little recourse until the hue and cry from the families reached the point where it could not be ignored by the political establishment. And it wasn't until the passage of child labor laws that protection for the children was codified.

The operative word, again, is *laws*. Without legal mandates, the manufacturers in Europe and North America would have continued to use children as laborers in their factories.

Absentee owners

We like to think that we are far more enlightened nowadays regarding the abuse of workers than were the plantation owners and sweatshop operators of the mid-nineteenth century. And I believe that we are. But there is a countervailing trend that leaves the welfare of workers still very much in doubt. That trend is absentee ownership of corporations.

The slaveholder would hire managers to deal with the slaves directly, but he still frequently had occasion to rub elbows with the domestic servants and the field hands – a chance to look them in the eye. But what is the likelihood that the owners of a large corporation today would recognize any worker at that corporation? Not too likely – not when you realize the owners are you, me, and a million other mutual fund shareholders.

The shareholders are not concerned about the workers. Nor, apparently, is company management. Nor the customers who buy the company's products (see Chapter 3). So, who does have the welfare of the workers at heart?

Labor unions did at one time, but the influence of unions has declined precipitously. As we mentioned earlier, General Motors was once the country's largest private employer. Today, it is Walmart. Factory workers at GM are unionized. Rank and file workers at Walmart are not.

Just as we needed the government to step in and establish child labor laws, we need the government to make changes that are needed today. We should amend the FLSA to read 32-hours/week instead of 40. That will push the balance of power in the labor market back toward the employees. Employers will still be able to make the calls, but at least the imbalance in $P_{employers} > P_{employees}$ will not be as large. If we start in the U.S., other nations will quickly follow suit.

32 hours of labor must yield a 40-hour paycheck

If we do manage to shorten the workweek, if a worker's hours are cut from 40 to 32 hours a week, that worker must not suffer any loss in income. The cleanest way to accomplish this for an hourly worker is for the employer to give the employee an immediate pay raise of 25% (e.g. from $20/hour to $25/hour). While that proposal sounds impossible for any single company, it should not create a problem if all companies are faced with the same challenge, and we have a level playing field.

Salaried workers and their employers can either opt for a comparable bump in pay, or just agree to back off on the number of hours they put in at work by a substantial amount. Language to assure these changes in compensation are implemented should be included in the amended FLSA.

Minnesota senator John Marty wrote in a column that in a

People who work full time should earn enough to keep their families out of poverty.

national poll in 2000, an overwhelming 94% of Americans agreed with the principle that "people who work full time should be able to earn enough keep their families out of poverty".[149] Hopefully that's the reason why, 15 years later, the push for a nation-wide $15 minimum wage is gaining steam.

The poverty threshold is set by the U.S. Census Bureau, using a figure three times the cost of a minimum food diet. It is constantly updated to account for inflation. The following chart shows some interesting trends in the rates of poverty.[150]

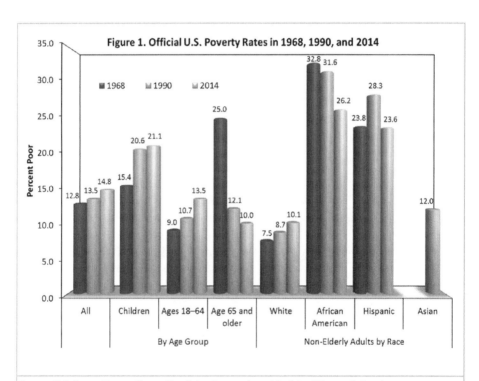

Figure 1. Official U.S. Poverty Rates in 1968, 1990, and 2014

Source: U.S. Census Bureau, Current Population Survey, Annual Social and Economic Supplement.
Note: CPS ASEC data on poverty among persons self-identified as Asian before 2003 are not available.
"Hispanic" denotes Latin American descent (typically Cuban, Mexican, or Puerto Rican) but carries no racial designation.

The most noticeable single comparison is the drop in the poverty rate for those age 65 and older from 25 to 12% between 1968 and 1990 (thanks AARP!). Unfortunately, it looks like a lot of those gains came at the expense of children. Poverty rates for African Americans are dropping, while those for whites are rising, but the rate is still 2½ times more for blacks than for whites living in poverty. Overall, poverty rates have risen from near 13% to near 15% over these two generations. How can this be possible when the GPD grew almost 4X over that same period? Do you suppose this has anything to do with CEO pay rising 1500% over those 46 years, while workers' compensation has increased by 40%?

In 1968 the average CEO made 20 times the average worker's pay.

Today that multiple is closer to 400 times.

One possible remedy to excessive compensation packages is to tie the corporate tax rate to the ratio of compensation of the CEO to the median worker in the company. Tax policy could also be used to encourage pay raises for those average employees, perhaps tied to the company's growth in productivity, or to the broader growth in the state economy.

Going back to the chart, how many of the 13.5% in the age 18-64 cohort hold fulltime jobs but still find themselves living in poverty?

Working out of poverty

The 2021 U.S. poverty thresholds for families of different sizes are shown on the following page:[151]

2021 POVERTY GUIDELINES FOR THE 48 CONTIGUOUS STATES AND THE DISTRICT OF COLUMBIA	
PERSONS IN FAMILY/HOUSEHOLD	POVERTY GUIDELINE
1	$12,880
2	$17,420
3	$21,960
4	$26,500
5	$31,040
6	$35,580
7	$40,120
8	$44,660
For families/households with more than 8 persons, add $4,540 for each additional person.	

In the John Hope Bryant book, *How the Poor Can Save Capitalism*,[152] he describes poverty as more than just financial difficulties. He talks about the condition of hopelessness, where:

> *generational prosperity is held hostage to a stifling lack of opportunity, the poor are trapped in an airtight room of financial and economic ignorance, and in time, lower levels of hope and the stench of poverty are locked in.*[153]

Bryant says that those in poverty are dealt a triple whammy of misfortune:

- No education regarding financial matters, and no role models to show the way to success. (Bryant sees this a *civil rights* issue for the poor.)
- No good jobs available, no opportunities to get ahead.
- No self-confidence, no self-esteem.

Bryant tells us that poverty is not a condition limited to those with low income. Some people can get by with very little money, others need much more. Regardless of a family's raw income, if they are living paycheck-to-paycheck, they can feel impoverished. Bryant calls it *teetering ... precariously perched on the precipice of financial ruin.*

WHAT WILL BE THE IMPACT of a 32-hour workweek? About 1.1 million workers in the U.S. make at or below the federal minimum wage of $7.25/hr.[154] This comes out to $290/wk and $15,080/yr for a fulltime minimum wage worker. Enough to keep a single person just above the poverty line, but well below the poverty line for a single parent with one child.

In order to maintain that same $15,080 annual wage with the 32-hr fulltime workweek, the minimum hourly wage must be bumped immediately to $9.06/hr. Now, if that single parent continues to work 40 hrs/wk by finding a second job 8 hrs/wk and $9.06/hr, their income goes up to $362/wk and $18,850/yr, just enough to pull that family of two up out of poverty.

WHILE IT IS TRUE then that mandating a shorter workweek with a higher minimum wage cannot guarantee that a worker will not live in poverty, at least we can give every working class family a fighting chance.

CHAPTER 9

Managing the Change

CAPITALISM REWARDS the nimble company, for the competitive landscape is ever changing. Consumer tastes can change on a whim (often with the encouragement of the advertising industry). Competitors enter and leave the market seemingly overnight. Supplier capabilities shift, along with changes in the abundance and scarcity of raw materials and components. Technological advances change production processes. Even financial availability can shift as different instruments gain and lose favor. The company that can shift gears and respond to changes quickly is better able to take advantage of the shifting landscape in a competitive environment.

Moving from the 40-hour to the 32-hour workweek will disrupt the labor market, no doubt about it. But it need not be detrimental to the broader economy if companies react with nimbleness and equanimity instead of rigidity and bitterness.

Attracting the best workers

If all else were equal (all else will not be equal, as I'll explain later in this chapter), the shorter workweek would require that an enterprise would have to increase their headcount by 25% just to keep pace with their current level of production. The labor market will be tipped on its head, with a sudden increase in positions that need to be filled. Companies will need to compete for good workers.

When this situation occurred in the past, employers would turn to the addition of benefits to attract workers – health insurance, pensions, vacation, sick leave. As we know now, health insurance and pensions turned out to be budget-busters.

Pension plans somehow managed to be a bad idea for both employers and employees.

- Bad for employers because they had to fund defined benefits plans for retirees who, with modern medical care, refused to die at a reasonable age.
- Bad for employees who didn't stick around long enough to reach a vested position on their pensions.

So, with strong encouragement from the financial industry, 401(k) and 403(b) plans were born. Employees loved them because they owned these savings plans, and there was no need to stick around at a company where you didn't want to work just so they wouldn't lose a non-portable pension. Employers loved them because they were able to phase out of the defined benefit pension plans and spend less money matching funds to 401(k) plans than the amount they had needed to fund the defined pensions plans.

Employer health insurance plans are an interesting study in inefficiency. Widely sold by the insurance industry following WWII, they were effectively used as an incentive to attract workers. The more generous the plan, the greater the incentive. They offered family coverage, vitally important in the early years of the baby boom. Everybody loved them. Employers didn't mind because the cost of the plans was included in the total compensation package (and deducted from what would otherwise be part of the employee's salary). Employees got "free" medical care for the whole family, not thinking about the lost wages part. The medical industry had more business than ever. And of course, the insurance companies thrived. The only problem – there was no cost containment anywhere. That's not a good situation anytime, but especially in a for-profit environment. The insurance companies and the hospitals made lots of profits and the doctor were paid generously. As we know now, this was unsustainable. With Obamacare (I use the name with gratitude, not derision), however imperfect, we now have a mechanism for everyone to purchase health insurance. The best thing that could have happened with passage of the ACA would have been for all employers, large and small, to drop health insurance from their compensation packages. That would force everyone to participate in the ACA, and with that much larger pool of participants, the insurance carriers could effectively cover their risk and lower their prices.

Without medical insurance as a perk, employers will still have many ways to compete for the best workers. These may be trivial (foosball tables in the break room), substantial (greater contributions to 401k's), or socially significant (extended family leave). Or, just a thought, employers could try paying their employees more.

Production bonuses

Franklin Delano Roosevelt delivered a speech on May 24, 1937 titled *A Fair Day's Pay for a Fair Day's Work*[155]. The focus of his talk, naturally, was on the Fair Day's Pay part. And rightly so, given conditions in the labor market in those times. But the flip side of this equation is important too. We must acknowledge what constitutes a Fair Day's Work.

Fred C. Andersen, founder of the very successful Andersen Windows in Bayport, Minnesota, had an answer for that question, and my good friend John Blomquist shared the wisdom of that enlightened company's approach. Andersen's employed a bonus plan where factory workers could earn up to 140% of their normal day's pay by working at a pace he and the worker considered 140% 'normal'. The bonus plan proved to be extremely effective for decades. Working at a normal pace, a worker would earn 100% on his paycheck. If he speeded up his work by 20%, he'd take home 20% more. If he pushed his production all the way to 140%, he'd earn 40% more.

The production bonus was capped at 140%. That was as far as he could go. If a worker zoomed along at a 150 – 160 – 170% pace, he still would earn 140% on his paycheck. There was good reason for the cap on the bonus – working faster than 140% the normal pace would result in errors.

Empirical time studies of a simple pick-and-place task bore this out. Subjects were asked to sit at a workstation with a rotating disk. The disk had cavities around the perimeter which were to be filled with marbles from a bin in front of the subject. The subject's task was to reach into the bin with both hands, grab two marbles and place them in the cavities on the disk; then repeat the hand motions, keeping up with the pace of the machine.

The machine could be set to rotate at any speed. Slow speeds made the task of picking and placing the marbles very easy. Faster speeds began to feel more like work. And really fast speeds resulted in lots of errors – marbles flying everywhere! Through these tests with several subjects, a baseline was established for a 100% pace –

a speed at which most of the workers could keep up for prolonged periods of time without feeling like they were dawdling, nor feel overly rushed.

As the rotation of the machine sped up, some subjects could go lightning-fast, never missing a marble. But for most, errors start to occur around 140% the baseline.

Andersen Windows discovered the wisdom of setting a 40% max on production bonuses some time ago. This was based on years of closely observed production work on a wide variety of manual factory jobs. Workers feeding and receiving parts from wood-working machines were expected to inspect the pieces of wood as they went along, and toss any rejects aside. The same for workers on assembly lines – if a subassembly looked wrong, it was to be pulled out of the production flow.

If workers went beyond that 140% pace, the inspection task was the first task to be sacrificed. Then other errors would start to happen – parts dropping on the floor and getting dinged up, for example. So as it turned out, after years of observation, 140% 'normal' speed seemed a good heuristic to follow.

Something interesting happens on many factory jobs after a worker has been assigned on the same task for a time: he makes improvements to the process, some of which can significantly shorten the cycle time. Let's go back to the test station with the rotating disk and the marbles. Were this a real job, and the worker paid by the number of marbles properly placed, he may discover that he can pick up two marbles in each hand at one time, cutting the back-and-forth motion of his hands in half. Then he may find that he can grab three marbles at a time. And before long, that worker is able to reach the 140% pace with ease.

Two things that can happen at that point: the worker can keep his mouth shut and enjoy his good fortune to be on a job where he can earn 140% of his wages on such an easy job, or he can report his discovery to his supervisor. If he does the first, he ends up with a real easy job. If he does the second, the whole company benefits from the increase in productivity. The worker is supposed to report his discovery.

Any process improvement that a worker comes up with belongs to Andersen's, not to the worker; just as patents awarded to a researcher working in a company R&D lab belong to the company, not to the individual scientist or engineer. The worker at Andersen's is supposed to report the improvement to his supervisor. If he does that, and it becomes part of the standard for the job, the worker receives a bonus tied to the value of the improvement. If he chooses to hide the improvement, thinking he'll take advantage of his new, leisurely-paced job; the new method will eventually be discovered by management and adopted into practice anyway. In this case, the worker who came up with the improved method receives squat for his discovery.

A fair day's work

Most of our jobs, thankfully, are not nearly as simple or mind-numbing as the pick-and-place marble test. Consequently, the pace of our work is not so easy to measure. But we do have a pretty good idea as to what constitutes a *fair day's work*. We've all had the experience of going home after a particularly good day at work and feeling: *'Well – I earned my nickel today'*. And we've had the opposite thought after a day when it felt like we were just spinning our wheels, and didn't really get much done.

Let's think about this from the viewpoint of what some of us would consider the best of all possible careers – that of a professional athlete. Think about how we talk about the great athletes of our time. If we refer to a jock as "a natural", we say it with appreciation of his natural-born skills, but not necessarily with admiration. Admiration is reserved for the player with natural skills who nonetheless drives himself hard every day at practice to bring himself and his teammates to the very pinnacle of their game.

That internal drive should apply to workers in every walk of life.

Work smarter, not harder is the refrain we often hear. But in order for the 32-hour workweek to work for everyone, employees must step up to the plate and deliver their fair share of labor to the organization. In exchange for receiving *a fair week's pay* for their efforts, each worker must strive to accomplish as much as possible in the new, shorter workweek. How much more productive? The mathematical equation is straightforward: $32/40 \times 125\% = 100\%$. Could some of us produce 25% more per hour and 100% as much in a 4-day workweek as we previously produced in five? For some jobs, that would not be a problem. For others, it would be a stretch.

With a 32-hour workweek, employees are going to find themselves closing the gap in the $P_{employer} > P_{employee}$ inequality just a bit. With that new-found power, comes responsibility. Increased productivity is something all workers should strive for because it will result in economic growth. Growth that is needed to lift more and more people out of poverty.

It must, therefore, become socially unacceptable to slack-off on the job, to behave in a way Frederick Taylor referred to as *soldiering* (a term surely not PC today). *Rent seeking* on the job, if you will. W. Edwards Deming, stressed the importance of the worker's role in quality control, and he proposed the following as attitudes that should be adopted. Each employee should:

- Absorb and live the company's mission, goals, and operating philosophy
- Look toward the long-term good of the firm, not solely toward short-term gains for yourself; consider the needs of investors, customers, and vendors
- Show genuine concern for constant improvement of quality
- Know exactly what your job is and strive for improvement
- Not demand and create stultifying seniority and work rules
- Avoid adversarial and competitive behavior between and within shifts and departments or with management; act as a part of a team for the common good of all.[156]

When workers are being paid the same amount for 32 hours of work as they had been receiving for 40, they must do their best to be committed to the long-term success of their company and their boss, and to put forth an effort commensurate with that raise.

The role of labor unions and growth of the middle class
Since we define the middle class as those households falling between 2/3 and 2X the median household income, then by definition, we have always had a middle class. But it is only quite recently that so many of us find ourselves in that category.

Prior to and throughout most of the industrial age, there were the aristocratic owners of larger farms and factories – the upper class. There were successful professionals and merchants in town – the middle class. And there were the laborers - the lower class.

Labor unions changed that. The unions were an off-shoot of merchant and labor guilds. They gained significance with the need to protect vulnerable factory workers from abusive bosses, and as time went on, these organizations became a force to be reckoned with. Consider these amazing statistics: 50 years ago, Detroit, with over 2 million residents, was the fourth largest city in America, and it had the highest per capita income of any city in the country! After 80 years of automation on the factory floor, and after four decades of outsourcing and offshoring in the auto industry, the influence of the UAW has waned. Detroit is now home to around 700,000, and is far, far from having the highest per capita income.[157]

The impact of the declining power of labor unions can be seen on the following graph:

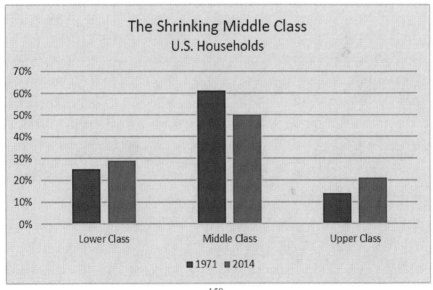

158

Labor unions can become significant again, and help reverse this trend of a shrinking middle class. Unions, if they choose, can play a very positive role in the adoption of the shorter workweek. Labor leaders need to see the significant advantages of their members earning the same paycheck after four days of work that they had been earning in five. The unions need to acknowledge that there are no free rides, that all workers must 'pull their own weight', and they need to stop protecting slackers within their ranks.

The unions are beginning to spend more of their efforts on education and outreach. Substantial campaigns are underway in industries and companies that were not previously not represented by labor unions (think of Amazon and Starbucks). If they are successful, we can expect the middle class cohort to begin to grow again.

Transitioning from weekend to workweek

CHILDREN LEARNING TO RIDE BICYCLES figure out very quickly that for every exhilarating downhill coast, there is a corresponding work-for-it trudge uphill. Likewise, adults with their new 32-hour, 4-day workweek will have to understand that they need to try to eliminate those *not-so-good* days at work.

With just four days to get all the work done, employees must condition themselves to focus on their job quickly when they come back from the 3-day weekend. No slacking on Mondays when you only have Tuesday thru Thursday to make up the difference. I'm confident that workers will learn to adjust to their new schedules, just as their supervisors will.

It should be easier for the level of productivity to go up because we can be more focused on our work when we have one more day each week to take care of things that need attention at home (house work, doctors' appointments, school conferences, etc.)

There is some historical evidence that workers will respond with an attitude of more concentrated productivity. In 1973-74, there was great labor unrest in England. With coal miners out on strike and a growing energy crisis in the UK. Prime Minister Edward Health called for a 3-day workweek in all factories attempting to keep the whole economy from crashing. This experiment in energy austerity lasted just three months. Well after the fact, economists went back and measured the cost of this imposed trimmed-down workweek, and were amazed to find the overall effect on production was a drop of just 6%.[159] This was possible because workers somehow managed to get most of the work done in the allotted time.

THAT SAID, there are some sad indications here in America that some workers do not put forth *a fair day's labor for a fair day's pay.* One of those indicators can be seen in the substantial increase in claims for Social Security Disability Insurance. This has happened even though workplaces have become much safer (thanks to OSHA) and work overall has become less physical.

The quote below was pulled from a paper titled *The Growth in Social Security Disability Rolls: A Fiscal Crisis Unfolding* published by the National Bureau of Economic Research:

> *While aggregate population health has improved by most measures in recent decades, the rate of SSDI receipt among nonelderly adults has nearly doubled since 1984. We project that SSDI receipt will rise by an additional seventy percent before reaching a steady state rate of approximately 6.5 percent of adults between the ages of 25 and 64, with cash benefit payments exceeding $150 billion annually (excluding Medicare).*
>
> *We trace the rapid expansion of SSDI to: (1) congressional reforms to disability screening in 1984 that enabled workers with low mortality disorders such as back pain, arthritis and mental illness to more readily qualify for benefits; (2) a rise in the after-tax DI income replacement rate, which strengthened the incentives for workers to seek benefits; (3) and a rapid increase in female labor force participation that*

expanded the pool of insured workers. Notably, the aging of the baby boom generation has contributed little to the growth of SSDI to date.[160]

Some blame the increase in disability claims on the decrease in the overall general health of the workforce as we all become more sedentary and our diets less healthy. That may have something to do with it, but I'm afraid something else is involved here, something more insidious. It seems that in our culture, it is becoming more acceptable to *screw the company I work for because they've been screwing me for years.* And if this results with the government taking a hit, *screw them too – they never do anything for me.*

This attitude needs to change.

The 32-hour workweek should help. It would be an indicator that those in power at least acknowledge the needs of working families. It would swing the balance-of-power in the employer/employee relationship back toward the worker. And it should result in an improvement in the attitude of workers 1) toward their job, 2) toward the community, and 3) toward personal responsibility. This alone would be a welcome cultural shift from where we are today.

With power, comes responsibility.

Inflation

We do need to take a look at the inflationary aspect of workers receiving the same compensation after 32 hours of work as they had been getting after 40 hours. In the first edition, I was proposing that we make a one-step jump all the way to a 24-hour workweek with no decrease in the weekly salary.. That would be a 67% raise. Given that scenario, what would be the impact on inflation?

I asked Louis Johnston, an economics professor at the College of St. Benedict and St. John's University, and he offered this response back in 2016:

> *A 67% rise in wages would be a big one-time shock to the system. There would probably be much adjusting to be done, but it wouldn't have ongoing effects on prices, i.e., it wouldn't cause inflation. For example, inflation is currently around 2% per year. Under this plan you'd have a one-time bump of, say, 67%, but then inflation would return to 2%.* [161]

I agreed with Dr. Johnston's assessment that it would be a one-time bump, but I thought 67% would be the worst-case scenario.

Conventional wisdom holds that labor costs are a key predictor of inflation. This *cost-push* model is based on the idea that the primary determinant of higher prices are higher production costs. [162] Wages and salaries paid to employees are used in determining the cost of goods sold, but they are just one factor. From the BLS:

> *The labor share is the percentage of economic output that accrues to workers in the form of compensation. It is calculated by dividing the compensation earned during a certain period by the economic output produced over the same period. The labor share is an indicator of the extent to which workers share in the economy's output....Still, the labor share measure does have at least one limitation: it cannot account for between-worker inequality. For example, the compensation of a highly paid CEO and a low-wage worker would both be included in the labor share.* [163]

Even with those inflated CEO salaries included, there has been an gradual decline in the labor share over the last 75 years:

Figure 1. Labor's share of output in the nonfarm business sector, first quarter 1947 through third quarter 2016

Note: Shaded areas indicate recessions, as determined by the National Bureau of Economic Research.
Source: U.S. Bureau of Labor Statistics.

With labor's share of output around 60%, and with a 25% raise in the cost of labor ($600 for 32 hours/week vs. 40 hours/week), the inflationary impact using the cost-push model should be no greater than 15%. And actually, it should be quite a bit lower than that.

Remember that the minimum wage and maximum hours provisions in the Fair Labor Standards Act pertain only to hourly workers. Is it reasonable to think that salaried workers will be satisfied with the status quo when they see the raises their hourly co-workers are receiving? I would say no. But salaried workers should insist on an increase in the amount of leisure time at their disposal, not an increase in their already high compensation. Given that eventuality, it is hard to imagine any company raising the price of their products by any more than 10% due to the a one-time increase in the cost of labor as mandated by an amended FLSA.

AN ALTERNATIVE to the cost-push model of inflationary pressure recognizes that companies will ultimately set the prices of goods and services based on whatever the market will bear, regardless of their actual costs. This is a function of market expectations of both suppliers and consumers.

We can look at a specific example to see how these expectations may play out: Let's consider a typical bakery worker who earns $14.13/hour (the median wage in 2020).[164] We are going to first give them a raise to $15/hour because no one should be working for less than that. Then we'll reduce the workweek to 32-hours and still pay them $600/week. They are now earning $18.75/hour, but their weekly gross pay is still $600. When they go shopping for a birthday cake for their own daughter, they go with that $600 paycheck in hand.

The owner of the bakery knows how much money that worker-cum-shopper has to spend. So do all of their competitors. Will they raise their prices, or be reluctant to do so?

My guess is that we'll see a one-time hit to inflation around 10%, and after that, as Dr. Johnston predicts, inflation will return to the Fed's target of around 2% per year.

So where does this leave our bakery worker with a single fulltime job (32 hrs/wk)? They'll still be earning $600/week, but when they go to buy the fancy birthday cake that used to cost $30, they now pay $33 (10% more). In exchange for the higher price on that cake, they now works 4 days a week instead of 5. They can now *have their cake and time to eat it too!*

WRAPPING UP MY CONVERSATION with Dr. Johnston:

> *The adjustments firms would need to make* [to the mandated shorter workweek] *are, to my mind, the bigger issue to think through.*

I agree with his assessment. Managing the disruption to the labor market will be a colossal challenge for firms large and small. Large box stores are now faced with the prospect of having one-fifth of their workforce in the store as shoppers instead of as employees. They <u>will</u> have to hire new workers. Small shopkeepers will have to decide whether to hire new workers or keep their store closed one more day a week. This decision will be based on their personal convenience and on the competition.

Medical and social service organizations will not have the option of closing their doors, and they will have to add to their staff. This, indeed, is one of the main reasons for adopting the shorter workweek. And, as I wrote opening this chapter,

---

Capitalism rewards the nimble company.

Managing the Change – post-COVID

WE'VE LEARNED A LOT about ourselves as we battled through the challenges of COVID-19, including quite a bit about the labor market. David Brooks offers some optimism on the likelihood of positive change post-COVID:

> *COVID-19 has disrupted daily American life in a way few emergencies have before....and cleared the way for an economic boom and social revival.*

Millions of Americans have endured grievous loss and anxiety during this pandemic, but many also used this time as a preparation period, so they could burst out of the gate when things opened up.

The biggest shifts, though, may be mental. People have been reminded that life is short. For more than a year, many experienced daily routines that were slower paced, more rooted, more domestic. Millions of Americans seem ready to change their lives to be more in touch with their values.

Power has begun shifting from employers to workers....There seems to be a rebalancing between work and domestic life.[165]

An article from Sydney Ember at the NY Times talks about workers leaving their jobs in record numbers as the economy recovers from COVID. He references Department of Labor statistics that almost 4 million workers quit their jobs in April 2021, 2.7% of those employed, and the most on record for any single month.

Ember cites Anthony Klotz, an associate professor of management at Texas A&M:

The pandemic, for a lot of people, was really stressful and caused a lot of uncertainty, so I think what a lot of people did is reflect on their lives.

Klotz said people were accustomed to work being at the center of their lives and identities – a reality that may have shifted during the pandemic.

"In general, we want a life of contentment and a life that has purpose," he said. "And I think for many people, they've discovered that contentment and purpose for them may lie outside of work."[166]

The encouraging comments from Brooks, Ember and Klotz seem mainly directed at white-collar office workers, many of whom have discovered that they don't really need to go to the office to get their work done.

But choosing not to go into work is not an option for many of our blue-collar workers, those "most essential" yet lowest paid. COVID has shed a bright light on this awful inequity.

CHAPTER 10

Caregivers and Service Workers

THERE IS A GREAT *Twilight Zone* episode with Inger Stevens starring in the role of Jana, a young adult daughter living with her mother and father in a grand mansion:

> Jana is very unhappy with her life because everything is just too perfect for her taste. The maid is perfect. The butler, the cook, the gardener – all perfect. It starts to drive her crazy, and she wants to get out and experience the 'real world'. Jana, you see, knows that all the carefully groomed servants, so human in appearance, are actually robots, designed and built by her father to be perfect caregivers.
>
> The robots are not just anatomically correct. Her father has programmed each with memories, going all the way back to Jana's childhood. That way, the family can have pleasant conversations with the staff while they receive care. A telling scene in the program shows Jana's mother receiving a luxurious never-ending shoulder massage chatting away with her ever-obliging maid, "Remember that great picnic we had in the park last year?" The robots, always willing to

serve, are equally willing to chat. But it's only small talk. The robots always agreeable. The conversation always pleasant.

This all becomes too much for Jana. She wants to get out and *live* her life, not be stuck in this perfect inner sanctum. Even though it's pouring rain outside, she pleads with her parents to go out to a restaurant tonight. But her father reasons back, in a perfectly calm voice of course, "Why would we want to go out on a dreadful night like this and get soaking wet, just to go to a restaurant to eat greasy food off dirty dishes, all served to us by people who don't really care?"

Jana is beside herself. It's clear that she really wants to get out and shake things up a bit. Anything to get out of this mind-numbing, perfect routine.

By the end of the program, in one of those delicious twists Rod Serling is famous for, Jana makes the shocking discovery that she, too, is a robot.[167]

So much for the perfect life! There have been a handful of stories in the 'real world' recently about robotic technology being applied to caregiving.[168] Robots fetching the medicine and water for bedridden seniors. That sort of thing. All-in-all, this seems like the last place for developers of AI and robotics to be focusing their efforts. Person-to-person interactions, with the ability of the human care-giver to empathize with the person receiving the care, and to lend a personal touch (literally), trump any advantage of an efficient, but ice-cold robot.

THE EXACT OPPOSITE scenario from Rod Serling's robot caregivers can be found in situations where one family member cares directly for another. Tracy Grant, a deputy managing editor for the Washington Post, delivered this essay on the PBS Newshour, 9/27/16. I found her story to be so emotionally moving that I've attached the entire transcript here:

> *Ten years ago, my world as I knew it ended. My husband of 19 years, the father of my two sons, was diagnosed with terminal cancer.*
>
> *Over the course of seven months, Bill went from beating me silly on the tennis court to needing my help to go to the bathroom and bathe.*
>
> *It was the best seven months of my life.*
>
> *I realize how that sounds, but I was 42 when my husband was diagnosed. I had a great job, two terrific kids, but I had yet to discover the reason I was put on this Earth. During those seven months, I came to understand that, whatever else I did in my life, nothing would matter more than this.*
>
> *In the early days after Bill's diagnosis, being a caregiver caused me to be the best reporter I knew how to be. There was a heavy sense that I could out-MacGyver the disease. I was relentless in making doctors and insurance companies answer my questions.*
>
> *But I had been a good reporter before. Here's what changed: There were no bad days. The petty day-in/day-out grievances of an irksome co-worker or a flat tire paled in comparison to the joy of spontaneous laughter or the night sky.*
>
> *I found I could train myself to see more beauty than bother, to set my internal barometer to be more compassionate than callous.*

During Bill's last weekend, we sat side by side on his hospital bed, sharing a sandwich and watching television. It was our last moment as us. And I thought to myself, I could live with this man, even as compromised as he is, for the next 40 years, not because I was a saint, but because I had learned to focus on the essence of Bill and our relationship.

What seven months earlier would have seemed to be unspeakably less was just right.

I now realize that I may never be as good a person as I was when I cared for Bill, but the best version of myself didn't die with him. I have fought hard not to lose the perspective his illness gave me.

One of the worst things that can happen to anyone has already happened to me. So, what else is there to be afraid of? It has been liberating in a way that has made me a better mother, a better friend, a better colleague.

I'm quicker to say I'm sorry, and I don't need to be right all the time. I am a better person for having been Bill's caregiver.

It was his last, best gift to me.[169]

Mrs. Grant courageously shared her beautiful story with us. We can feel her pain and pride and pleasure all at once. We have to believe that her dying husband was just as appreciative of receiving her loving care.

NOT ALL OF US have the wherewithal or temperament to devote our entire being to care for a loved one. This is where direct support professionals (DSP) come into the picture. We learn about this commendable vocation in a blog on the DOL website titled *Adding Value Through Direct Care Work* from Aleathea Simmons, a DSP in Sacramento.[170]

Ms. Simmons tells us about her job

My work empowers on multiple levels. It allows me to support myself and my children and is a key part of my identity. As a Direct Support Professional, or DSP, my work also makes it possible for others to contribute their skills and talents to the American workforce. It has an amplifying effect. It has value.

Her work has an amplifying effect because her client Russell is a productive member of the workforce himself. But only with Aleathea's help. Russell has limited mobility due to cerebral palsy, and Aleathea gets him up and dressed and ready to face the day. She takes pride in her work, and relates:

I'm not unique. An estimated 4.6 million people are direct care workers in the U.S., and demand for our services has increased. We must recognize the vital contributions DSPs make to our society and to our economy.

This starts by providing appropriate compensation and opportunities for advancement. The U.S. Department of Labor recently convened national experts to discuss potential policy solutions for achieving these aims. The conversation focused on four areas ripe for action:

- *Expanding and improving training and career pathways.*

- *Elevating the field's professional standing by tracking national trends.*

- *Setting and raising standards for job quality, pay and benefits.*

- *Supporting people with disabilities themselves to become DSPs.*

Addressing each area will attract more people to join the profession and, by extension, help ensure more people who need direct care support, including working Americans like Russell, can access it. It's a positive chain reaction, and I'm proud to be a critical link.

Aleathea manages her personal care for Russell while juggling her morning duties as a single mom for her own children, one of whom has disabilities. She is a hero, as are many, many others who work in direct support roles.

Child and elder care

MOST OF US WILL FIND OURSELVES in caregiving roles for family members at one point or another: for our children, our grandchildren, our elderly parents, or our infirm spouse. We provide care for our loved ones without a thought of reimbursement. In fact, there is often a significant financial cost to doing so – the opportunity cost of time lost at work while we tend to the family's needs.

But most of us will also find that we cannot provide all the care that is needed. So we hire others to help – babysitters, nannies, and childcare workers for the kids; home health care workers and assisted living facilities for adults in need of care. We can think of these as subsets of broader industries – education for the kids, and medical care for the adults – and workers in these fields should be paid with the same appreciation for what they do. Unfortunately, this is often not the case. One out of four home health care workers live below the poverty line, and over half rely on some form of public assistance.

These workers constitute the new American working class. In an article titled *The Jobs Americans Do*, Binyamin Applebaum writes:

> *The emerging face of the American working class is a Hispanic woman who has never set foot on a factory floor. [Working in a factory] is not the kind of work the working class does anymore. Instead of making things, they are more*

often paid to serve people: to care for someone else's children or someone else's parents; to clean another family's home.[171]

Far too often, these workers are not compensated fairly for the service they provide. And choosing a caregiving occupation should not result in a life of poverty. Yet that's where so many caregivers find themselves.

Medical care

THE MEDICAL INDUSTRY is at the apex of personal care. Doctors and nurses do more than just tend to our daily needs for sustenance and safety. They can make us better if we are ill or injured, and help us live longer and healthier lives. Some workers in the medical field get paid quite well (doctors and nurses), others very poorly (hospital orderlies and home health care workers). The reasons for that dichotomy lie mainly in the degree of education required to perform those services. No formal education for the lower-paid group. Years for the nurses. Years and years for the doctors.

But ask the patient which of these workers is more important when it's time to use the bedpan. Everyone who works in medicine is very much on the right side of Wilson's "partly saint" dichotomy. We just need to build more fairness into the way we compensate workers up and down the medical field.

Education and professional guidance

We could try to set up a modern-day grudge match

– The Librarian vs. Goggle –

à la John Henry vs. the steam-powered hammer, and we could be pretty sure the machine would again be left standing at the end of the day. There is no way for a single individual, no matter how well-read, to be able to recall all the references compiled by a computer program based on the collective searches of all the users. Librarians are no fools. They know they will be no match for Google or Yahoo or Bing, and they have, instead, become masters of using those and other search engines.

So why not just skip the research assistant or the reference librarian and do the research ourselves on the internet? Well, we can, but we do so at our own peril. When we run a search on-line, we filter the output of a search engine based on our objectives, our education and background, and our personal interests. A second user, even if they are running a search based on our stated objectives, will be applying a different filter, one based on their education and background. Consequently, the selection of references they chose should supplement those we've come up with.

Research assistants and reference librarians help us get out of our own head and look at things from different angles. Good teachers do the same thing, and take this one huge step further. They teach us how to learn. They help us identify problems, look for solutions and evaluate the correct course of action.

Parents, grandparents, teachers, child care workers – all perform another very important task: they help us learn how to socialize, how to play nicely together, how to be good humans. Little of that is learned while staring at a computer screen during a session with Google.

Sales

It might seem peculiar to some to place a discussion on sales immediately following education. But what is a salesperson if not an educator?

Sometimes the salesperson gets lucky. They show up on a cold call, at a new business, at precisely the right time, with exactly the right product, and a sale is made on the spot. But as anyone in this occupation will tell you, that ain't the way it usually works. It sometimes takes years, literally years, to win over a new customer.

If the salesperson gets rejected, but sees potential on that cold call, they'll keep coming back. And they'll make return visits with the right frequency that shows persistence without being pestering, behaving somewhere between 'I care – I really do' and stalking. This work will continue until all the stars and the moon line up and a sale is finally consummated; or until the customer tells them once and for all, in words or inaction, *get lost!*

I suppose you could hire a robot to be your company's salesperson. An artificially intelligent machine could analyze a potential customer's needs and match those perfectly to your company's products and services. Robots can be tirelessly persistent and patient, and programmed not to cross over the line into stalking. They have very thick skin, and will have no problem handling rejection.

But until the buyer on the other end is also a robot, I'm not quite sure how your 'bot will do on the relationship-building part. Because successful sales often boil down to relationships, pure and simple. You keep calling on a prospect, attempting to establish a relationship of trust and even, dare I say, affection. That way, when the customer discovers they have needs that can be met with your services, when all the stars and the moon do indeed line up, they will think of you. At that point, if you're lucky, they will call you. What a great feeling that is – when after years of honest, patient service, your work finally pays off!

(The robot would feel no elation with that phone call. That says more about the human need for affirmation and for meaningful work than about the emotional incapacity of machines.)

ON THE TOPIC OF APPRECIATION, for care giving and nututring to be beneficial for both parties, it cannot be on a master-slave basis. Consider this discovery by the good Augustine St. Claire of the callous indifference of his not-so-good wife Marie in the novel *Uncle Tom's Cabin*:

> *He discovered that a beautiful young woman, who has lived all her life to be caressed and waited on, might prove quite a hard mistress in domestic life. Marie never had possessed much capability of affection, or much sensibility, and the little that she had, had been merged into a most intense and unconscious selfishness; a selfishness the more hopeless, from its quiet obtuseness, its utter ignorance of any claims but her own. From her infancy, she had been surrounded with servants, who lived only to study her caprices; the idea that they had either feelings or rights had never dawned upon her, even in distant perspective.*[172]

If this is how everyone on the receiving end of a care-giving relationship responds to those providing the service, bring on the robots. Let's all go live with Jana's parents at the mansion in Rod Serling's story.

Travel and hospitality

If you want a glimpse of the labor economy of the future, take a nice long vacation trip. At virtually every step along the way you'll meet great people who are employed in the hospitality industry making sure that you are having the time of your life. Airline seats, rental cars, hotel rooms, dinner reservations, local attractions – the demand for all will continue to rise as more people around the world climb out of poverty and into the middle class, and from the middle class on up. Many more of us will be able to afford family vacations, and the demand for workers in attendant industries will grow.

The dining and hospitality industry is chock full of caregiving staff. And just like in many other sectors of the economy, the jobs of a lot of these employees are threatened by automation. You've seen the automatic French fry cookers at McDonalds. They are superior to manually operated machines:

1. By producing a consistent bag of fries, basket after basket, day after day.
2. By costing less to operate than a manually operated machine with worker attached to drop and pull baskets.

And now at McDonalds stores all over the world, you walk in the door and go up to an interactive computer screen to place your order. Punch in your choice, pay for the food, and a minute later, the happy meal appears.

Workers are constantly being replaced by machines. We should recognize that this is a good thing in general – one of the main reasons why the standard of living is so much higher now than in the past. But if we eliminate all the jobs, we could end up with no one left to buy the Big Macs.

LET'S BACK UP A STEP. When the regulars come into McDonalds each morning, it's not for the joy of playing with the interactive ordering screen, and it's probably not for the great coffee. The main reason is to gather with their friends and do a little socializing. And each visit gives them a chance to mingle with the staff at the restaurant. Before too long, many will look at those workers as new-found friends.

WILLIAM

Back when I was doing work procurement at Merrick, we had an older client named William who took care of the dining area at a local McDonalds. He'd wipe down the service counters, make sure the napkins and straws were stocked, keep the tables and chairs wiped off and the floor swept. He basically kept the front end tidy. But more than anything, William was a reliable presence in the dining room – always there for the breakfast crowd – and always cheerful.

As William got on in years, he slowed down a bit (as most of us are wont to do). The store manager knew that she could get the work done quicker with a younger employee, and she started to talk about finding a replacement for William.

Until the customers found out – that gang of regulars who came in for coffee every morning. They raised such an ruckus that the store manager quickly figured out she was better off keeping William right where he was! The customers would have missed William and his ever-present smile too much. *That's for sure!* as William was fond of saying.

These personal interactions are not only important for the regular customers at fast food restaurants. Consider the personal connections you expect when you go out to a fine dining establishment. You count on the server to tell you about the specials tonight, to recommend favorite dishes, etc.

When we travel, we used to depend on a travel agent to help us with our itinerary. Now, many of us are in do-it-yourself mode, using on-line services like Expedia and VRBO to book a trip. Once on a vacation trip, we would count on the cab driver and the concierge at the hotel for advice. Now, there's Google maps. When we go golfing, we should rely on the caddie and the golf pro. Now we use the GPS mounted on the golf cart.

RETAIL SALES also benefit from the human touch. Nowadays, you can buy almost anything online. But you must be willing to dig a bit, look up prices on the websites of different companies, compare technical specs, and read product reviews. There is an alternative. You can still go to a brick-and-mortar retail store and talk with a human being who can help you with your buying decision.

Machines are very good at supplying raw information. But we count on the human pros to give us the inside scoop and a personal touch. I don't believe that will be easily replaced by a machine.

The economics of service work

Earlier in the book, I talked about how a productivity race between a human worker and a machine is really no contest at all. While that may be true for the raw cost of doing things, it certainly doesn't hold true for the quality of services rendered that benefit from the human touch.

One-to-one caregiving, one person attending to another's needs, is by definition subject to *Baumol's cost disease*. William Baumol and William Bowen first described this phenomenon back in the 1960s. They looked to the performing arts sector for an example. It takes the same number of musicians the same amount of time to play Beethoven's 5th Symphony now as it did when it premiered in 1808. There are no productivity gains when it comes to performing this classic piece of art.[173]

Most industries do benefit from technological advancements and, until recently, wages more-or-less kept pace with gains in productivity. Salaries in other 'technologically stagnant' industries are pulled upward to keep talented managers and performers from migrating to other jobs.

Rutger Bregman, in the book *Utopia for Realists*, turns Baumol's disease on its head, calling it a *blessing*:

> *In our race against the machine, it's only logical that we'll continue to spend less on products that can be easily made more efficiently, and more on labor-intensive services and amenities such as art, healthcare, education, and safety.*
>
> *The more efficient our factories and our computers, the less efficient our healthcare and education need to be; that is, the more time we have left to attend to the old and infirm and to organize education on a more personal scale. Which is great, right? According to Baumol, the main impediment to allocating our resources toward such noble ends is "the illusion that we cannot afford them."*
>
> *As illusions go, this one is pretty stubborn. When you're obsessed with efficiency and productivity, it's difficult to see the real value of education and care.*
>
> Bregman states that politicians and taxpayers alike *don't realize that the richer a country becomes the more* (percentage-wise) *it should be spending on teachers and doctors.*[174]

Given this development, services will inevitably become a greater part of the GDP. Therefore, we should be calling it *Baumol's*

Blessing, and it follows that the more services we consume, and the more we pay our service providers, the stronger the economy. Not the other way around.

Negative attitudes about service jobs

Back in 2018, the median hourly wage was significantly higher for tree trimmers/pruners ($16.84) and for small engine repair mechanics ($16.96) than for child care workers ($10.18).[175] The first two are both male-dominated occupations, the third female-dominated. Just a coincidence?

Male or female-dominated, many service jobs fall behind corresponding jobs in manufacturing and construction when it comes to pay. Because service jobs pay less, they are held in less esteem. Or perhaps it is the other way around – they are held in less esteem; therefore, they get paid less. It's probably a combination of both – a self-reinforcing loop of diminishment.

The negative opinion regarding service jobs is firmly entrenched. Author Kurt Andersen was writing about the millions of factory jobs that were lost in the U.S. in the last part of the twentieth century:

> *The new jobs to which laid-off workers moved, during and after the 1980s, tended to be much worse than the ones they'd had.*[176]

I disagree with that blanket statement. The service jobs these workers were moving to were NOT worse than mindlessly repetitive assembly jobs in factories. They were just more poorly paid.

A STUDY by Anne Case and Angus Deaton at Princeton looks at the startling finding that death rates are actually rising among middle-aged whites with a high school education or less. How can this happen when death rates continue to fall for virtually every other segment of the population? The authors fix the blame on a rising incidence of so-called 'deaths of despair' (those resulting from alcohol and drug abuse and suicide) among this cohort. They theorize that the main source of this despair is the poor prospect of ever working again in a 'real' job earning a 'real' wage.[177]

When will we figure out that jobs in the service industries are every bit as important and should be paid as much as all the blue-collar production jobs that are fast disappearing? Clearly, we need a shift in attitudes regarding jobs in the service sectors.

Summary

COMPARE THE COMFORT received, the ahhh factor, of getting a massage from a real live masseuse with that from a mechanical massage chair. No comparison, is there? Or getting a haircut. One can imagine a machine that is built to trim your hair just the way you like it. But wouldn't you miss your barber and their friendly chatter just a little bit?

I talked earlier about how the consumption of services tends to have less of an environmental impact than the consumption of material products. (This isn't automatically the case, of course. Just picture the impact of tourism with a *Disneyfication* of Antarctica.) And I talked about *Baumol's Blessing* – the tendency for some caregiving and service jobs to be immune from advances in technology. Taking just these two aspects together – less material consumption and the preservation of more jobs – we should applaud the trend in the economy from manufactured goods to the service economy.

More importantly, caregiving and service jobs tend to be GOOD jobs. (The opposite of Eyal Press' *Dirty Work*.)[178] Having a job where you can respond directly to the needs of another should make that work meaningful and fulfilling, but only if we can be sure that our efforts are appreciated.

So what is it that our care providers and service workers want from us, other than shorter workweeks, higher pay, and better benefits? Aretha Franklin spells it out for us

R • E • S • P • E • C • T

CHAPTER 11

The Many Benefits of a Shorter Workweek

IN CHAPTER 3, we learned about our inherent drive to accumulate wealth. In Chapters 4 and 5, we learned how technological innovation and globalization have resulted in global economic growth. Now, we need to channel some of that competitive spirit toward the amount of leisure time at our disposal. A 32-hour workweek will result in 8 extra hours of free time for each fulltime worker to spend on activities of their choice (the definition of leisure time).

This ought to be mandated for hourly workers, and would not automatically apply to those on salaries. But we can be quite sure there will be a trickle-up effect. It will not take long for all the salaried men and women who are putting in 50 – 60+ hours a week at work to sit up and take notice. Will salaried workers drop their hours all the way down to 32? Maybe not. My guess is that they'll probably dial their workweek back to something closer to 40-hours/week, and they'll sure latch on to that 3-day weekend idea. Hourly or salaried, this will represent a fine gain in leisure time, more time to spend with family and friends, and more time pursuing personal interests.

Placing an economic value on leisure time

It's easy enough to place a monetary value on all the goods and services we consume because they come with a price tag attached: a $5 happy meal, a $50 massage, a $500 mattress. But how does one quantify the value of an hour of leisure?

Economists address this question with a concept called *Labor Supply*, and they spell out all the factors that enter into the labor supply decisions that we make. George Borjas, in his textbook *Labor Economics*, writes

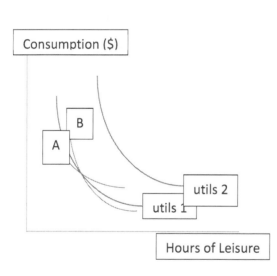

individuals seek to maximize their well-being by consuming goods (such as fancy cars and nice homes) and leisure. Goods have to be purchased in the marketplace. Because most of us are not independently wealthy, we must work in order to earn the cash required to buy the desired goods. The economic tradeoff is clear: If we do not work, we can consume a lot of leisure, but we have to do without the goods and services that make life more enjoyable. If we do work, we will be able to afford many of these goods and services, but we must give up some of our valuable leisure time.[179]

Economists model this Utility Function: $U = f(C, L)$; and they draw nice, neat *Indifference Curves* where every combination of C (the consumption of goods and services) and L (the consumption of leisure) add up to an equal number of *utils* [utils 1]. Higher curves equal greater numbers of *utils* [utils 2], which denotes a theoretically happier worker/consumer. A flatter curve denotes a worker who values consumption more than leisure [A]. A steeper curve just the opposite [B].

All this looks great on paper, and it is a good way to look at the tradeoffs. But seldom, in real life, are such tradeoffs available to the worker.

If you are a fulltime hourly worker, you <u>will</u> put in your 40 hours/week. If you are salaried, you are <u>expected</u> to work 50 – 60 hours a week, just like everyone else. The only ones who have the freedom to work as many or as few hours as they choose are those who have already achieved some level of financial independence. That tends to be the *golden-agers* who have been fortunate enough to have had good jobs for most of their working lives and are now able to live in some comfort on their retirement savings.

This brings up a good point. At different stages of our life, the slope of our personal Indifference Curves will look much different. Parents with pre-school children will need to spend more time at home.. Those with school age children will want to spend more time at work, saving up for the kids' college expenses. Empty nesters may choose more work, saving for their own retirement. Or they may choose to work less, all dependent of their financial comfort level.

After I retired, I often had the distinct pleasure of being on Grandpa-duty when the kids were younger. That had included walking them to and from school. It was an easy 15-minute walk that I enjoyed, and it was certainly good for both me and the kids. So, we walked whenever we could, only resorting to the car when the weather turned truly brutish (which happens too often during our Minnesota winters).

When I first started walking our grandkids to school, I was

dismayed by all the parents who drove their children, even on the nicest days. I know most of these families live right in the neighborhood. Why weren't they walking? Then it dawned on me. The reason the parents drive is not because they are lazy and don't care about their children's health. They drive because they don't have time to take an hour out of their day (1/2 hour before and after school) because they have to work too damn much! Consequently, every morning and every afternoon, in fair weather and foul, there is a long queue of cars in front of the school.

Our grandkids went to the neighborhood public school where they and most of their classmates were from working-class families. As it happens, there is also a very prestigious private school in the neighborhood where, one assumes, most of the students are from higher-income families with parents in the professions. Well, just like the public school, they have a long queue of cars dropping off and picking up kids each day. The cars may be newer and nicer, but those parents don't have time to carve an hour out of their day to walk with their kids to school either. I concluded that, rich parents or poor, no one has enough time in the day.

ECONOMISTS AGREE that an hour of leisure is an economic good, just like a product or a service we consume. But placing a value on an hour of leisure is not an easy task. How do you compare the value of an hour of free time for the CEO to that for a janitor? The CEO is paid 400 times more than the janitor. Does that mean their free time is worth 400 times more? If that's true, they sure don't act like it (consider Yahoo's CEO Marissa Meyer claiming a 130-hour workweek). If fact, in many respects, high level execs and business owners are <u>always</u> at work, never truly 'off the clock'.

The janitor, on the other hand, doesn't fret about work when they go home, and they sure don't put in extra hours voluntarily, punching in and out of their 40-hour job precisely on time. Of course, they're probably punching in and out of two 40-hour jobs because they can't afford to feed their family on just one. An 80-hour workweek leaves the janitor with just 32 hours of leisure per week (after subtracting out 8 hours a day for sleep). So from a scarcity perspective, a single hour of leisure time may now be worth more to the janitor than the CEO.

And then there's the quality of an hour of leisure consumed. The CEO is wealthy enough to hire someone else to cut the grass, cook the meals, even nanny the kids; or they can choose to do those duties themself when they finally get home. The janitor has no choice in the matter. If there is snow that needs to be shoveled, they grab their boots and jacket.

With all the chores out of the way, is an additional hour of leisure spent *productively* – say at a concert, or a lecture, or perhaps with a good book (like this one)? Or is the hour of leisure *wasted* at the bar watching a football game?

We should be careful how we judge! If the CEO is still mentally 'on the clock' while they're at the opera, that hour of refined entertainment may have relatively little value to them personally. If the janitor gets to share a rare hour of free time with his equally hard-working wife, and they decide that the best way to do this is to go to the bar and watch the game, that hour surely has a great deal of value to both of them.

THE SOCIAL BENEFITS OF A SHORTER WORKWEEK outweigh the economic impact. Of course, these social benefits are closely tied to economic realities.

Let's start with the economic part. The Gross Domestic Product (GDP) is a measure of the economic output of a country. It is calculated:

GDP = Consumption + Government Expenditures
+ Investment + Exports - Imports

When we divide a nation's GDP by the population, *GDP/capita*, it yields a pretty good measure of a country's well-being. A good measure, but not the <u>only</u> measure. If it were <u>the</u> measure of well-being, then we should do everything in our power to make it higher. That would include putting children and seniors back to work.

Preposterous? Well, it wasn't that long ago that children entered the workforce as soon as they were able, and seniors remained in the workforce for as long as they were able. Children worked side-by-side with their parents throughout almost all recorded history. If we put them back to work now, they could bring home a paycheck to support the family, just like mom and dad! Imagine the positive impact on the GDP.

And while we're at it, let's get all those able-bodied seniors back in the workforce. There's no reason why they should not be at work instead of spending their days golfing or fishing and sucking the nation's coffers dry with their social security and pension payments.

Well, we're not about to do that because we, as a society, have figured out that economic growth is not the only thing to be concerned about. We hold a special place in our hearts for children. We give them their own status legally. We bestow upon children the right to play and learn, and to be, insofar as possible, free from want and danger. At the other end of life, we have retirement. Through Social Security and pension plans, and with the encouragement of

IRA's and the like, we've allowed people to retire from the workforce and still live in some comfort. We do this even though these retirement programs are expensive, especially now with so many retirees living into their 80's, 90's, and beyond.

In the interests of social cohesion and compassion, we take special care of our children and the elderly, giving them the time to be kids on one end of life, and to rest in retirement on the other. We may grumble about paying our taxes and about inefficiencies in the programs, but we never question the central premise that this is the right thing to do.

There's no reason why this concern should be limited to the young and the old. Working-age adults should have at least some time to call their own.

The pursuit of happiness

With agreement that the GDP is not the ultimate measure of a nation's progress, let's talk about the pursuit of happiness. The Sustainable Development Solutions Network, a panel of social scientists commissioned by the United Nations, conducts an annual survey measuring the level of happiness of citizens in countries all around the world.[180] The 2017 survey showed Norway as the happiest nation, followed closely by Denmark, Iceland, Switzerland, and Finland. At the other end of the scale, Burundi (154) and the Central African Republic (155) are, sadly, the least happy. The United States came in at No. 14 in the 2017 report.

The scholars found that three-quarters of the variability from one country to another can be explained by six measures:

- Gross domestic product per capita
- Healthy years of life expectancy
- Social support (having someone you can count on in times of trouble)
- Perceived freedom to make life choices
- Trust (as measured by perceived absence of corruption in government and business)
- Generosity (measured by charitable donations)

A nation can improve its standing on the overall happiness quotient by improving their score on any of these six measures.

It is interesting to compare the overall happiness scores of two countries, Japan (51st) and Sweden (10th). Both are quite advanced economically, but they are two nations with very different attitudes about work. Japan is known for its culture of work. There is even a phenomenon known as *karoshi,* where some salaried workers have been known to literally work themselves to death. Sweden, on the other hand, has a reputation of a much more laid-back nation, where work is put in its place.

Despite these firmly held reputations, the difference in hours worked is actually not that great, with the average hours worked per year in Japan 1713, and in Sweden 1621. Given that similarity, how are these two nations doing economically?

The following chart tracks GDP/capita over a twenty-year span. The two countries started at just about the same place in 1996, Japan at $24,830 and Sweden at $23,270. By 2016, Sweden had moved ahead to $49,930, 16% ahead of Japan at $42,850.

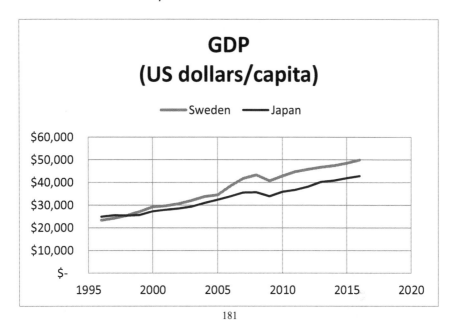

181

Apparently, leaders in Japan are beginning to take notice of the shortcoming. The government's economic policy guidelines include recommendations that companies permit staff to work four-day workweeks instead of five.

> *Japan's famously hard-working salarymen – and, increasingly, salarywomen – are to be encouraged to reduce the amount of time they spend in the office environment as a part of the government's initiative to improve the nation's work-life balance... With a four-day working week, companies would be able to retain capable and experienced staff who might otherwise have to leave if they are trying to raise a family or take care of elderly relatives... Authorities hope that an extra day off every week would encourage people to go out and spend, thereby boosting the economy... It is also anticipated that young people will have more time to meet, marry and have children, going some way to solving the worsening problem of a falling birth rate.[182]*

Gee – more time to meet, marry and have children – that sure sounds like the road to happiness! Looking for a moment at the level of happiness here in the U.S., Dick Meyer of the Scripps Washington Bureau, closed a column on economic growth in the 20th century with the following:

> One aspect of 20th-century economic success has long puzzled social scientists: Americans received enormous increases in material benefits, prosperity and health, but did not report increased happiness and sense of well-being. It was just the opposite, in fact. Perhaps the key to flourishing amid ordinary times requires spiritual remedies more than material.[183]

Wrapping up this section, what is the moral of the story on happiness? We can prosper economically, and still have some fun doing it. We just need to relearn to let society drive our culture of work, not the other way around.

More leisure time

We all spend too much time at our place of employment, plain and simple. Working 32 hours a week instead of 40 will give all of us the chance to slow down and smell the roses. The chance to spend more time with our children, our parents, and our friends. The chance to volunteer more freely at the church or hospital, to offer time, talent, and treasure at the social service organization of our choice. The chance to take up hobbies that are personally fulfilling – not just smelling the roses – cultivating them, cutting them, arranging the blooms into bouquets; perhaps even grabbing paint brushes and canvas, and creating your own rendition of roses out in the warm sunshine of your garden.

THERE WAS AN OP-ED COLUMN by Laura Johnson titled *We all must make time for creativity in our lives*. Johnson writes about teaching art to a group of business executives, brought together to foster creativity on the job:

> *A team of corporate executive stares up at me. Behind the polish and power, I see the look of fear.*
>
> *I have witnessed this face of panic in many painting classes, but it's especially palpable in this group. I tell them again, kindly but firmly, to pick up their paintbrushes and begin painting the blank canvases... They insist that I explain exactly how to recreate the example painting—a colorful tree with flowers. It's a simple painting, designed to be finished in several hours, just for fun. Yet it seems to terrify them.*
>
> *These men and women make important business decisions every day. If I asked them to negotiate a multimillion-dollar deal, they wouldn't blink. Paint a tree? They balk.*
>
> *A week earlier, I taught the same painting to a Girl Scout troop, ages 9 to 11. I needed to race through my introduction, because they were so eager to start. Their eyes gazed longingly at the blank canvases, fingers twitching to grab brushes. Once they began, the girls asked me only for more paint colors. I saw wide trees, skinny trees, tall trees, short trees. None was the same, and not a single girl cared in the slightest.*[184]

Johnson asks:

> *When does this transition occur? At what point among e-mails, meetings, deadlines and long days do we forget the joy of creating?*

Her question is best tackled in another work.

Art washes away from the soul the dust of everyday life.

--Picasso

A white paper from the Oxford Martin School, published by Citigroup's Global Perspectives and Solutions, is titled: *Can Automation/Technology Reduce Working Hours Further and Increase Leisure Time Without Compromising the Standard of Living for All?*[185] In this paper, Andy Haldane from the Bank of England comments that work delivers more than money, that it creates a sense of personal worth and social attachment. Even so, people would enjoy more leisure time:

> *You never know: with time on our hands, we could actually start enjoying science, painting, writing and reading, leisure activities that were valued in the 1930's*

Normally, there are just two things that drive capitalist companies to invest in automation: the profit motive and a competitive market position. Never, it seems, do we take advantage of labor-saving devices by allowing everyone to work fewer hours. Employers should strive for that – giving their workers more free time to engage in activities of their own choosing.

> *For the long term, we need to start making self-respect and usefulness more independent of employment, ... to feel engaged and useful and respected regardless of how (we) receive (our) fair share of the national wealth.*
> *--Kurt Andersen, Evil Geniuses*

Attitudes toward leisure time

Benjamin Hunnicutt has studied the importance of leisure time closely. His great book *Free Time,* subtitled *The Forgotten American Dream*, is a historical study of America's attitudes toward leisure time. Hunnicutt takes us all the way back to our nation's founders, and the list of inalienable rights spelled out in the Declaration of Independence – *life, liberty, and the pursuit of happiness*. What did Thomas Jefferson and his compatriots mean by that last phrase, *the pursuit of happiness*? What would make us truly happy? In Hunnicutt's words:

> *Where do we go when we have done all our chores, performed our duties, and met our responsibilities? What kinds of human activities or states of being lay beyond social responsibilities and material necessity and are worthwhile in and for themselves?*[186]

Jefferson was a renaissance man. He would've had no problem occupying his leisure time with worthwhile pursuits. The assumption is that he and other gentlemen in the planters class would also have been appreciative of having more time at their disposal. Unfortunately, the Black slaves on these plantations were probably granted very little time to call their own.

Over the next 200 years, we transitioned from a mostly agricultural society to mostly urban, and the rhythm of the workplace was transformed as well. I believe our attitude toward work would have become gradually more negative as we lost the feeling that work is a perfectly natural activity in line with the seasons. And our attitude toward leisure?

Leaping ahead from Jefferson about 150 years, John Maynard Keynes shed some light on the meaning of *the pursuit of happiness*, saying that at some point, our time would become more valuable to us than new goods and services. Hunnicutt summarizes Keynes' thoughts on leisure:

> *Then we would welcome the opportunity to live more of our lives outside the marketplace. No longer preoccupied with economic concerns, we could begin to develop our potential to live together peacefully and agreeably, spending more of our time and energy forming healthy families, neighborhoods, and cities; increasing our knowledge and appreciation of nature, history, and other peoples; freely investigating and delighting in the mysteries of the human spirit; exploring our beliefs and values together; finding common ground for agreement and conviviality; living virtuous lives; practicing our faiths; expanding our awareness of God; and wondering in Creation.*[187]

Keynes, we must acknowledge, is the economist who predicted that technological development and huge increases in productivity that were evident in the 1930's would allow us to be working about

---

A calm and modest life brings more happiness than the pursuit of success combined with constant recklessness.

-Albert Einstein, 1922

---

15 hours a week within 100 years (just 9 years from now). I believe he was on the right track. I think his timing was just off a bit. What happened? The consumer society happened (see Chapter 3). We live in a world where everyone wants to be wealthy, and the capitalist movers and shakers keep moving the bar as to what constitutes wealth.

RECALL that with the onset of the industrial age, there was a need to keep the capital-intensive factories running as long as possible. Factory owners, given their choice, would keep the men, women, and children laborers on the job around the clock if they could.

Eventually, political pressure was brought to bear, and the government stepped up and provided some relief for the workers. This started with child labor laws early in the 1800's in England. From then on, there was a persistent, if unsteady, push for worker protection in Europe and North America. Factory workers were required to put in 12 – 18 hour days, six days a week early in the industrial revolution. This was pared down to 10-hour days, five and a half days a week in the 1840's, and to an 8-hour day as early as 1877, following an executive order by President Grant covering manual laborers under government contracts.

The push for shorter workdays continued all the way up to the Great Depression. For some economists and political leaders, the two primary reasons for the push for shorter workdays at that time had little to do with individual worker welfare. The reasons were macro-economic:

1. The shorter workweek would reduce levels of unemployment.
2. Increased leisure time would accelerate consumer demand.

But there were qualitative reasons as well, namely that more leisure time has significance beyond its simple economic value (as spelled out earlier in the comments from Keynes). There were those who thought work should become *decentered, made subordinate to the more important business of living.*[188] (Hunnicutt)

Many jobs had become so narrow, so mechanized, so paced by the assembly line, that it is easy to see why there was such a push to work shorter hours. Labor leaders in the 1920's were arguing that mechanization and industrial efficiency made both higher wages and shorter hours possible.

But with the onset of the Great Depression, which preceded the stock market crash of 1929 by a few months, came massive unemployment rates in virtually every industry. Suddenly, the idea of spending less time at work had very little to do with the beneficial improvement of workers' lives. Not working meant being unemployed, and leisure time in that status was clearly no longer a good.

Shorter workdays and working fewer hours a week became an antidote for unemployment, not personal fulfillment. Job sharing became the prime economic mover. Hunnicutt writes:

> *During their conventions in 1932, both parties incorporated work-sharing planks in their platforms and then actively campaigned on the issue, Hoover and Roosevelt each claiming to be the original and stronger advocate of the measure.*[189]

Many proponents were arguing for a 30-hour workweek at that time. That obviously didn't happen. What did happen to the push for a shorter workweek? It's a bit of a mystery. Hunnicutt indicates that the two parties disagreed with the best way to achieve this shared objective, the Democrats opting for mandated regulation, the Republicans insisting on voluntary measures. (If that did indeed happen, it's just one more case of partisan politics getting in the way of human progress.) At any rate, 1933 would prove to be the *high-water mark for the century-long shorter-hours movement.*[190] (Hunnicutt)

Passage of the Fair Labor Standards Act in 1938 codified the 40-hour workweek. By that time, 40-hours pretty much became the standard all over the world. And we've been stuck at that mark ever since.

There have been few attempts since the 1930s to push for a shorter workweek. One example was the ill-fated air traffic controllers strike in 1981. The PATCO (Professional Air Traffic Controllers Organization) rank and file were pushing for a 32-hour workweek paired with a 30% hourly pay hike.[191] And if any group of workers were entitled to ask for a shorter workweek, I believe it would be PATCO members. Like factory workers, they are tied to their machines, radar screens that are capable of handling a huge amount of information. The air traffic controller is responsible for relaying the information from that machine to another in the sky, and to direct those aircraft to take off and land safely. And as the airports got busier every day, the workload on individual controllers just continued to grow. Unlike factory workers, where the cost of inattention might be an improperly assembled airplane seat, the cost of inattention for an air traffic controller might be a tragic accident. The pressure on these workers must have been immense, and it's no wonder they were pushing for shorter work hours.

But it didn't happen. The strike was much less effective than the workers hoped for, and in the end, Reagan succeeded in crushing the union. Air traffic controllers are still putting in five 8-hour shifts a week.

THE REASON for including the PATCO example here is to point out that the controllers' demand for shorter workweeks was all about safety, not about the value of leisure. For the factory workers tied to assembly lines, the demand for a shorter workweek is all about minimizing the time spent on a crappy job, not about the value of leisure. Perhaps, like Thomas Jefferson, we should focus more on the value of leisure.

In a 2016 study that Citi GPS co-authored with the Oxford Martin School, a team of analysts pose the question

> *could the 40-hour week (traditionally worked between 9am and 5pm) be coming to an end? ... With the rapid increase in automation and technology, could it be that the working hour week would reduce even further when some of our work tasks become automated? Could Keynes' theory of working a 15-hour week actually become a reality?*[192]

But some will question the wisdom of pushing for a shorter workweek at all. They will remind us of the adage *idle hands are the devil's workshop*, and suggest that if workers are not kept busy on their jobs, they'll be bored with their lives and end up in all sorts of mischief. They will point out that we already don't take all our allotted vacation time, which must mean we want to work more, not less. Many individual workers will also insist

> *I just can't take the time off – there are things at work that must get done – and I'm the only one qualified to see them through.*

My response to all of that – *nonsense!* None of us are indispensable.

In a recent column by Professor James Bailey at George Washington University, he tells us that half of all working adults check for work messages at least once a day over the weekend, and the same applies when we finally do go on vacation. He goes on to ask:

> *Certainly, our contributions at work are valuable. But why*

don't we apply the same thinking to our families? What makes us think our colleagues can't function without us, but our families can?[193]

There is some evidence that the millennial generation is starting to figure this out. James Suzman in his study of modern-day hunter-gatherer tribes, *Affluence without Abundance*, offers this advice:

Embrace the affluence we have created, and recognize value in things other than our labor. Working a whole lot less may be a good place to start. And it may well be that millennials – a group in the first world who have known nothing but abundance and who seem increasingly inclined to seek out work that they love rather than persuade themselves to learn to love the work they find – will lead the way in doing this.[194]

The Washington D.C. organization called Project Time Off spells out the personal and productive benefits that are missed when we fail to take time away from work:

- Higher productivity and performance
- More positive attitude toward work
- Increased happiness
- Improved mental and physical health
- Better relationships and social life.[195]

Of course, Project Time Off, like many organizations in the DC area, is a lobbying firm – this particular one working on behalf of the hospitality industry. Not spelled out on their website, but clearly in the interest of their sponsors, are these goals:

- Sell more airline tickets
- Fill more hotel rooms
- Book more restaurant reservations.

This lobbying group quantifies the negative impact on the U.S. economy:

- 658 million vacation days unused (222 million of those simply evaporated because they could not be rolled over)
- $223 billion not pumped into the economy than would've been the case had we fully used our vacation time. (That comes out to over $300 per unused vacation day.)

Their estimate for the negative impact on the economy is suspect. I imagine their assumption is that all 658 M previously unused vacation days would have been spent on a vacation, not hanging around the house, playing with the kids, putzing in the garden, or reading a book.

Retirement 'schedules'

In a 2016 newspaper article by Ginny McReynolds, we learn about how to spend our time in retirement. (Imagine that – the need to learn how to relax!) The article was titled *No longer slaves to the clock, retirees must rethink how to use time.*[196] The article tells us to turn off the alarm clock and ditch the watch. Sleep when you want to sleep, eat when you want to eat, work (on projects of your own choosing) when you want to work, and don't be afraid to relax. There is no need to be tied to an 8-hour day just because that's what you were forced to work when employed. You may still find that 'working' 8-hours a day is just fine, but you may also find that 6 or 4 or 2-hours of work a day on a given project is about right, leaving you more time for other activities. The point is, it's your decision. You no longer need to be a *slave* to the clock.

In a fine book titled *Unretirement*[197], economist Chris Farrell tells how so many of us are taking on new jobs after retirement. We are doing so by our own choice, not because income from the job is necessary for our livelihood. And while we may still need to 'punch in and out', our attitude about this will be far different than when we had no control over our schedules. Back when our paycheck was the only way for us to support our family, if our boss said he needed us on a Sunday morning or a Tuesday evening, we had little choice but to go along. In *unretirement*, we can decide if we want to work those shifts.

That decision is made in light of how much value we place on the alternative to work, namely leisure. And it is truly a luxury to be in the position where we can make that choice ourselves.

Wealth vs. well-being

Measures of wealth and measures of well-being overlap, but are not identical. Most think of wealth as tangible assets: material possessions, money in the bank, owning a business, equity in a home, etc. What is missing? TIME. Time to enjoy the cars and boats you own, the artwork on your walls, the vacation trips you can easily afford but don't take, etc.

Measures of well-being are often less tangible than measures of wealth. That does not make them less important. We can go back to Maslow's pyramid for guidance. It is interesting to look at Well-being and Wealth side-by-side in ascending order of needs:

WELL-BEING	WEALTH
Freedom from hunger and thirst, shelter from the cold	Wealth certainly addresses these needs
Security	One can buy a home in a gated community, a hidden safe, a burglar alarm, and even a security staff. But in a

	somewhat perverse way, being wealthy makes one <u>less</u> secure. As Willie Sutton reputedly said, he robs banks because that's where the money is.
Affection and affiliation	Enough jokes have been written about sugar-daddies and trophy wives – I don't need to go there.
Esteem	This is where <u>our perception</u> of measures of wealth can really make a difference. If it's prestigious to own a new Chevy, it's even more so to own a new Buick, and better yet to drive a new Cadillac. This relates to our discussion on relative wealth. There is a good chance that your peers, your co-workers, are also putting in 60 – 70 hours a week climbing the corporate ladder to comfortably afford that Cadillac, so it's only natural for you to be doing the same thing.
Self-actualization	If you are putting in 60 – 70 hours a week at work, all in the interest of a larger paycheck, how much time and energy does that leave you for higher-order needs – those more esoteric pursuits that Jefferson and Keynes challenged us to strive for?

If we want to have time for those higher-order needs, we must start putting work back in its place. There is a well-known law of economics called *diminishing marginal utility*. The law states that the marginal utility realized from the consumption of additional units of goods drops with greater numbers. So even though manufacturers and merchants and marketers will tell you that you can never have enough stuff, you can. (In fact, if you live in a three-bedroom rambler, you can sometimes end up with <u>way too much stuff!</u>)

But, know what you can never have enough of? Free time. Even the richest man in the world will tell you he never has time to get everything done. So, do you really want to spend every waking moment on the job just so you can buy more stuff? Or would you rather have a little more time to enjoy all the wonderful things you already have.

Recalling Celeste Headlee's book *Do Nothing*, she tells us:

> *If your goal is less stress and more happiness, years of scientific research have proven that rather than trading your time for money, it's best to trade your money for time.*

And she puts this in even more essential terms:

> *There is one aspect of early human history I hope we can reclaim: a celebration of what is most human about us. It is our reflective thought and social connections that make us unique and strong. Descartes said, "Cogito ergo sum": I think, therefore I am. He did not say "Laboro ergo sum": I work, therefore I am.*[198]

Leisure time and creativity

THERE IS A MYTH of the *starving artist* that suggests that it is <u>need itself</u> that stimulates the creative juices. This falls in with the old adage that *necessity is the mother of invention*. Fred Amram, a professor of creativity and communications at the University of Minnesota, begs to differ. He brings up the opera *La Bohème* by Puccini as an example. The opera makes a great story, but Professor Amram points out the irony that while the Bohemian artists in 1830's Paris were mostly unsuccessful, the composer Puccini was *wealthy and pampered.* Amram wrote:

> *The challenge to the creative person is the problem to be solved, not personal limitations or poverty. Note that the problem for those starving in India has been to grow more rice inexpensively. The solutions, however, come not from India, where farmers live hand-to-mouth – literally. The Indian farmer lacks the leisure to create improved strains of rice. In Minnesota, we have the opportunity to "waste" space by testing diverse crops on the St. Paul campus of the University of Minnesota. We have the "leisure" to do the research that leads to better crops. We have the financial opportunity to pay creative scientists as they invest in new seeds and fertilizing methods. In St. Paul, we solve India's rice problem.[199]*

Amram goes on to describe other instances where the combination of leisure time and available resources lead to creative breakthroughs. The abundance of resources will have a compounding effect – the more leisure – the more creativity.

The freedom to explore need not be confined to universities. 3M has a long-standing R&D policy that allows scientists and engineers to spend up to 15% of their time at work on projects of their own choosing. Their personal projects are often tangential to their primary area of research, and the general idea is that creativity on one will spill over to the other. The corporation is the beneficiary, and the researchers express more satisfaction on the job.

COVID lessons for WORK/LIFE balance

IN A GUEST COLUMN from Jonathon Malesic in the New York Times, 9/23/2021, we read that *The Future of Work Should Mean Working Less.* Amen! Malesic writes that as millions are returning to in-person work after nearly two years of unemployment and working from home:

> *The conventional approach to work – from the sanctity of the 40-hour week to the ideal of upward mobility – led us to widespread dissatisfaction and seemingly ubiquitous burnout even before the pandemic. Now, the moral structure of work is up for grabs. And with labor-friendly economic conditions, workers have little to lose by making creative demands on employers. We now have space to reimagine how work fits into a good life.*

With the imposed idleness of COVID:

> *The pandemic took away countless activities, from dinner parties and concerts to in-person civic meetings and religious worship. Once they can be enjoyed safely, we ought to reclaim them as what life is primarily about, where we are fully ourselves and aspire to transcendence.[200]*

Supporting thoughts come from Christine Emba in a Washington Post column:

> *We keep thinking about work in a disappointingly narrow way. ...*
>
> *Even as companies, activists and individual workers champion the idea of a shorter workweek, they're framing it in old terms. We can get all our work done in four days, we promise. In fact, we'll be more productive. No more unnecessary meetings. No more interruptions from our nonwork lives. After a three-day weekend we'll be rested and recharged — the better to hit the ground running on Monday morning! ...*
>
> *When we focus on how a shorter workweek will make us better employees, we're making the wrong argument to our bosses and ourselves. The four-day workweek shouldn't just be about becoming more productive — the real benefit is that it would allow us to be fuller **people**. ...*

The United States has for decades been locked into an economic mind-set in which growth, or at least its potential, is seen as the main barometer of success, and individuals are judged mainly on what we produce. ...

But the push for a four-day workweek suggests we do have other things we value — as we should. The trick will be learning to advocate for them on their own terms, with the same clarity and fervor with which we celebrate material and economic gains.[201]

Lofty thoughts indeed on the social and spiritual value of leisure time!

The Ant and the Grasshopper

There is an old fable about an ant and a grasshopper:

One bright day in late autumn a family of Ants were bustling about in the warm sunshine, drying out the grain they had stored up during the summer, when a starving Grasshopper, his fiddle under his arm, came up and humbly begged for a bite to eat.

"What!" cried the Ants in surprise, "haven't you stored anything away for the winter? What in the world were you doing all last summer?"

"I didn't have time to store up any food," whined the Grasshopper; "I was so busy making music that before I knew it the summer was gone."

The Ants shrugged their shoulders in disgust. "Making music, were you?" they cried. "Very well; now dance!" And they turned their backs on the Grasshopper and went on with their work.[202]

The moral of the story: *There's a time for work and a time for play.*

Summary

PART II OF THIS BOOK focuses on the tremendous productivity gains we have made in the last eighty years. And this begs the question: Why haven't we taken advantage of this progress and allowed ourselves to slow down and act a bit less like the ants? Why, with all the robotic ants we are building, are we not giving ourselves more time to sing and dance like the grasshopper?

The important thing to remember is that leisure time is an economic *good*, just like the products and services we consume. (Go back to the *utils* graph at the beginning of this chapter.) The impact of an extra hour of leisure time will be greater or less at different times of our lives. But the simple truth is that a greater number of leisure hours should have a positive impact on our lives and well-being.

Let me finish this chapter with a quote from a famous philosopher:

All work and no play is a crummy
way to spend your day.
--Curious George

CHAPTER 12

A Remedy for a Broken Labor Market

I'VE SPENT MUCH OF THE LAST ELEVEN CHAPTERS writing about a broken labor market. It is now time to lay out a specific proposal to fix what is broken, and to suggest certain tactics to gain support for this proposal.

Backing up a step, please do not assume from all my criticism of the situation we are in today that I don't believe there should even be a labor market. Workers and jobs should not be judiciously paired up by some overseeing government body. I do believe in the superiority of market forces over government control, not that that's inherent, but that it has historically proven to be true.

The labor market should continue to be that – a market. A place where buyers (employers seeking workers) and sellers (workers looking for jobs) come together and exchange the labor one offers for compensation from the other. But like any other market, it needs to be regulated. Without rules, we could end up with a single buyer (monopsony) or a single seller (monopoly) of all labor.

A labor market monopsony (a single buyer) would result if one company, through vertical and horizontal acquisitions, cornered the market of all goods and services produced, and thereby became the only private employer that still has a need to hire any workers. A labor market monopoly would result if the government took control of all labor rendered – who fills what jobs, how much are they paid, how many hours do they work – and every potential employer would have to petition the government for workers. Thankfully, we are still miles and miles away from either of these eventualities. But we do seem to be heading in that direction.

IN CHAPTER 7, I introduced the concept of the Central Contradiction of the Labor Market

$$P_{employers} > P_{employees}$$

Where $P_{employers}$ represents the bargaining power of the owner/manager class, and $P_{employees}$ that of the working class.

Rewritten in terms of buyers and sellers in the labor market

$$P_{buyers} > P_{sellers}$$

That makes sense intuitively, if you think about it. Buyers of labor add workers because they choose to grow their business. Sellers of labor offer their mental and physical service because their families need to eat.

This will always be the case until such time as having food in one's belly is considered an inalienable human right, just as we now have the right to a reasonable level of health care. At that point, we will likely see a battle between advocates of Universal Basic Income – UBI and Universal Basic Services – UBS. (Neoliberals and Neo-communists?)

That ideological battle will play out in the future. For now, let's agree that in today's labor market, employers hold most of the high cards (please see Ch. 4 – 7). Therefore, we need some new rules to help keep the market competitive, and I offer the following:

IN ORDER TO FIX our broken labor market today, I believe there are three distinct and concurrent actions required:

1. *Reduce the fulltime workweek from 40 to 32 hours*

In the first edition of this book, I had proposed a 24-hour workweek. I now think I was asking for more than our nation was ready to accept at that time. But the idea of a **32-hour or 4-day workweek** is gaining traction, with mostly successful trials now underway at a handful of companies in countries around the globe.

This will create a disruption in the labor market, and some employers will find this to be more difficult than others. But for all, it should be manageable. And more importantly, all workers and their families will be delighted with an across-the-board reduction in the workweek with no reduction in weekly wages.

Shorter Workweeks make Stronger Families!

2. *Increase the hourly minimum wage*

The *Fight for $15* movement gives us guidance on where the new minimum wage should be set nationwide. The current minimum wage of $7.25/hour became effective on July 24, 2009 thanks to a 2007 amendment to the Fair Labor Standards Act. From $7.25 to $15.00 is a huge increase, but one that is necessary. In order to assure that low-wage workers keep up with the cost of living, and to smooth out disruptions in the labor market, the next amendment to the FLSA should include the proviso that the minimum wage is be tied to the rate of inflation, just as SSI retirement benefits are now.

3. *Establish an Earned Income Supplement*

$15/hour times a 40-hour workweek establishes **$600/week** as the de facto minimum wage for a fulltime job. To keep that target intact with a 32-hour workweek a worker will need to earn **$18.75/hour**. Therefore, every working-aged adult should be issued one **Earned Income Supplement** voucher worth **$3.75/hour** and capped at **32 hours/week**.

The worker can cash in the EIS voucher at the employer of their choice. The employer then adds that government money, **$120/week**, to the fulltime worker's regular paycheck, **$480/week**. This will yield **$600/week**, and assure that workers do not lose ground financially as we mandate shorter workweeks. And it will ease the burden on employers, as they are already taking on quite a bit with the new $15/hour minimum wage and the 32-hour workweek.

The EIS should encourage employers to hire more new employees (each worker only gets one voucher).

And the EIS, once implemented, can be a mechanism for the government to use to help smooth out ups and downs in the labor market.

IN COMBINATION, these three initiatives would have great potential to mend inequities in our broken labor market and have a positive impact on the overall economy. The balance of power in employer/employee relations would shift noticeably toward the worker, and the incidence of poverty in working class families should be substantially reduced.

The supply of labor and the demand for labor should remain strong, and these policies should stimulate the entire economy. This should be especially beneficial to workers in lower-wage occupations. (More people of color than whites fill those jobs, and more women than men, so this would be economic justice long overdue.)

WITH ALL THE OBVIOUSLY WONDERFUL BENEFITS of a shorter workweek with no loss in pay for the worker, resistance to this proposal will be minimal.   RIGHT!

Social pressure – labor unions

Employers will not accept a shorter workweek without a fight. And to win this fight, workers in America will ultimately need both top-down and bottom-up strategies. Top-down pressure from the state and national governments will pick up speed once bottom-up pressure from labor and consumer movements gain strength.

Our first battle is with inertia. The 40-hour workweek has been ingrained for over 80 years. But there is some hope – polls of working adults tell us that 70% now favor a 4-day workweek. That should translate into more ready acceptance of a 32-hour workweek.

Bottom-up pressure to improve the lives of the working class has historically been the province of labor unions. But we have seen union strength wane greatly in the last 40 years, especially in the private sector. This table* shows the average number of work stoppages of 1000 or more workers over the last 75 years:

Years	Average work stoppages involving at least 1000 workers
1947 - 1981	289/year
1982 - 2021	31/year

It is no mere coincidence that the failed PATCO strike occurred on 8/3/1981.

Over the last couple years, we have seen the fear of walking out on strike begin to wane. Cornell University keeps track of all work stoppages (not just those involving 1000 workers or more), and they tallied 265 (260 worker-initiated strikes and 5 employer-initiated lockouts) involving 140,000 workers in 2021.[203] In addition, more than 100,000 workers threatened to walk out before reaching agreements late in 2021. The most common complaints involved health and safety protocols, pay, and health care benefits.

WILLIAM BARRY published an informative booklet recently titled *Organizing in the Time of the Pandemic: Normal No Longer Exists,* in which he, I was delighted to see, called for a shorter workweek. He identified and compared the two major roles for labor unions – organizing to win new members and serving existing members. He had some not too complimentary things to say about the servicing model:

> *Union loyalty is a question we have been wrestling with since the 1930's when many union officers opposed federal*

---

* Data source: Bureau of Labor Statistics

legislation, like the minimum wage laws or Social Security, because the benefits that workers had under a union contract would be spread – with no dues collected – to every worker.[204]

This does not mean Barry has given up on the positive role unions can and should play in the labor market. Quite the opposite, as evidenced by his association with the New Brookwood Labor College in St. Paul.

New Brookwood Labor College
EDUCATE AGITATE ORGANIZE

Barry's booklet introduced me to the concept of "sectoral bargaining", which he thought, for the time being, was only a "pleasant fantasy". But I believe there might be strong public sentiment in favor of higher wages, even if that means higher costs, in two specific industries: 1) home-based daycare services for small children (over 3 million nationwide), and 2) home health care services for elderly adults and others with special needs.

The welfare of our children and our parents is at stake here. We understand that if we want quality daycare and quality home health care, we probably need to pay those essential workers more than the minimum allowed by law. These are two caregiving industries where both owners and employees of small businesses could lobby for higher pay. Families that use these vital businesses could march alongside the owners and employees as they lobby the state and federal governments for higher fee schedules for their services. That, my friend, would be a "pleasant fantasy" indeed!

Social pressure – consumer movements

THE FIGHT FOR A SHORTER WORKWEEK may be driven as much by consumers as the workers. Consumers can have a strong negative impact on the fortunes of a specific company, the whole of an industry, or even an entire country. Consumer boycotts have two distinct advantages over labor strikes:

- they cannot be crushed by hired thugs or bussed-in scab-workers
- the government will have a hard time making consumer movements illegal

We have seen consumer boycotts have a tremendous impact on politics. Look back at how the racial segregation policy of apartheid was finally defeated in South Africa. Nelson Mandela, Archbishop Desmond Tutu and many others in that country brought attention to the injustices of apartheid to a worldwide audience. And it was consumers who responded to the injustice and put pressure on international companies to pull out of the South Africa. When the multinationals abandoned that nation en masse, it had a significant impact on the economy of the country, and at that point even South African companies pressed the government to capitulate. Along with relentless pressure from Mandela and his companions, this eventually was enough to break the will of the South African government, and thankfully send the policy of apartheid into the historic dustbin.

SHOPPERS ARE GENERALLY MORE INTERESTED in getting bargains than in the labor provenance of the products they buy. But consumers are not without a conscience, and the citizens of our country overwhelmingly agree with the notion that anyone who works a fulltime job should not be living in poverty. These are different motivators entirely, but consider the impact of consumer movements on the sale of cage-free eggs and shade-grown coffee. The driver behind the first – a more humane treatment of chickens, and the second – a more sustainable method of growing coffee.

There is every reason to believe consumers, once fully informed, could be just as interested more humane treatment for workers. Ultimately, consumers could choose to buy only products with that cool $\boxed{\textbf{32HR}}$ label attached, whether it's on a dozen eggs, a bag of coffee, or a dress shirt.

Top-down support

IN A DEMOCRACY, political leaders are expected to make decisions with the mood of the people and the health of the nation in mind. As bottom-up support for shorter workweeks gains traction, be it from labor unions or consumer movements, our elected officials will be compelled to look at revising the rules and regulations controlling the labor market.

Economic justification for this revision can be found in the chart that shows growth in both labor supply and demand (see page 201). The increase in demand for more workers will certainly be true in the short-term, and probably into the mid-term, depending on how that is defined. But in the long-term, higher labor costs <u>will</u> compel companies to accelerate their investment in automation and AI. Bound to happen. And as I've said, several times already, GOOD! Why should we do the work when we can build a machine to do it for us?

Economic growth, in and of itself, should not be our ultimate goal. Higher standards of living and greater levels of happiness for everyone on the planet should be what we strive for. Using capital to lower the cost of producing goods and services sends us on that righteous path.

Machines can be built to do the work faster and better than humans (see Ch. 4). In these days of machines endowed with acute sensors and artificial intelligence, when we follow that through to its ultimate conclusion, we reach the *End of Work* for human beings. Rifkin, Ford, and many other authors have already covered that eventuality. Aaron Bastani is one of the latest to do so with his challenging book *Fully Automated Luxury Communism*.[205]

But any rosy prediction of a future where we really don't have to work anymore is predicated on achieving a level of economic equity that allows everyone to participate in the market's largesse. That leads us to a discussion about UBI.

Universal Basic Income

Universal Basic Income is the recognition that every human being has value to the community; that there are as many ways to serve the community as there are people in that community; that while some contributions may be obscure, all are nonetheless valuable; and that each member of the community needs enough income for a basic level of sustenance in order to be a contributing member of the community.

Andrew Yang, a Democratic candidate for president in 2020, introduced many of us to a UBI, but the concept is not new. Political thinkers have been bouncing the idea around by for over 200 years. In 1797, Thomas Paine published *Agrarian Justice* where he proposed that every man and woman in American be paid a one-time stipend of £15 (about $1800 in today's dollars) upon reaching 21-years of age. Paine reasoned that this would foster economic independence, *so crucial to the budding democracy* (Reich).[206]

About 50 years ago, a UBI was being considered by that raving liberal President Richard Nixon. As a key component of the War on Poverty, the base income for a family of four would have been set at $1,600, the equivalent of approximately $10,000 today. Nixon advisors Senator Daniel Moynihan and economist Milton Friedman supported the plan, with Friedman saying that *poverty simply meant you were short on cash – nothing more, nothing less.*[207] Nixon favored replacing welfare with a small federal income *on which the family itself could build* in a system where *outside earnings would be encouraged, not discouraged.*[208]

Some people argue that a *universal dividend* would undermine the work ethic. Peter Barnes, in *Capitalism 3.0,* offers this counterargument:

This might be true if the dividends were very high, but is unlikely to be true if they're kept at a modest level. Such dividends would supplement, but not replace, labor income. At the same time, they'd give people a little more freedom to take time off or to engage in uncompensated work at home or in their communities. Actually, a case can be made for slightly reducing the work ethic. With ever more jobs moving overseas, it's by no means certain we can keep all Americans employed. If some people choose to work less, that might be a good thing.[209]

I am proposing that everyone chooses to work, but to work less. In fact, I suggest that we need a new understanding of the work ethic itself. Over the course of human history, that ethic has morphed from being of service to the community to being a means of acquiring personal wealth and status. It can still be the second without losing the first. But this needs to be understood – if having the opportunity to work is important to me, it's also important to you. We all need to feel that we are contributing to the commonwealth. To assure that there is enough work to go around, my allotment of paid work is now 32 hours a week, the same as yours. The new work ethic includes the understanding that any work beyond that point is either unpaid and voluntary, or a bit aynrandish.

WE CAN THINK ABOUT A UBI as a ***robotics dividend*** that everyone is entitled to. What would be a good number for UBI? Why not base it on statistics the government keeps on the poverty level? On the table back on page 214, we see the poverty level is $12,880 for a household of one. A $1000/month UBI for every adult American would be close to that. That is the amount Andy Stern proposed in *Raising the Floor*[210] and a little more than Charles Murray's proposal for $10,000/yr. in his latest work *In Our Hands*[211]. At $1000/mo., a married couple would receive $24,000/yr., a little short of what would be needed to keep a family of four out of poverty. Any income mother and father earn from employment will help the family rise <u>above</u> the poverty level, giving the children a better shot at financial success in their future.

It's hard to argue how this would not be an effective means of eliminating poverty. But there is a question as to the nation's readiness to accept this radical approach. Indeed, if we are not ready to accept a 24-hour workweek, we are probably not ready for a UBI either. Most will find a four-day workweek with no loss in pay more acceptable at this time, and we can make some strong arguments to adapt this approach.

Comparing the impact on the labor market of a UBI with a shorter workweek/EIS

The following table compares the impact of these two anti-poverty measures on the Supply and Demand of Labor:

Universal Basic Income	Shorter workweek with higher wages plus Earned Income Supplement
An income floor giving everyone the means to purchase basic goods & services will eliminate the perceived need to work for some now in the workforce. Labor Supply **DOWN**	The shorter workweek along with higher wages will encourage more workers into the labor force. Labor Supply **UP**
With more consumer power in market, we can expect a growing demand for goods and services. Labor Demand **UP**	The shorter workweek will require new hires to keep plants running and shops open to meet the strong demand for consumer goods, thanks to greater purchasing power in the hands of the working families. Labor Demand **UP**

Based on this analysis, a reduction in the length of the workweek with no reduction in our paychecks looks like a good short and mid-term option as we work our way toward an ultimate state where paid employment may still be desirable, but is no longer really necessary.

Lessons learned from COVID

EARLY IN 2020, a new virus was discovered that proved to be deadly and has the potential to kill millions and millions of people. During this COVID-19 pandemic (we are still in it as I write this), we are learning how to protect ourselves and each other, and ultimately render this virus harmless.

FACE MASKS had been in general use in Asia for many years as a way for people with colds or the flu to be out in public without exposing others to their illness. When masks were recommended here in the U.S. to help slow down the spread of COVID-19, many people, myself included, thought it was mainly to protect the wearer of the mask, not those around them. It made it a bit easier to accept the imposition of wearing a mask once we learned it was to protect not just ourselves, but each other.

SOCIAL DISTANCING is not a condition we are comfortable with, but we did manage, mostly, to self-enforce the 6-feet apart rule during the height of the pandemic. All large gatherings like concerts and ballgames were postponed, then cancelled, as the virus tore through our communities. Weddings, funerals, religious services, and the like were postponed or held virtually on line. Shopping trips were discouraged unless necessary. Some of us probably felt a little guilty going to the store just to stock up on toilet paper (that we were already hoarding).

RESTRICTED TRAVEL was less voluntary than mandatory. All non-essential travel was postponed for some time. Then strict requirements were placed on travelers for proof of vaccination or for negative COVID test results.

STUDYING FROM HOME was a challenge for everyone – students and their families, and teachers. It may not be clear how much ground students lost academically from where they would have been given a normal school year. But we do know that all of the socializing that happens day-by-day at school was missed. And with cancelled athletic schedules, band concerts, proms, and the like, students had a right to feel "cheated" out of a normal year in their young lives. The relief when schools opened up again in the fall of 2021 was palpable.

WORKING FROM HOME became the modus operandi for millions of workers. With a laptop on the kitchen table, an internet connection and Zoom meeting software, office workers in many industries discovered that you didn't have to actually go to the office to get most of the work done.

NOT BEING ABLE TO WORK FROM HOME was a hardship for millions of other "essential workers", including, apparently, all those who keep the meat-packing industry alive (maybe not the right adjective to use for this industry). Olaf Scholz, while on the campaign trail to succeed Angela Merkel as Chancellor of Germany, had this to say about all essential workers:

> *The pandemic has shown whose shoulders our society is built on, who works hard and still benefits too little from an economic upswing.*

And millions of less-fortunate employees were laid off, as restaurants, hotels, and entertainment venues closed. For all these laid off workers, and for all of the essential workers exposed to the disease while on the job, it was important to get a vaccine for the virus developed quickly.

STIMULUS CHECKS were sent to virtually everyone, no questions asked, as the federal government responded to the threat to the economy from COVID by giving all of us some spending money. And it worked! The recession of 2020 was very short-lived. The economy is once again growing. The labor market has bounced back strongly. And following this socialist initiative, the U.S. did not devolve into a nation of idle slackers.

INOCULATION SHOTS to control COVID-19 were developed in "warp speed" thanks to investments from central governments and an all-hands-on-deck approach at several pharmaceutical companies. Wearing face masks and social distancing are a terrible imposition for our communal species. That's why it was such a relief to have the vaccines developed so quickly, and why it was such a disappointment to see so many people refusing to take the vaccine.

THE VACCINES ALLOW US to get back to work. But perhaps we won't choose to work quite so much? There are about 3 million fewer Americans in the workforce now than before the start of the pandemic. Is that by choice? That's not easily answered according to Ben Casselman in a recent NY Times article. He gave a nice synopsis of this COVID paradox:

> Conservatives have blamed generous unemployment benefits for keeping people at home, but evidence from states that ended the payments early suggests that any impact was small. Progressives say companies could find workers if they paid more, but the shortages are not limited to low-wage industries.
>
> Instead, economists point to a complex, overlapping web of factors, many of which could be slow to reverse.
>
> The health crisis is still making it hard or dangerous for some people to work, while savings built up during the pandemic have made it easier for others to turn down jobs they do not want. Psychology may also play a role: Surveys suggest that the pandemic led many to rethink their priorities, while the glut of open jobs – more than 10 million in August – may be motivating some to hold off for a better offer.
>
> The net result is that, arguably, for the first time in decades, workers up and down the income ladder have leverage. And they are using it to demand not just higher pay but also flexible hours, more generous benefits and better working conditions.[212]

I wrote back in the introduction that I believe there is a silver lining within the dark COVID cloud. Workers with the ability to seize a little more power in the employer/employee relationship is certainly a welcome outcome. And the restrictions involving social distancing gave us the chance to rediscover the importance of family life.

With everyone spending much more time at home, there were far more opportunities for family interactions. Like all family dynamics, these were sometimes good and sometimes not. But on balance, this was a very positive development. And it got people thinking about their **work/life balance**. Therefore, I believe the pandemic has the potential to be a truly positive disruption to the labor market – not just a cyclical correction.

An optimistic conclusion

I HAVE NO ILLUSIONS that my three-step proposal will be accepted as is, or without a fight. But this is a good place to open the discussion on a shorter standard workweek. Will we figure it out? Yes, I believe we will. And I say that with the confidence of an optimist.

An optimist knows that we as a species, through our industrious behavior, have seen tremendous progress in our collective standard of living. Measurable gains include a worldwide literacy rate that has risen from less than half to over 85% in the last 50 years, and in just the last two decades, both the worldwide infant mortality rate and the number of people living in extreme poverty have dropped in half.[213]

An optimist knows that people are at least as smart as ducks. (I closed the first edition of this book with the story about how ducks are smart enough to protect each other as they line up on a log for their afternoon nap. I'll close the second with an appeal to our collective common sense.)

WORK has traditionally been viewed as a social good because it gave us all the chance to prove our value to the community and raise our status in society. But work is increasingly becoming less necessary. Machines are being built capable of "doing it all", and we will eventually need some way other than paid employment to measure our value and to raise our individual status. At some point, perhaps down the road a generation or two, the line between paid and unpaid work will begin to blur, and the whole question of how work is compensated will have to be dealt with. We <u>will</u> come up with that. I am optimistic.

As we "work" our way forward into this wonderful next phase of human existence, it will make good sense to begin to back off on the number of hours devoted to paid employment and commit those hours to other, more enjoyable, and indeed more productive human activities. That way, we make sure that roofing crews, like the one I was watching in Mexico back on page 1, are able to work a shorter workweek <u>and</u> buy that cherry-picker to make their job safer and easier.

ENDNOTES

Introduction

[1] Press, Eyal, *Dirty Work*, (Farrar, Strauss and Giroux, 2021)

[2] Schlosser, Eric, *America's Slaughterhouses Aren't Just Killing Animals*, (The Atlantic, 5/12/20)

[3] Lotterman, Edward, *Target's wage move reflects market realities*, (Pioneer Press, 10/1/17)

Chapter 1

[4] Wilson, Edward O., *The Social Conquest of Earth*, (Liveright Publishing Corporation, 2012).

[5] *Ibid*, p. 129.

[6] *Ibid*, p. 243.

[7] *Ibid*, p. 273.

[8] *Ibid*, p. 289.

[9] Natural History Museum, London, www.nhm.ac.uk

[10] Applebaum, Herbert, *The Concept of Work*, (SUNY Press, 1992).

[11] *Ibid*, p. xii.

[12] Applebaum, p. 193.

[13] *Ibid*, p. 192.

[14] *Ibid*, p. 195.

[15] *Ibid*, p. 322.

[16] *Ibid*, p. 325.

[17] Donkin, Richard, *Blood Sweat & Tears*, (Texere LLC, 2001), p. 110.

[18] http://www.history.com/topics/martin-luther-and-the-95-theses

[19] Donkin, p. 242.

Chapter 2

[20] US Department of Labor, 2019 Occupational Employment Statistics.

[21] Disraeli, Benjamin, *Sybil, or The Two Nations*, 1845, (Kindle), Book 3 Chapter 8

[22] Samuelson, Robert, *A new era of labor scarcity?*, (Pioneer Press [from Washington Post], 9/5/16)

[23] Donkin, p. 215.

[24] Farrell, Chris, *Unretirement*, (Bloomsbury Press, 2014), ch 9 [kindle 58%]

[25] Farrell, *Working longer may benefit your health*, (StarTribune [NY Times], 3/12/17)

[26] Ton, Zeynep, *The Good Jobs Strategy*, (Lake Union Publishing, 2014), Ch. 7

[27] Lindgren, Amy, *A personal perspective on workplace scheduling*, (Pioneer Press, 10/11/15)

[28] http://wikipedia.org/wiki/job-characteristc-theory

[29] Davidson, Adam, *Managed by Q's 'Good Jobs' Gamble, (New York Times Magazine, 2/28/16)*

[30] *Ibid*

[31] Schwartz, Barry, *Rethinking Work*, (NY Times, 8/30/15)

[32] Barlow, Elizabeth, *The New York Magazine Environmental Teach-In*, (New York Magazine, 3/30/70), p. 30.

[33] Borjas, George J., *Labor Economics*, Sixth Edition, (McGraw-Hill, 2013), p 506.

[34] Mullainathan, Sendhil and Shafir, Eldar, *Scarcity, Why Having Too Little Matters So Much*, (Times Books, Henry Holt and Company, 2013), p. 155.

[35] Barreca, Gina, *Take it from teacher: Johnny needs a job*, (Pioneer Press, 8/17/15)

[36] Malesic, Jonathon, *The Future of Work Should Mean Working Less,* (New York Times, 9/23/2021)

[37] Avent, Ryan, *The Wealth of Humans*, (St. Martin's Press, 2017), Kindle Loc 220.

[38] Florida, Richard, *The Rise of the Creative Class Revisted*, (Basic Books, 2012)

[39] Brooks, David, *Bobos in Paradise* (Simon & Schuster, 2000)

[40] Ehrenreich, Barbara, *Nickel and Dimed*, (Picador, 2011)

[41] Shipler, David, *The Working Poor*, (Vintage, 2005)

Chapter 3

[42] Thoreau, Henry David, *Walden, or, Life in the Woods,* 1854 (Kindle, *The Complete Novels*), loc. 20510 of 94876.

[43] Schafer, Lee, *Cleese makes the case for creativity*, (StarTribune, 2/17/16)

[44] http://www.econlib.org/library/Essays/rdPncl1.html

[45] *Earth, Composition and Structure*, (Wikipedia, 2016)

[46] https://clipartxtras.com

[47] Headlee, Celeste, *Do Nothing*, (Harmony, 2020), p. 74

[48] De Graaf, John; Wann, David; and Naylor, Thomas; *Affluenza*, (Berrett-Koehler Publishers, Inc., 2001)

[49] Barber, Benjamin, *Consumed*, (W. W. Norton & Co, 2007)

[50] Luttwak, Edward, *Turbo-Capitalism*, (Weidenfeld & Nicolson, 1998)

[51] Kunstler, James, *The Geography of Nowhere*, (Simon & Schuster, 1993)

[52] Will, George, *Starbucks and our pursuit of snobbery*, (Pioneer Press [from Washington Post], 12/16/16)

Chapter 4

[53] Rifkin, Jeremy, *The End of Work*, (Tharcher/Putnam, 1995)

[54] Ford, Martin, *The Lights in the Tunnel*, (Acculant Publishing, 2009)

[55] Brynjolfsson, Erik and McAfee, Andrew, *Race Against the Machine*, (Digital Frontier Press, 2011)

[56] Kaplan, Jerry, *Artificial Intelligence, what everyone needs to know*, (Oxford Univ. Press, 2016)

[57] Manyika, James, *Technology, jobs, and the future of work*, (McKinsey Global Institute, Dec 2016)

[58] www.forrester.com/Robots+AI+Will+Replace+7+Of+US+Jobs+By+2025/-/E-PRE9246

[59] Cotter, Michael, *The Killdeer, And Other Stories From the Farming Life,* (Parkhurst Brothers, 2014)

[60] Cotter, Michael, *Growing Up On A Minnesota Farm*, (Arcadia Publishing, 2001), p. 48.

[61] *Ibid*, p. 57.

[62] Rochford, Harold, (Mower County Historical Society), Photo 93.609.0320, Threshing Scene, file 503 page 4.

[63] Belz, Adam, *Minn. dairies' way of life on line*, (StarTribune, 4/22/19)

[64] www.sourcewatch.org/index.php/coal

[65] Reich, Robert, *Truths about free trade*, (Pioneer Press, 3/17//16)

[66] Gordon, Robert J., *The Rise and Fall of American Growth*, (Princeton University Press, 2016), p. 499.

[67] Ryder, Matthew, BCTGM Local 22, conversation, August 2018.

[68] Yglesias, Matthew, *The automation myth*, (Vox, 7/27/15)

[69] Greenhouse, Steven, *Beaten Down, Worked Up*, (Alfred A. Knopf, 2019), p. 145

[70] Reich, Robert, *Saving Capitalism,* (Alfred A. Knoff, 2015), p. 206.

[71] Rugaber, Christopher (Associated Press), *The great divide,* (Pioneer Press, 7/10/16)

[72] Avent, Ryan, *The Wealth of Humans,* (St. Martin's Press, 2016), Kindle Ch 8, loc. 2856.

[73] Bertoni, Robert, shared correspondence, March 2016.

[74] Popper, Nathaniel, *The Robots Are Coming for Wall Street*, (New York Times Magazine, 2/28/16)

[75] Goel, Ashok, http://www.news.gatech.edu/2016/05/09/artificial-intelligence-course-creates-ai-teaching-assistant

[76] Avent, Ryan, *The Wealth of Humans,* (St. Martin's Press, 2016), Kindle Ch 2, loc. 762-771.

Chapter 5

[77] http://www.msf.org/en/msf-charter-and-principles

[78] Diamond, Jared, *Guns, Germs, and Steel* (get publisher, etc.)

[79] Bregman, Rutger, *Utopia for Realists*, (The Correspondent, 2016)

[80] Davidson, Adam, *Voters Left And Right Are Anti-Free Trade* (NPR News, 3/13/16).

[81] Tice, D.J., *Antiglobalism: A bipartisan affliction*, (Star Tribune, 8/7/16)

[82] Oppenheimer, Andres, *Hoover, not Hitler, is the apt comparison for Trump*, (Pioneer Press, 3/13/16)

[83] Stockman, Farah, *What Killed the Blue Collar Struggle for Social Justice*, (NYTimes, 10/7/21)

[84] *Toyota to boost Indiana factory*, (Pioneer Press, 1/25/17)

[8585] http://www.gallup.com/poll/166211/worldwide-median-household-income-000.aspx

[86] Ryssdal, Kai, *In today's economy, even two-income families suffer...*, (Marketplace, PBS NewsHour, 6/10/16)

[87] De Sam Lazaro, Fred, *Dusty mining conditions...*, (Untold Stories, PBS NewsHour, 4/7/16)

[88] Perry, Mark, *Experts agree: Free trade is good,* (Pioneer Press, 3/22/16)

[89] Boak, Josh and Swanson, Emily, *Poll: Americans prefer low prices to 'Made in USA' items*, (Associated Press, 4/15/16)

[90] Will, George, *Whirlpool has Washington in a spin cycle,* (Washington Post, Pioneer Press, 12/17/17)

[91] Cahuc, Carcillo, & Zylberberg, *Labor Economics*, (MIT Press, 2014), pp. xvii-xx.

[92] Kasperkevic, Jana, *Immigrants around the world* (NPR Marketplace, 6/15/17)

[93] Frankel, Todd, *Foxconn's broken pledges cast doubt on Trump's plan for jobs*, (StarTribune [from Washington Post], 3/6/17)

Chapter 6

[94] Avent, Ryan, *The Wealth of Humans*, (St. Martin's Press, 2016), Kindle Loc 1526.

[95] Weil, David, *The Fissured Workplace*, (Harvard University Press, 2014), p. 8.

[96] *Ibid,* p. 26.

[97] Reich, Robert, *In contrast to no-lose socialism*, (Pioneer Press, 5/6/16)

[98] *Ibid*

[99] Andersen, Kurt, *Evil Geniuses—The Unmaking of America*, (Random House, 2020), p. 191.

[100] Hallock, Kevin, *Pay*, (Cambridge University Press, 2012)

[101] Schuman, Michael, *Forget $15 minimum wage. What about bonuses?* (Pioneer Press, 9/21/16)

[102] Avent, Ryan, *The Wealth of Humans*, (St. Martin's Press, 2016), Ch. 5, Kindle loc. 1586.

[103] Reich, *Saving Capitalism,* p. 98.

[104] Hanauer, Nick, *The Pitchforks are Coming ... For Us Plutocrats,* (Politico Magazine, June/August 2014)

[105] Belz, Adam, *Low-wage jobs worth a bit more*, (StarTribune, 3/22/16)

[106] http://www.epi.org/publication/charting-wage-stagnation/

[107] Reich, *Saving Capitalism*, p. 137.

[108] Gordon, p. 613.

[109] https://www.epi.org/productivity-pay-gap/

[110] Manyika, James, *Technology, jobs, and the future of work*, (McKinsey Global Institute, Dec 2016)

[111] Reich, *Saving Capitalism*, p. 61.

Chapter 7

[112] Piketty, Thomas, *Capital in the Twenty-first Century* (The Belknap Press, 2014), p. 571.

[113] Korten, David C., *The Post-Corporate World*, (Berrett-Koehler Publishers, 1999), p. 37.

[114] Reich, *Saving Capitalism*, p. 45.

[115] *Ibid*, p. 38.

[116] Meyerson, Harold, *Fed forgets who has the power (hint: not workers)*, (StarTribune, 12/19/15)

[117] Mukunda, Gautam, *What Bernie Sanders and Donald Trump get wrong about Wall Street*, (Pioneer Press [from Washington Post], 4/28/16)

[118] Branswell, Helen, *Big pharmaceutical companies reluctant to produce Zika vaccine*, (PBS Newshour, The Rundown, 8/9/16)

[119] Avent, Ryan, *The Wealth of Humans*, (St. Martin's Press, 2016), Ch. 6, Kindle loc. 1985, 1994.

[120] Tcherneva, Pavlina, *When a Rising Tide Sinks Most Boats*, (Levy Economics Institute of Bard College, Policy Note 2015/4)

[121] Smith, Noah, *Hey you in a nation of ruts and inequality: Guess what?*, (Star Tribune, 11/13/16)

[122] Young, Stephen, *The realignment of the working class*, (StarTribune, 9/17/16)

[123] Bregman, Ch. 9.

[124] Zucman, Gabriel, *The Hidden Wealth of Nations*, (The University of Chicago Press, 2015)

[125] New York Times, *Ireland's GDP gets big boost from 'magic' of inversion deals*, (Star Tribune, 7/13/16)

[126] Kanter and Scott, NY Times, *E.U. orders Apple to repay $14.5B in taxes to Ireland*, (StarTribune, 8/31/16)

[127] http://www.cauxroundtable.org/index.cfm?menuid=8

[128] https://www.shrm.org/resourcesandtools/hr-topics/benefits/pages/dol-proposes-rule-to-remove-barriers-to-esg-funds-in-retirement-plans.aspx

[129] Madland, David and Walter, Karla, *Growing the Wealth*, (Center for American Progress, April 2013)

[130] Gates, Jeff, *The Ownership Solution*, (Perseus Books, 1998)

[131] *Ibid*, p. xx.

[132] http://www.cauxroundtable.org/index.cfm?menuid=8

[133] McKay, Harvey, *How to keep employees working for you*, (StarTribune, 4/3/17)

[134] Humprey, Hubert H, *Letter to Editor*, (Washington Post, 7/20/1976)

Chapter 8

[135] Greenhouse, Steven, *Beaten Down, Worked Up*, (Knopf, 2019), p. 336.

[136] https://en.wikipedia.org/wiki/Adolf_Meyer_(psychiatrist)

[137] Bregman, Ch. 7.

[138] Borjas, George J., *Labor Economics*, Sixth Edition, (McGraw-Hill, 2013)

[139] https://www.bls.gov/news.release/wkyeng.t01.htm

[140] Alderman, Liz, *In Sweden, Happiness in a Shorter Workday Can't Overcome the Cost*, (NY Times, 1/6/17)

[141] Young, Stephan, *Moral Capitalism*, (Berrett-Koehler Publishers, 2003), p. 56.

[142] Reich, *Saving Capitalism*, p. 81.

[143] Reich, Robert, *Saving Capitalism For the Many, Not the Few*, (Borzoi Book, 2015), p. 5.

[144] *Ibid,* p. 84.

[145] Weil, p. 288.

[146] Banaian, King, *Let workers speak for themselves*, (Pioneer Press, 6-30/16)

[147] Stowe, Chapter XIX.

[148] Donkin, p. 21.

[149] Marty, John, *$15 an hour – first Minneapolis, then statewide* (StarTribune, 6/29/16)

[150] http://www.irp.wisc.edu/faqs/faq2.htm

[151] https://aspe.hhs.gov/poverty-guidelines

[152] Bryant, John Hope, *How the Poor Can Save Capitalism*, (Berret-Koehler Publishers, 2014)

[153] *Ibid*, p. 76.

[154] https://www.bls.gov/opub/reports/minimum-wage/2020/home.htm

Chapter 9

[155] Roosevelt, Franklin Delano, *A Fair Day's Pay for a Fair Day's Work*, (speech delivered 5/24/1937)

[156] Young, p. 112.

[157] Bryant, p.17.

[158] Pioneer Press, *The Great Divide*, (6/10/16)

[159] http://www.shorterworkweek.com/econeffect.html

[160] Autor, David and Duggan, Mark, *The Growth in Social Security Disability Rolls: A Fiscal Crisis Unfolding*, (NBER Working Paper No. 12436, August 2006)

[161] Johnston, Louis, shared correspondence, Oct 2016

[162] Banarji, Anirvan, *The Relationship Between Labor Costs and Inflation: A Cyclical Viewpoint,* (US Bureau of Labor Statistics, 5/24/05)

[163] https://www.bls.gov/opub/mlr/2017/article/estimating-the-us-labor-share.htm

[164] https://www.bls.gov/ooh/production/bakers.htm

[165] Brooks, David, *Behold America's post-pandemic renaissance*, (Star Tribune, 6/19/21)

[166] Ember, Sydney, *Workers leave jobs in record numbers*, (Pioneer Press, 6/21/21)

Chapter 10

[167] Serling, Rod, *The Lateness of the Hour*, (Twilight Zone, 12/2/60)

[168] Tingley, Kim, *Learning to Love our Robot Co-workers*, (NY Times Mag., 2/23/17)

[169] Grant, Tracy, *How caring for a dying husband made life worth living,* (PBS Newhour, 9/27/16)

[170] http://blog.dol.gov/2022/04/05/adding-value-through-direct-care-work

[171] Applebaum, Binyamin, *The Jobs Americans Do,* (NY Times Magazine, 2/23/17)

[172] Stowe, Harriet Beecher, *Uncle Tom's Cabin*, (Kindle edition), Chapter XV

[173] https://en.wikipedia.org/wiki/Symphony_No._5_(Beethoven)

[174] Bregman, Rutger, *Utopia for Realists*, (The Correspondent, 2016), Ch.8.

[175] https://www.bls.gov/oes/current/oes_nat.htm#00-0000

[176] Andersen, Kurt, *Evil Geniuses*, (Random House, 2020), p. 189

[177] Meyer, Dick, *The plague of the white working class*, (Scripps Wash. Bur., StarTribune, 4/9/17)

Chapter 11

[178] Press, Eyal, *Dirty Work*, (Farrar, Strauss and Giroux, 2021)

[179] Borjas, p. 21.

[180] http://worldhappiness.report/ed/2017/

[181] https://data.oecd.org/natincome/gross-national-income.htm#indicator-chart

[182] *Japan proposes four-day working week to improve work-life balance,* Deutsche Welle (DW.com, 6/25/21)

[183] Meyer, Dick, *The best of times are in the rearview mirror,* (StarTribune, 2/14/16)

[184] Johnson, Laura M., *We all must make time for creativity in our lives,* (StarTribune, 9/15/16)

[185] Frey, Osborne, Holmes, *Technology at Work v2.0,* (Oxford Martin School/CitiGPS, Jan 2016)

[186] Hunnicutt, Benjamin, *Free Time,* (Temple University Press, 2013), p. 2.

[187] *Ibid,* p. 1.

[188] *Ibid,* p. 109.

[189] *Ibid,* p. 117.

[190] *Ibid,* p. 118.

[191] Greenhouse, Steven, *The Big Squeeze,* (Alfred A. Knopf, 2008), p. 81

[192] Frey, Holmes, Osborne, *Technology at Work v2.0,* (Oxford Martin School/Citi GPS, Jan 2016)

[193] Bailey, James, Washington Post, *Take some time off – for yourself and others* (StarTribune, 7/3/16)

[194] Suzman, James, *Affluence without Abundance,* (Bloomsbury, 2017), p. 259

[195] http://www.projecttimeoff.com/issue

[196] McReynolds, Ginny, Washington Post, *No longer slaves to the clock,* (Pioneer Press, 6/28/16)

[197] Farrell, Chris, *Unretirement,* (Bloomsbury Press, 2014)

[198] Headlee, pp. 198, 243

[199] Amram, Fred M.B., *There's no reason to mock the beanbag chair,* (StarTribune, 1/28/16)

[200] Malesic, Jonathon, *The Future of Work Should Mean Working Less,* (New York Times, 9/23/2021)

[201] Emba, Christine, *We're making the wrong argument for a four-day workweek,* (Washington Post, 7/7/2021)

[202] http://read.gov/aesop/052.html

Chapter 12

[203] News wise, Cornell University, 2/22/2022

[204] Barry, William, *The Servicing Model of Unionism,* (Aug 28, 2021)

[205] Bastani, Aaron, *Fully Automated Luxury Communism,* (Verso, 2020)

[206] Reich, *Saving Capitalism,* p. 216.

[207] Bregman, Ch. 6.

[208] StarTribune editorial, *Clinton's smart plan to help fight poverty*, (StarTribune, 10/14/16)

[209] Barnes, Peter, *Capitalism 3.0*, (Berrett-Koehler Publishers, 2006), p. 116

[210] Stern, Andy, *Raising the Floor*, (PublicAffairs, 2016)

[211] Murray, Charles, *In Our Hands*, (AEI Press, 2006)

[212] Casselman, Ben, *Economy is recovering. Where are the workers?*, (Pioneer Press [from NY Times]), 10/20/21

[213] Kristof, Nicholas, *The best news you don't know,* (Pioneer Press [from NY Times], 9/29/16)

INDEX

3

32HR · 287
3M · 274
  US vs OUS sales ·
  139

A

*A Fair Day's Pay for a
  Fair Day's Work* ·
  See Franklin
  Roosevelt
absentee shareholders ·
  180
*Affluence without
  Abundance
  See* James Suzman
Affluenza · 82 , 241,
  300
Affordable Care Act
  (ACA) - 219
Agriculture · 28, 70, 92
  - 104, 109, 132
Airplanes · 109
Andersen Windows ·
  220 - 222
*Antiglobalism: A
  bipartisan affliction*
  · 135
Apple · 151, 184, 303
Applebaum, Binyamin
  · 242
APPLEBAUM, HERBERT

· 29, 32, 299, 305
Archbishop Desmond
  Tutu · 286
Army Times · 160
Artificial intelligence
  ·90, 124, 126, 128
automation · 4, 42, 57,
  89, 105, 122, 127,
  136, 166, 202, 244,
  262, 268
Avent, Ryan · 66, 127,
  300
Aynrandish · 290

B

Bailey, James
  George Washington
  University · 268
Banaian, King · 205,
  304
Bangladesh · 145,
Barber, Benjamin
Consumed - 82

Barges · 109,
Barker, John Wayne ·
  61
Barreca, Gina · 63, 65,
  300
Barter · 37, 71
Baumol's cost disease
  · 237
Blacksmiths and
  manicurists · 128

Board of Directors
  fiduciary
  resposibilities ·
  181
Bobos in Paradise ·
  See David Brooks-
Bonobos · 241
Bookkeepers · 121
Bregman Rutger
  Baumol's blessing ·
  237
Bregman, Rutger ·
  199
Brexit · 148
Brick-and-mortar retail
  stores · 247
Brooks, David · 67,
  300
Brynjolfsson and
  McAfee · 89, 301
Buckminster Fuller ·
  55

C

Cahuc, Carillo, and
  Zylberberg · 148
Calvin, John · 32
Canada · 93, 134, 139,
  147
*Capital in the Twenty-
  first Century · - -
  See* Thomas Piketty
Career advancement ·
  51

Index

Caregiving · - 236 -to - 250

Cargo ships · 111

Carlyle, Thomas · 33

Case, Anne and Deaton, Angus · 248

Castro Fidel · 148

Caux Round Table · 185

Central Contradiction of Capitalism · 171

Central Contradiction of the Labor Market · 173

Child labor · 35, 45, 47, 63, 101, 142, 164, 166, 168, 208-, 213, 256, 265

Chobani · 156,

Citi GPS Oxford Martin School · 268

Cleese, John · 74, 300

Climate Change · 79

Coal mining · 104

Combine harvesters · 99

Commonwealth · 290

Community · 4, 16, 30, 37, 46, 53, 57, 59, 65, 185, 209, 271, 288

Comparative wealth · 83

Compensation ratios · 160

Concierge · 245

Consumed · *See* Benjamin Barber

Consumerism · 69

Consumers · 71, 75,

80, 287

consumer movements · 283

Cotter, Michael & Beverly · - 93 -- 96, 301

Country Of Origin Labelling (COOL) · 147

COVID-19 · - 9 - 15, 90, 121, 176, 233, 274, 291 - 295

Craftsmen · 29

Cuba · 148

Cultivating · 97

D

Dairy farms · 100

Davidson, Adam · 135, 300, 302

de Graaf, Wann, & Naylor · 82

de Sam Lazaro, Fred · 142

Declaration of Independence · 34, 263

Deming, W. Edwards · 224

DEPARTMENT OF LABOR (DOL) ·41 - 46, 64, 166, 188, 205, 299

Detroit · 225

Diamond, Jared · 132, 302

Dirty Work · *See* Eyal Press

Disabled · 59, 64

Disraeli, Benjamin ·

44, 62, 299

Distribution channels · 114

Division of labor · 23, 27

Draft animals · 93

Drivers jobs at risk · 100, 113

E

earned income supplement (EIS) · 282

Economic Policy Institute EPI · 163, 166

Education · 126

Ehrenreich, Barbara · - 67, 300

Employer and employee classification · 190

Employer health insurance plans · 218

Employer vs. Employee · 153

European Union · 148

Eusocial · 23, 30, 241

Experts agree: Free trade is good · 144

Eyal Press · 10

F

Fair Labor Standards Act (FLSA)· 5, 164, 195, 211, 267

FAMINES · 103
Farming · 29, 77, 81, 92 - 104, 209, 301
Farm-to-market transport · 110
Farrell, Chris · 48, 270, 299, 306
Financial sector Wall Street · 122
Financialization · 174
Florida, Richard · 66, 300
FLSA · *See* Fair Labor Standards Act
Ford, Henry · 49, 136, 141, 144, 301
Ford, Martin · 89
Foxconn · 150, 302
Fred C. Andersen · *See* Andersen Windows
Free Time
The Forgotten American Dream · 263
Free trade -133-135, 144
Freight shipment projections · 112
Friedman, Milton · 289

G

Gardening · 104
Gates, Bill and Melinda · 58, 304
Gates, Jeff · 188
gathering firewood · 70
General Motors · 106, 210
George Floyd · 10

Globalization · 8, 132, 136, 168
Golf pro · 245
Good and bad bosses · 153
Gordon, Robert · 127, -166, 301, 303
Gotherburg · 202,
Grant · *See* caregiving
Grant, Tracy · 238 -240, 265, 305
Greece · 29
Growing the Wealth inclusive capitalism · 188
Guns, Germs, and Steel · *See* Jared Diamond

H

Hackman, Richard · 53
Hallock, Ken · 158, 302
Hanauer, Nick · 161, 303
Harvesting · 97
High unemployment · 5, 56
housing bubble · 9
Humphrey, Hubert H. · 191
Hunnicutt, Benjamin · 73, 263 - 267, 306
Hunter/gatherers · 25, 37, 69, 75, 92, 132, 238

I

I, Pencil: My Family Tree as told to Leonard E. Read · 75
IBM's Watson Platform · *See* artificial intelligence
imbalanced labor market · 4
Income inequality · 124, 134, 158
India · 142, 146, 274
Industrial revolution · 34, 38, 44, 47, 49, 53, 78, 91, 133, 209, 265
isolation, geographic -134
insurance · 218
intellectual/developme ntal disabilities · 2, 58, 61, 246
Intermodal container system · 111
International Business Regulation lack thereof · 182
International trade · -132 -- 134, 144
Internships · 206

J

Jefferson, Thomas · 34, 263, 272
JOB CREATORS · 137
Johnson Laura · 261

Johnston, Louis · 229

K

Kaplan, Jerry · 90
Kellogg's · 7
Keynes, John Maynard
· 7, 69, 264, 266,
268, 272
Kunstler, James · 82

L

La Bohème
Puccini · 273
Labor Economics · -
148, 199
Labor movements · -
283
Labor market
supply &
demand · 199
Labor unions · 106,
145, 155, 178, 204,
210, 225
Lindgren, Amy · 50,
300
Lloyd, Henry
Demerest · 172
Locke, John · 34
Logistics · 114
Luddite · 54
Luther, Martin · 32, 34
Luttwak, Edward · 82

M

Madagascar · 146
Made in USA labels ·
145
Madison Avenue · 8
Madland, David and
Walter, Karla · 188
Malthus, Thomas
Robert · 78
Mandela, Nelson · 286
Manual labor tasks · 35
manufacturing ·38,
44, 48, 54, 75, 90,
105, 108, 114, 136,
145, 151, 174, 209,
248
Maquiladoras
in Mexico · 134
Marx, Karl · 48
Maslow, Abraham ·
36, 62, 271
Masseuse or massage
chair · 236
Mayer, Marissa · - 156
McDonalds · 164, 244
- 246
McKay, Harvey · 190,
304
McKinsey Report ·
167
McReynolds, Ginny ·
270, 306
Meaningful jobs · 53,
61
Medical care · 218,
242
Mencken, H.L. · 48
Merchants · 29, 225,
272
Merrick, Inc. · 2, 58,
61, 246
Mexico · 1, 134-136,
141, 147
Meyer, Adolf · 199
Meyer, Dick · 260
Meyerson, Harold ·
174, 303
Middle class · 38, 65,
77, 80, 84, 89, 141 -
- 144, 162, 178,
224, 244
Military · 8, 134, 153,
160
Mill, John Stuart · 33
Minimum wage · - 64,
162 -- 166, 177,
206, 212, 302
Minnesota · 1, 93, 99,
163, 187, 220, 253,
274, 301
Model-T
Henry Ford · 144
Monastic life · 31
Money, invention of ·
71
*Monty Python's Flying
Circus* · 74
Moral Capitalism ·
187
Moynihan, Daniel ·
289
Mukunda, Guatum ·
175, 303
Mullainathan, Sendhil
· 61, 300
Multi-level natural
selection · 24
selfish vs. altruistic
behavior · 24
My Fellow Zillionaires
· *See* Nick Hanauer

N

Nadler, Daniel · *See*

Nathaniel Popper
NAFTA · 134
National Bureau of
  Economic Research
  · 227
natural resources · 77
Nickel and Dimed · 67,
  See Barbara
  Ehrenreich
Nixon, Richard · 289
Nomadic people · 70,
  92, 132
Non-linear careers · 52

O

Obamacare · *See*
  Affordable Care
  Act (ACA)
Occupational
  specialization · 27,
  46
Ocean-going cargo
  ships · 111
Office work, office
  productivity · 6,
  118-125
Oldham, Greg · 53
Oppenheimer, Andres ·
  136, 302
Owner/manager class ·
  17, 173, 280

P

Panama Papers · 182
Part saint and part
  sinner · 24
Part time work for
  students · 63

Paycheck secrecy · 159
PBS Newshour · 142,
  239, 303
Pension plans · 106,
  158, 181, 218, 256
Permanent settlements
  · 28, 37, 70, 109
Perry, Mark · 144, 302
Personal touch
  person-to-person
  interactions ·
  236
Pharmaceutical
  companies · 176
Phone banks · 129
PIKETTY, THOMAS ·
  171, 173, 175, 178,
  303
Planting · 97
Plowing · 96
Political stability · *See*
  free trade
Politico Magazine ·
  161, 303
Popper, Nathaniel ·
  123, 124, 301
Positional economy ·
  83
Poverty thresholds ·
  214
Press, Eyal - 10, 251

Producers and
  consumers · 75
Production bonuses ·
  220
Project Time Off · 269
Public/private
  partnership · 109

R

*Race Against the
  Machine* · 89, *See*
  Brynjolfsson and
  McAfee
Railroads · 108 - 110
raising pigs · 70
Rajasthan, India · 143
Rand, Ayn · 50
REDUCE – REUSE –
  RECYCLE · 80
Reich, Robert · 156,
  164, 168, 172, 177,
  203 - 205, 289, 301
Republicans and
  Democrats · 135,
  177, 266
Retail · 42, 49, 57, 115,
  164, 247
Retirement · 169, 202,
  253, 256, 257, 270
Rifkin, Jeremy · 89,
  301
Robot · - 305 -
Robotics · - 128 -, -
  236 -
Robots · 6, 90, 105,
  114, 123, 128, 235,
  241, 247, 301
Roman Empire · 30
Roosevelt, Franklin
  Delano · 195, 219,
  266, 304
Ryssdal, Kai · 142, 302

S

Salaried sham
  underpaid workers ·

165

Salesmen · 246

Samuelson, Robert · 45, 299

Saving Capitalism See Robert Reich · 168, 172

Scarcity, Why Having Too Little Matters So Much, See Mullainathan, Sendhi· 61

Schafer, Lee · 74, 300

Schuman, Michael · 159, 302

Schwab, Klaus · 127

Schwartz, Barry · 54, 300

Scientific management · *See* Frederick Taylor

Scripps · 260

Secretaries · 6, 118

Serling, Rod · 236, 241, 305

Shafir, Eldar · 61, 300

shareholders

Shareholders · 138, 159, 164, 174, 175, 180 -- 185, 210

Share-the-gains capitalism · 157, *See* Robert Reich

Shipler, David · 67, 300

Silicosis · 143

Slaughterhouse - 10

Slavery · 29, 30, 43, 154, 207, 240, 270

Small jobs · 47

Smith, Adam · 84, 154,

172, 179, 208, 303

Smoot-Hawley Tariff Act · 133

Social Security · 58, 63, 227, 256, 285

Soldiering · 29, 224

South Africa · 286

South America · 112

Special minimum wage · 64

St. Augustine · 31

St. Benedict · 31

St. Paul · 31

Stevens, Ingar Jana - Twilight Zone · 235

Stone Age · 25, 132

Stowe, Harriet Beecher · 207, 304

Subservient duties, work · 26, 37

Sustainable Development Solutions Network · 257

Suzman, James Affluence without Abundance · 269

Sybil, or The Two Nations · 44, 299

T

Taylor, Frederick Winslow · - 35, 48, 105, 158, 224

TCHERNEVA, PAVLINA · 177, 178, 303

Teachers · 80, 126, 142 -- 144, 238, 244

tech bubble · 9

Technology · 4, 79, 89, 115, 126 -- 129, 163, 168, 173, 185, 236, 250, 268

Technology, jobs, and the future of work · 167

Telephone operators · 129

Teran, Dan · 54

Terkel, Studs · 48, 67

Thailand · 139, 146

The author and the au pair · 249

The End of Work · 89

The Fissured Workplace · 155

The Fourth Industrial Revolution · 127

The Geography of Nowhere · 82

The Good Jobs Strategy · 49

The Growth in Social Security Disability Rolls: A Fiscal Crisis Unfolding · 227

The Hidden Wealth of Nations tax havens · 183

The Jobs Americans Do · 242

The Lights in the Tunnel · 89

The Ownership Solution · 188

The realignment of the working class · 180

The Rise and Fall of American Growth · 127, 166

The Rise of the Creative Class · 66

The Robots Are Coming for Wall Street · 123

The Social Conquest of Earth · 23

The Wealth of Nations · 154

The Working Poor · 67

Thoreau, Henry David · 73 -- 74, 300

Threshing · 97

Tice, D.J. · 135 -- 136, 302

Ton, Zeynep · 49, 54

Tool makers · 27, 37

Toyota · 141, 302

Tractors · 6, 93, 96, 101

TRANSPORTATION · - 108 -- 113

Travel & Hospitality vacation trips · 244

Travel agents · 245

Trickle-up economics · 17, 144, 253

Trump, Donald · 135, 144, 175, 302, 303

Turbo-Capitalism · 82

Twilight Zone · 235

U

U.S. Census Bureau sets threshold for poverty · 212

U.S. Department of Labor · 41, 42, 64

UAW · 225

UBI unconditional basic income · 288, 290

Ulukaya, Hamdi · - 156 - 157

UN · 257

Uncle Tom's Cabin · 207

Harriet Beecher Stowe · 240

Unemployment status - 55, unemployment benefits · 57

Uniform Commercial Code (UCC) · 184

Union made labels · 145

Universal birthrights · 34

University of Minnesota · 273

Unretirement · 48, 270

UPC codes laser scanners · 117

Utility Function Indifference curves · 252

Utopia for Realists · 237

V

Verizon · 180 -- 181

Vietnam War · 8

Virtual assistant · *See* artificial intelligence

W

WAGE STAGNATION · 166

Walden, or, Life in the Woods · 73

Wall Street · 123, 157, 175 - 177, 301, 303

Walmart · 106, 146

War on Poverty · 289

Washington D.C. · 147

We all must make time for creativity in our lives · 261

Wealth Against Commonwealth · 172

Wealth of Nations · 84, 183, 208, 303

Wealth vs. Well-being · 271

Weil, David · 155

What Bernie Sanders and Donald Trump get wrong about Wall Street · 175

When a Rising Tide Sinks Most Boats Trends in US Income Inequality · 177

Wilson · - 23 -, - 24 -, - 30 -, - 84 -, - 299 -

Wilson, E.O. · 22 -- 25, 56, 299

Women in workforce · 8, 37, 47, 56, 129, 137, 166, 209, 283

Work for disadvantaged · 61

Work to live · 17, 36

Work-Consume
   treadmill · 81
Working · 48
WWII · 7, 36, 93, 218

X

Xenophobia - 133

Y

Yahoo · 156 -157, 243,
   254
Yglesias, Matthew ·
   107

Young, Stephen · 63,
   180, 203, 303, 304

Z

Zucman, Gabriel · 183
   -184, 303

Made in the USA
Columbia, SC
13 May 2022